THE FIGHT TO SAVE JUÁREZ

The Fight to Save Juárez

LIFE IN THE HEART OF MEXICO'S DRUG WAR

■ ■ ■

By Ricardo C. Ainslie

University of Texas Press ◆ Austin

Author's Note: All quotations in this book are from public documents, newspapers, press conferences, personal interviews, or first-person observations. For Mexican sources, I drew most heavily from the newspapers *El Diario* (the Ciudad Juárez paper with the highest circulation), *El Norte* (Ciudad Juárez), *Reforma* (Mexico City), and *El Universal* (Mexico City), and *Proceso* magazine, among others.

Copyright © 2013 by the University of Texas Press
All rights reserved
Printed in the United States of America
First edition, 2013

Requests for permission to reproduce material from this work should be sent to:
    Permissions
    University of Texas Press
    P.O. Box 7819
    Austin, TX 78713-7819
    http://utpress.utexas.edu/about/book-permissions

♾ The paper used in this book meets the minimum requirements of ANSI/NISO Z39.48-1992 (R1997) (Permanence of Paper).

Library of Congress Cataloging-in-Publication Data

Ainslie, Ricardo C.
The fight to save Juárez : life in the heart of Mexico's drug war / by Ricardo C. Ainslie. — 1st ed.
    p.   cm.
    Includes bibliographical references and index.
    ISBN 978-0-292-73890-4 (cloth : alk. paper)
1. Drug traffic—Mexico—Ciudad Juárez.   2. Drug control—Mexico—Ciudad Juárez.
3. Violent crime—Mexico—Ciudad Juárez.   I. Title.
    HV5840.M42C5822 2013
    363.450972'16—dc23   2012035822
    doi:10.7560/738904

For my wife, Daphny, who has shown me the meaning of courage

Contents

There's no one thing that is true. They're all true.

—Ernest Hemingway

Acknowledgments

I wish to thank my wife, Daphny Ainslie, for the many ways that she has supported me in this effort, from champagne upon landing key interviews, to reading drafts, to enduring my many trips to Juárez and so very much more. I also wish to thank my children, Roberto, Gabriella, and Jorge, whom I love dearly and whose love nurtures me and gives me strength.

My agent, Jim Hornfischer, has a keen eye and worked tirelessly on my behalf. My dear friend Steve Harrigan, over countless lunches, helped me find the solutions to the puzzles and challenges I encountered in writing this complex story and read the manuscript with his exquisite sensibility. I owe him a great deal for these and other acts of kindness he has shown me over the years.

John Burnett, a dear friend, National Public Radio correspondent, and fellow bandmate in WhoDo, our Austin-based "blues collective," was extremely generous in sharing his insights as well as his contacts in Juárez and El Paso. We shared many conversations about this book and about Mexico's drug war over the course of the three years that I worked on the book. Roberto Newell, of the Instituto Mexicano para la Competitividad, opened many doors for me in Mexico, helping me get interviews that would no doubt have been out of reach without his intercession. He is a lifelong friend—our parents were friends as well—and I am grateful for all he did to support this project. Another childhood friend, Gary Richmond, has been a foundation for all of my work in Mexico, always extending his friendship, advice, and hospitality during my many stays in Mexico City. My cousin Alejandro Ainslie and his wife, Monica, have given me excellent advice, suggestions on translations, insights into the Mexican political process, and bottomless support. My brother Robert Ainslie was a steady beacon throughout and has always been an enthusiastic supporter of my projects. My niece Cristina Ainslie is part of our (that is, my wife's and my) "kitchen cabinet," and her wisdom and advice is extremely valued on many fronts. My friends Jim Magnuson, Robert Bryce, and Larry Wright have been helpful and generous with their insights. "Brother Bill" Ferris, Tom Palaima, Bryan Roberts, and John Phillip Santos wrote me letters of support that readers found sufficiently compelling to grant me life-changing awards. I really appreciate the generosity of time and spirit from these friends.

I'm grateful to Jake Silverstein of *Texas Monthly*, Julián Aguilar of the *Texas Tribune*, Clay Smith of the Texas Book Festival, and Bill Booth of the *Washington Post* for their ideas, leads, and conversations about the project.

Richard Schmidt, federal judge in Corpus Christi, and Omar Zamora, a former DEA agent, helped me make important contacts related to this story. Peter Ward and Charlie Hale helped me secure an interview with Alejandro Poiré; Hugo René Oliva, deputy consul, Mexican Consulate, Austin, Texas, also played a role in this interview. Samuel Schmidt, PhD, Fundación Universidad de Guadalajara, EUA, was also generous with his views about key players in the Juárez political scene.

A very special thanks to Dave Hamrick, director of University of Texas Press, and my editor, Theresa May, both great people with a great commitment to the wonderful enterprise of the written word.

In the course of my research I have received support from many quarters, generous support that has, at times, left me breathless. The following institutions, foundations, and individuals have each played a very significant role in this effort and I thank them from the bottom of my heart: the John Simon Guggenheim Memorial Foundation; the Rockefeller Foundation Bellagio Residency; and at the University of Texas at Austin, the Department of Educational Psychology; Manuel Justiz, PhD, dean of the College of Education; the Lozano Long Institute for Latin American Studies; Ed Emmer, PhD, chair, Department of Educational Psychology (until 2011); Cindy Carlson, PhD, chair, Department of Educational Psychology; Linda Williams and Regina Smuts, administrative associates, Department of Educational Psychology; Jena Crim, executive assistant, Department of Educational Psychology; Paloma Diaz, Lozano Long Institute for Latin American Studies.

The following Mexican scholars have been writing about these issues for years. I was humbled to meet them, to have the benefit of reading their works, and to have the opportunity to talk with them about my work: Jorge Chabat, professor of international studies, CIDE (Center for Research and Teaching in Economics); and Luis Astorga, researcher at the Institute for Social Research, Universidad Nacional Autónoma de México (UNAM).

The following individuals were essential resources in helping me sift through the millions of words that have been written in American and, especially, Mexican newspapers, as well as in researching other aspects of the story: Molly Molloy, research librarian for Latin America and the border at New Mexico State University and creator of the Frontera List; and my doctoral students Alicia Enciso, Annie Farmer, and Luis Sandoval, who have been terrific. Finally, on several occasions Olga Valenzuela Ortiz of the Secretariat for Public Security was kind enough to take my fact-checking calls and clarify incidents, dates, and other elements.

THE FIGHT TO SAVE JUÁREZ

Prologue

The first time I saw José Reyes Ferriz was on March 16, 2009. The Mexican Army had just arrived in force and Reyes Ferriz, the mayor of Ciudad Juárez, was swearing in a new police chief, his third chief in less than a year. Security surrounding the event was tight and the tension in the expansive room at police headquarters palpable. The city was on the verge of anarchy. Dozens of Juárez police had been assassinated over the course of the preceding year and the force's collusion with the drug cartels was so intractable that Reyes Ferriz had found himself compelled to disband the force entirely. As I stood behind a phalanx of television cameras, photographers, and journalists, the thought occurred to me that I was watching the most beleaguered man in all of Mexico.

It would be some months later before I had the opportunity to interview Reyes Ferriz. The interview took place in his office at the Presidencia Municipal, the Juárez city hall. That day the offices of the mayor's communications director, Sergio Belmonte, were chock-full of journalists from all over the world waiting in queue to speak to the mayor. When it was my turn, I was escorted past armed guards and into an ample office on the second floor. The interview covered the typical topics: his understanding of the origins of the drug war in Juárez, the impact of the Mexican military patrolling the streets of the city, his aims for rebuilding the fractured police force. I had the impression that this was well-traveled terrain for the mayor, but for me it was a useful overview for understanding how the city's leadership was engaging the present crisis.

On prior visits I'd had the opportunity to observe the mayor being interviewed by others in impromptu encounters at public events. That day in March 2009, when the mayor had sworn in the new police chief, stood out. The director of a German documentary film crew had slammed Reyes Ferriz hard about the fact that the Juárez municipal police was rife with corruption and challenged the legality of using the military to intervene in the city. The interviewer was accusatory, hostile, and confrontational. While that wasn't my style by temperament, or perhaps by profession (as a psychologist-psychoanalyst my reflexive instinct is to find an empathic engagement with my subject, whether or not I agree with their actions or worldview), I also had the feeling that it wasn't good journalism; the assumptions at work were too evident and facile. There was something else, as well. My gut instinct about Reyes Ferriz, as I observed him at these public events, was that this man was not the evil, corrupt politician that I, too, had expected. Quite to my surprise, I found that I liked the man.

By the time of that first interview in the summer of 2009, Reyes Ferriz had already been the object of numerous death threats. As events unfolded in the city, the cartels periodically threatened to kill the mayor and to behead him and his family. The heavily armed bodyguards that accompanied Reyes Ferriz's every move were ample evidence that the threats were taken seriously: Juárez was a city where officials were being executed routinely.

An exchange occurred during my interview with the mayor that opened the door to an opportunity to understand what was taking place in Juárez through his eyes. It came toward the end of the conversation, when I asked him about the death threats against him. He was circumspect about them, but I pressed the point, saying, "I imagine that there must be moments when you must feel terribly afraid." The mayor played it off as just a part of his job, although he acknowledged that he'd moved his family across the river to El Paso for security reasons. My impression was that there was something in that interaction, in that gesture toward his humanity, that seemed to have caught him by surprise. Whatever it was, it went unspoken, but I was granted a second interview upon my next visit to Juárez. Subsequently, I took advantage of every opportunity to interview the mayor or to observe functions at which he was presiding—press conferences, public ceremonies, speeches, and the like. It was in this way that José Reyes Ferriz gradually emerged as the central character of this book.

■ ■ ■

There are many who see in Mexico's present drug war the shadows of age-old culprits: government corruption and official collusion with the cartels. Stereotypes die hard. That's especially true when they draw from an infinite array of experiences and observations that reiterate and reaffirm the same truth. Given those facts, it is difficult to arrive at a conclusion other than what one has always known. So it is with the view that Mexico is a corrupt nation run by corrupt people whose primary interest is to engorge their bank accounts and to position themselves, their families, and their friends so as to profit from opportunities that if not seized will simply be seized by others. The examples that populate this notion are endless and go back to the birth of modern Mexico, if not before. Mexican presidents, cabinet ministers, legislators, governors, and mayors have fed at the public trough so voraciously and with such abandon that the very notion of public figures who would be honestly motivated to serve verges on the incomprehensible.

In Mexico, there are few templates to draw from for this idea. The avarice has been indulged with such arrogance (the kind that comes from unfettered power), that the public's scorn saturates virtually every part of the political process and anyone associated with it. The same is true for many of the country's institutions, but none more so than law enforcement and the judiciary.

In Mexico, where it was once said that not even a leaf fell from a tree without the president's permission, the power of political office has eroded significantly over the last nineteen years. The first clear sign of this was a horrific act of violence. On March 23, 1994, Luis Donaldo Colosio, the presidential candidate for the Partido Revolucionario Institucional (PRI by its Spanish initials), was wading through a crowd of well-wishers on a campaign stop in a poor Tijuana neighborhood when a man walked up to him and shot him at point-blank range. Colosio's assassination shook the nation. It was partly the brutal act itself in a country where no president or presidential candidate had suffered such a fate in modern times, but it was also the fact that Colosio was enormously popular because he was campaigning on a promise: he would end the PRI's "anointing" process of selecting presidential candidates, the process that made the notion of democracy in Mexico a sham, a mere posture, a dissimulation that no Mexican failed to see through. Colosio was committed to transforming Mexico into a real democracy, and many believe that it was that ambition that forced the hand of the PRI's old guard, who felt their power eroding. In short, it is a commonly held view in Mexico that Colosio's democratic ambitions led to his execution.

Ernesto Zedillo, Colosio's successor in the campaign, became Mexico's next president, and he helped usher in the reforms that Colosio had championed. In the next Mexican presidential election, in 2000, Vicente Fox of the Partido Acción Nacional (or PAN by its Spanish initials) became the first president since the 1910 Mexican Revolution to come from an opposition party. The PRI's uncontested rule, with which it had governed Mexico for seventy years, was over. Felipe Calderón, the author of the current war against the drug cartels, assumed the Mexican presidency following Vicente Fox in December of 2006. He is also from the center-right PAN party.

The PRI continues to exert a powerful influence in contemporary Mexico. The majority of the thirty-two state governors are from the PRI, for example. But in the spring of 2012, the PAN had eight governors while the PRD (Partido de la Revolución Democrática by its Spanish initials), the other (center-left) main opposition party, had three governorships as well as the all-important Federal District, where Mexico City lies. The three parties have mayors in municipalities all over the country. Every election since 1994 has brought real shifts in the distribution of power among the political parties. Though brittle, fragile, and still rife with problems (including corruption), Mexico is emerging as a fledgling democratic state.

■ ■ ■

In 2009 I interviewed Fernando Castillo Tapia, the director of communications for the federal attorney general's office (Procuraduría General de la República, or PGR by its Spanish acronym). The meeting took place in Mexico City in a modern building near the Historic Center. Mr. Castillo was polite if circumspect, and he took umbrage at my referencing "Mexico's war against the drug cartels," making it a point to correct me. "This is not a war," he clarified. "It is a law-enforcement action."

The distinction was not convincing. For one thing, the main force being deployed around the country was the Mexican Army. In addition, at the very start of his six-year administration, while visiting a military base in his native state of Michoacán in December of 2006, Felipe Calderón, the Mexican president, had actually used the word "war" in declaring his intentions to go after the drug cartels. By 2008, throughout the country one had the feeling that Mexico was, indeed, at war. For example, while driving from Puebla to Mexico City in 2008, I was struck by the steady stream of public-service announcements coming over the radio waves, such as, "Your federal government reminds you that it is a federal crime to buy property in the name of another person or to carry large sums of cash for others." Or, "Your federal government reminds you that it is a federal crime to be in possession of weapons that are for the exclusive use of the military [a reference to assault weapons]." Or the listing of drug war–related arrests: "In the last month your federal government arrested the following lieutenants from the Sinaloa, Gulf, and Juárez cartels." For years now, print and electronic media have been awash with daily accounts of army and federal police operations taking place all over the country as well as the ever-present shock waves of bloody cartel actions that include hangings, beheadings, torture-executions, and mass killings.

This is a war by anyone's standards. By the spring of 2012 the PGR estimated that between December 2006 (the beginning of the Calderón administration) and the end of 2011, 47,515 Mexicans had been killed in the course of the drug war, a figure close to the casualties the United States suffered over the course of ten years of war in Vietnam. However, pundits and government critics assert that the actual number easily exceeds fifty thousand and may be closer to sixty thousand, given that government figures do not include people who have been "lifted" and thus have simply disappeared. Every month or so mass graves are discovered in the states bearing the brunt of the narco-war.

Almost none of the executions in Mexico have been adequately investigated or documented, making the specific circumstances surrounding the deaths all but impossible to tease out in many instances. Most of the victims have been executed as part of the schisms between cartels and attempts to take over rival territory in order to control smuggling routes. The bulk of the dead are young men between sixteen and twenty-five years of age, many of them members of the street-level gangs that the cartels increasingly employ to manage their retail drug markets. A smaller number of victims are civilians who have been killed because they have not paid extortions or because they have been caught in cross fires. Some of the victims have been killed in the course of firefights with the authorities, and at least a thousand Mexican Army and federal police members have been killed in the course of the war. But the tally of the dead also includes an unknown number of individuals who died while in police or military custody. Official accounts minimize these deaths because Mexican officials are sensitive to accusations of human rights violations, while opposition groups are eager to inflate the figures. We may never know their actual number.

The cartels have expanded their "business model" in recent years to include other criminal acts, especially extortion, kidnapping, theft of gasoline and petroleum products, and human trafficking, among other activities. Thus, while the majority of the tally of the dead reflects drug war casualties, it is sometimes difficult to separate those executions from criminal activity that is not specifically about the drug business. In addition, non–drug cartel criminal enterprises often emulate the cartels' criminal activities (extorting neighborhood businesses, for example). All of this makes it difficult to nail down exactly what is taking place in Mexico and who is doing what.

The bloodshed in Mexico occurs primarily in nine states. Four of these are border states (Chihuahua, Nuevo León, Coahuila, Tamaulipas); two are on the coast and have important ports (Guerrero and Veracruz); and two states form part of the "golden triangle"—the ancestral home of the Mexican drug trade and the families that created it (Sinaloa and Durango, with Chihuahua forming the third leg). Finally, Michoacán has also been a site of considerable violence. Eighty percent of the killings have taken place in but 162 of Mexico's 2,441 municipalities, according to the PGR's statistics.

■ ■ ■

There are many truths to be told about what is taking place in Mexico. This book braids together the lives of a Mexican mayor caught in the vortex of his city's unraveling; a midlevel cartel player's paramour who lived the narco-life on the inside; a human rights activist caught between the abuses of the authorities and the stories of their victims; and a journalist caught between the ideals of his profession and the police, the cartels, and the gangs who don't want stories told.

I spent three years exploring the tragedy that has befallen Mexico through the lens of its darkest place: Ciudad Juárez. I've seen many dead in Juárez, their bodies splayed out on the pavement midstreet or on sidewalks or caught as they desperately attempted to reach the sanctuary of their homes. I have been to cemeteries and to wakes where mourners are praying the rosary. I've interviewed the frightened neighbors of cartel victims (frightened that they might be next, frightened that someone might see them talking to me, frightened that the future no longer holds promise for them or for their children). I've spoken to the relatives of the executed at their kitchen tables and under their carports and I have driven around with them in hobbled cars, down trash-strewn, rut-filled streets that have never known pavement. I know the neighborhoods where the night belongs to the gangs. I have gone to these and other neighborhoods trying to understand, trying to comprehend the nightmare that has enveloped the life of every person in this city.

I have seen the many faces of Juárez. In researching this book I have gone to the site of mass narco-graves and I have gone to the police stations. I have interviewed Catholic priests whose lives are threatened because they care for the sick and impoverished in neighborhoods controlled by the cartels and their gangs. I know the efforts of leftist community organizers as well as people working for non-profit organizations, all trying to help young people from poor communities avoid becoming the rank and file of the cartel hit squads and the worker bees of the cartel business. I have interviewed Mexican journalists, many of whom have been personally threatened (and all of whom know colleagues who have been assassinated for covering the cartels' work). I have interviewed elementary-school teachers who describe the ways in which the ever-present deaths have shaped the worlds of their charges. I have also witnessed terror in the eyes of high-school students in their school uniforms, toting book bags as they walk around crime-scene tape a few feet from the bullet-ridden body of a man who has just been executed at the entrance to their school. I have talked to rich people and to poor people, I have talked to right-wingers who favor death squads if the government can't do its job, and I have talked to leftist neighborhood organizers who want the army and the federal police out of their city.

It is not only brute violence that signals to the people of Juárez that theirs is a city bordering on anarchy. Anarchy has many faces. In Juárez I have spoken to people who have been extorted by the gangs and I have seen their businesses burning in the night when they do not comply. I have spoken to assembly plant workers who are forced to pay neighborhood thugs a third of their weekly pay just to have safe access to and from their homes. I have interviewed professionals who lock their office doors with deadbolts during work hours and who monitor the entrances to their businesses with security cameras; they live under constant threat that they or their families will fall victim to kidnappings, extortions, or assassinations. In the course of my work I have come to know the fear that is lived in Juárez on a daily basis.

I have also seen the resilience of life: the teenagers playing their trumpets as they rehearse for a party and children playing in the parks and families having barbecues. I have driven the streets of the poorest neighborhoods as sunset falls on another scorching day in the desert and heard the music pouring out of the windows as people sit along graffiti-tagged walls in white plastic chairs escaping the heat trapped in their homes.

The city of Juárez is ground zero for the Mexican government's strategy against the drug cartels. Almost a quarter of the federal forces that Felipe Calderón has deployed in this war have at some point been sent to Juárez, and almost 20 percent of the country's drug-related executions have taken place in the city, a city that can be as unforgiving as the hardest places on earth. It is here that the Mexican government came to turn the tide, and the outcome of what happens in Juárez will have lasting repercussions for both Mexico and the United States.

CHAPTER 1

Christmas in Juárez

On a late December night in 2007, between Christmas and New Year's, the recently elected mayor of Juárez stood alone in his office staring out the window. The usual vibrant chaos of the border city's streets below had yielded to an almost ghostly absence of activity; in addition to the holidays, the violence was beginning to have a dampening effect upon Juárez life. With executions perpetrated by the drug cartels averaging one and sometimes two people a day that year, the weight of the dead upon the city was palpable. City hall was empty save for the bodyguard posted outside the mayor's door. Earlier that evening, José Reyes Ferriz had received an urgent call from the federal government's security representative in Juárez to say that it was imperative that they meet, which is why the mayor had come to city hall during the holidays and at such an unusual hour. The need for a face-to-face meeting only added to the sense of urgency, but it was also the case that no one in Juárez trusted their cell phones—it was too easy for someone to monitor them.

The window at which the mayor stood faced south and spanned nearly the entire length of the wall. Outside and below lay the city of Juárez. The more proximate buildings were readily discernible, but beyond them, in the desert night, the city was aglitter with twinkling lights, like so many diamonds cast upon a sheet of black velvet. Upon assuming office a few months earlier, Reyes Ferriz had instructed his people to remove the blinds and the wood panels that divided the window into sections. He wanted to optimize the view, and the vantage from this particular window was already the mayor's favorite. He loved the view, but it was also the light; he loved natural light.

The federal government's intelligence operative arrived shortly, escorted into the office by the mayor's bodyguard, who left them to talk in private. Reyes Ferriz greeted him at the door, next to the larger-than-life print of Benito Juárez, Mexico's revered first president (following the reign of Maximilian in 1867). The two men sat down in the chairs and couch that formed a small seating area at this end of the office, under Juárez's watchful eye. (During Mexico's war against French intervention, Benito Juárez had taken refuge from the French forces in what was then a remote hamlet called El Paso del Norte; Juárez's stay during that turbulent time eventually gave the city its name).

"What's going on?" Reyes Ferriz asked. It was evident that the intelligence officer had something pressing on his mind.

"Mayor," the federal officer said, "I have some disconcerting news." The agent proceeded to describe new intelligence indicating that in all likelihood a bloody war was about to erupt in Ciudad Juárez between the Sinaloa cartel and the Juárez cartel. "It will happen sometime this coming month," he said. He couldn't be more specific.

A corporate attorney by training with a master's degree from Notre Dame in international law with a specialization in international business, José Reyes Ferriz had only been in office since October. There was little in the mayor's curriculum vitae or in his appearance that would suggest him as a likely candidate to face off with the most violent cartels in the history of Mexico or cast him in the role of the would-be savior of Juárez. In addition to his law practice, he also held a part-time appointment teaching law at the Universidad Autónoma de Ciudad Juárez, arguably the best university in the city, something he'd done for years (he had decided to keep his classes notwithstanding his new responsibilities). A man of modest stature with a mild-mannered style and a jowly, rather cherubic face framed by wire-rimmed glasses, the forty-six-year-old mayor did not look the part of a border city politician, certainly not in the old-school Mexican sense of the role. His speeches were rarely strident, and some might even have described him as soft-spoken. The affable mayor dressed conventionally—blue or charcoal-gray suits, pressed white shirts with cufflinks, and muted primary-colored ties, his feet typically ensconced in loafers. None of it added up to the challenges that lay in store for José Reyes Ferriz and his city. Had he known, Reyes Ferriz might well have passed on the opportunity to run for mayor of Juárez. State and local politics were flush with intrigue, and there was no shortage of cutthroats and backstabbers, but being at the epicenter of his country's war against the drug cartels was another matter.

The intelligence officer's report pointed to something ominous looming on the horizon, adding a new dimension to the mayor's worries. Reyes Ferriz was not one given to overreaction, but alone again in his office, staring out upon the flickering lights of his city, the mayor felt a sense of foreboding.

■ ■ ■

José Reyes Ferriz had been elected on a platform that included cleaning up the city through a program he called the Municipal Accord of Order and Respect (AMOR, or "love" by its Spanish acronym). Reyes Ferriz planned to put an end to the proliferation of cars without registrations and license plates and address criminal impunity by shoring up the district attorney's procedures, among other things. One could safely say that the program's vision fell short of the earth shattering. In addition, however, the mayor had ambitious economic goals for the city. He wanted to increase its importance as a financial hub for business between the United States and Mexico. Mexico was already the United States' third-most important trading partner, but most of that trade centered on the maquiladora assembly plants along the border or the big Mexican companies like Bimbo and the Moctezuma Brewery. "Midlevel and smaller companies didn't know how to interact with U.S. markets," the mayor told me. He felt that the Juárez business community's expertise could make the city a key player in helping these midlevel companies find a home for their products in the U.S. Another initiative of interest to the newly elected mayor was medical tourism. "We have great hospitals in Juárez," he told me. "And the U.S. has a medical crisis."

Whatever its merit, the mayor soon discovered that his agenda for the city was easily derailed by unforeseen events. For example, a wave of car thefts in Juárez had produced this odd fact: the cars were turning up again, abandoned on the street, days or sometimes only hours after they had been stolen. The mayor and his police chief concluded that the cartels were using the stolen cars to ferry drugs across the river before driving them back and abandoning them. To disrupt these operations, the mayor decided that he would provide American customs officials with car descriptions and VIN numbers of stolen vehicles as soon as these were reported. Reyes Ferriz announced the new program one morning at 11 a.m.; that afternoon, while the mayor was at his private law office, one of his bodyguards rushed in to tell him that armed men had surrounded the building. When Reyes Ferriz peeled the curtain back to peer out he saw two Suburbans and a dozen or so men with assault rifles forming a perimeter around the office. With only four bodyguards, the mayor's security team was no match in either number or firepower: the mayor's men were armed only with pistols. "It was a clear threat," the mayor would later tell me. The Juárez cartel was letting the novice mayor know that there was a cost to interfering with their operations. He'd only been in office a month. "It was my initiation," Reyes Ferriz noted. The mayor increased his personal security team to six and arranged for them to be trained in the use of automatic weapons.

Not long thereafter, a series of mutinies occurred at the Juárez city prison, known as the CERESO (the Spanish acronym for Social Rehabilitation Center, as Mexican prisons are called). A local gang called Los Aztecas took over the prison and systematically killed rival gang members. Video footage from security cameras caught the bloodletting on tape and order was difficult to restore at the prison, where Los Aztecas were armed with automatic weapons that someone had smuggled in to them. The authorities conducted a systematic search after regaining control of the prison, but the weapons were never found. The incident underscored the extent to which gangs held sway in the Juárez prison.

While José Reyes Ferriz may have had plans for his city, others clearly had their own agendas. There were powerful forces at work in Juárez, and Reyes Ferriz's "initiation" was but the sparest of gestures intimating what lay ahead.

■ ■ ■

From his bunker at the Secretariat for Public Security on Avenida Constituyentes in Mexico City, Genaro García Luna, Mexico's top law enforcement official, had a vantage that was different from that of Reyes Ferriz. Since Felipe Calderón had assumed the presidency and declared war on the drug cartels in December 2006, García Luna had been a busy man. He was a key player in the president's security cabinet, and his federal police[1] were second in importance only to the Mexican Army in the now-declared war. Over the course of that first year other regions in Mexico had occupied García Luna's attention. For example, there was open warfare between the Gulf and Sinaloa cartels for control of Nuevo Laredo, across the river from Laredo, Texas. The violence in Nuevo Laredo had included many deaths, an ambush by municipal police on a column of federal police as it was arriving in the city, the execution of the Nuevo Laredo police chief within hours of his installation, and an assault on the offices of the city's main newspaper in which cartel hit men had thrown hand grenades and sprayed the newsroom with AK-47 fire. Nuevo Laredo was a major commercial hub between Mexico and the United States and thousands of commercial trucks crossed the border there every day. The Mexican government had been attempting to tamp down the violence in Nuevo Laredo, but the battle between the two cartels was raging full force.

And there were other hotspots in Mexico that were demanding García Luna's attention. In Michoacán, an important transit point for Colombian cocaine into Mexico, a new cartel had formed and was now at war with the Gulf cartel and its military wing, a group of former elite military troops who had defected over to the dark side and were known as Los Zetas. Michoacán was producing almost daily headlines in the national press because La Familia, as the new cartel was called, had taken to severing the heads of its victims and putting them on display. In the highlands town of Tepalcatepec, in August 2007, a note was pinned to one such head with the following message: "See. Hear. Shut up. If you want to stay alive." In another incident, in Uruapan, they had rolled the heads of five victims onto the dance floor at a nightclub. Such tactics had a kind of shock-and-awe effect and were spreading fear throughout the country. Similarly, a rift between the Sinaloa cartel and the Tijuana cartel was leaving a trail of blood and horrific acts of violence in Baja California, where hundreds had died. And there were other states in Mexico where grisly executions were taking place on a daily basis.

These battle zones were getting all the media attention and absorbing a great deal of García Luna's time. Ciudad Juárez remained far down on the list of priorities or concerns. American intelligence was not picking up much on Juárez, either. The Congressional Research Service's February 2008 report to Congress merely described the Juárez cartel as one of the four most important Drug Trafficking Organizations operating in Mexico and mentioned, almost in passing, that the Juárez cartel "may no longer be tied to the Federation due to murders committed by another Federation member" (the Federation was the name given to the Pax Mafiosa that had held Mexico's main cartels in a tenuous peace since 2006). That clause was the only reference in the CRS report that suggested that things between the Juárez and the Sinaloa cartels might be taking a different turn.

To be sure, there were rumblings. García Luna's people were picking up reports about Ciudad Juárez through the network of federal intelligence sources and what he heard worried him. He knew that in 2004 the Sinaloa cartel had executed Rodolfo Carrillo Fuentes, the brother of the head of the Juárez cartel, Vicente Carrillo Fuentes. An enraged Vicente Carrillo Fuentes had purportedly put in a call to Ismael "El Mayo" Zambada, a long-standing ally of both Vicente Carrillo Fuentes and of El Chapo Guzmán, the head of the Sinaloa cartel. Zambada was also a member of the so-called Federation to which the CRS report had made reference. "Are you with me?" Carrillo Fuentes is said to have asked. Zambada said he was. "Then I want you to deliver the head of that son of a bitch!" Carrillo Fuentes said, in reference to El Chapo Guzmán. But the head never came, and later El Chapo's son, Edgar Guzmán, was assassinated in a hail of AK-47 fire when Juárez cartel operatives ambushed him in the parking lot of a shopping mall in Culiacán, the capital of the state of Sinaloa. This was the assassination to which the CRS was referring in its report.

Squabbles and conflicts between the cartels were nothing new. It was in the nature of their business. The tit-for-tat aggressions between the Sinaloa and Juárez people had been going on for a while, but these flare-ups had a way of being short-lived, after which the cartels went back to their day-to-day work. At the same time, García Luna was keenly aware that in the world of the drug cartels incidents like these also did not simply disappear from the institutional memories. They remained part of the backdrop to what went on between them, pools of resentment and discontent that could be tapped and which could burst into the open like molten lava when triggered by a new incident or by shifting allegiances within the cartel world. What was surprising was that such resentments could be sealed over at all, given that what most often fueled them were the assassinations of blood relatives, close friends, or long-standing associates.

By December 2007, the Gulf cartel had succeeded in beating back the

Sinaloa cartel's attempt to seize control of Nuevo Laredo. As a result, the Sinaloa cartel had turned its sights on Ciudad Juárez. García Luna knew that the Sinaloa cartel was preparing to make its move. The intelligence suggested that war had been declared, although in Juárez a relative calm reigned, like the still waters that precede the arrival of the hurricane. It was a war that was partly fueled by revenge, but it was also mobilized by greed: the Sinaloa cartel believed that the Juárez cartel had become weakened because of rivalries and internecine conflict, and it saw in this weakness an opportunity to move on what all of the cartels knew to be prime real estate—the city of Juárez, which had long been one of the most important transit points for crossing illicit drugs into the United States. Factoring all of these threads together, García Luna had decided it was time to alert Mayor Reyes Ferriz about the coming storm.

The Christmas warning to Reyes Ferriz foretold a coming war, but even with the warning the mayor had no way of grasping what lay in store or how his life and the life of his city would be irretrievably transformed. "I couldn't imagine the possible scale of what was coming," Ferriz would later tell me. And it was precisely that failure of the imagination, that failure to grasp or to conceive, that amplified the feeling of apprehension. The mayor of Juárez knew that somewhere beyond his window lay a threat, but he could not yet fully fathom its contours.

Note

1. Until April 2009, when a new federal law expanded its powers and authorized its investigative functions, the federal police was called the federal preventive police. I use the term federal police throughout this book because it is otherwise awkward and confusing to shift between the two names, which, in any event, refer to the same law enforcement organization.

CHAPTER 2

The Saulo Reyes Affair

On the morning of January 1, 2008, *El Diario*, the Ciudad Juárez newspaper with the widest circulation, opened the new year with a tally of the dead for the year that had just drawn to a close. The story was written by one of the paper's most respected journalists, a man named Armando Rodríguez, who at the time had no way of knowing that before the newly christened year yielded to the next, the grim tallies that he chronicled so assiduously in his reportorial duties would come to include him, too.

El Diario reported that 301 people had been murdered over the course of 2007. The number was record-setting and created unease in the city. The 2007 tally exceeded the prior record of 294 deaths, registered in 1995, at the height of Juárez's infamous femicides, when poor working women were being brutally killed. For almost a decade the city had been trying to distance itself from those ugly and inconvenient facts, facts that had brought Juárez to the attention of the United Nations Human Rights Commission and generated considerable unflattering national and international press coverage. Armando Rodríguez's article in *El Diario* indicated that, of the violent deaths that had taken place over the course of the year, only nineteen had been women. Something else was now afoot in Ciudad Juárez, something that would soon displace the femicides as the city's defining mark.

The recently appointed Juárez chief of police, Guillermo Prieto Quintana, appeared at a loss to explain the record executions, resorting instead to platitudes: "This number [of deaths] is truly worrisome," Rodríguez quoted him as saying. "Even one death is unfortunate. With this record we are obligated to work on prevention in coordination with all of the police forces, and to reinforce a culture within the citizenry that will help us care for them and be vigilant."

The words seemed to hang from the page: even one death unfortunate . . . we are obligated to work on prevention . . . coordination . . . vigilance. They had the hollow ring of a public servant grasping at straws. If the people of Juárez drew any succor from the police chief's words it was short-lived. As the January days rolled on, Juárez seemed to be on the same grim trajectory as the year before, averaging one execution or so a day, each dutifully added to the new, fresh tally of the dead.

Mayor Reyes Ferriz attempted to go about his responsibilities as if nothing more were amiss, as if he had not received the Christmas warning that something grave and malevolent was coming. And as difficult as it was to preside over a city whose death toll had an inexorable insistence, there were other duties that required his attention: the incessant meetings, the petitioners to be received, the ribbons to be cut, the budgets to be examined, the city council members to be negotiated with, and the ever present city and state political currents with which to contend. There was no shortage of things to demand the mayor's attention, to take his mind off the prognostication that the federal intelligence officer had recently delivered that night in his office. And when his mind veered back to it, there was an enforced passivity that was disquieting: there was nothing for the mayor to do but to wait.

■ ■ ■

If on the surface Juárez had the look of any bustling border city, in early 2008 one event provided a window into the narco-world that lay just beneath that misleading appearance. On Wednesday, January 16, 2008, a vehicle loaded with 985 kilos of marijuana rolled out of Juárez and across the Bridge of the Americas into El Paso, Texas. The prior day, a man named Saulo Reyes had paid an individual posing as an Immigration and Customs Enforcement agent $4,250 in cash as a down payment to ensure the passage of the load. Reyes had been introduced to the man in November and for almost two months they had been negotiating the deal. Once safely across, the shipment had been delivered to a home in Horizon City, a suburb of El Paso.

The following day, near eight o'clock in the evening, Saulo Reyes and the would-be ICE agent met again, this time in an El Paso parking lot. Reyes paid the man an additional $15,000, which was the balance due for the load that had crossed the previous day. The two men lingered for a few minutes, discussing Reyes's plans for future shipments, when suddenly federal agents appeared as if from everywhere at once, swooping down to arrest Reyes. Unbeknownst to Reyes, over the course of the last two months all of the conversations between the two men had been recorded. The arrest of a man who was clearly a major player in the drug trafficking world made immediate headlines. However, one telling detail made the story all the more shocking: just three months earlier Saulo Reyes had been the director of operations of the Juárez Municipal Police Department.

■ ■ ■

I remember the first time I crossed from El Paso to Ciudad Juárez, walking across the Bridge of the Americas, or Puente Libre as it is known on the Mexican side, the same bridge Saulo Reyes's driver had used to ferry close to a ton of marijuana across to the U.S. By then the war had already begun. The city was low-slung on the horizon, and beneath me the fabled Rio Grande was but a pale version of itself as it flowed slowly toward the east down a concrete trough. From the bridge I could see the Immigration and Customs Enforcement security corridor along the American side of the river as one of their ever-present green-and-white SUVs moved at a snail's pace along the tamped-down dirt. Beyond, Ciudad Juárez lay spread out before me. The city seemed to be wrapped in a shroud of mystery and fear. From the apex of Puente Libre, Juárez's violence already felt more immediate. I knew that the city had become a dark crossroads where Mexico's narco-war was playing out, and that sinister reality permeated the air.

Juárez is spread out across the floor of the Chihuahua Desert, bounded on the west by a modest mountain range and on the north by the Rio Grande. In Mexico it has long enjoyed a reputation as a dynamic city whose people are innovative and entrepreneurial. A jump-off point for those wanting to cross the border into the United States, Juárez has no doubt drawn an unusually high mix of people with an adventurous bent. Juarenses are very attached to their city, even as it lacks the patina of glass and polished marble of downtown El Paso. In fact, prior to the eruption of the cartel war, even those with the requisite papers preferred their city to its U.S. counterpart.

Spring and fall can be glorious and temperate in the Chihuahua Desert but otherwise conditions in Juárez are harsh. Summers are interminable and hot; triple-digit temperatures parch the skin and all but the hardiest of drought-tolerant plants whither and die unless tended to daily. Winters are no better; cold and unforgiving, the desert winds blow through with a howl. Ironically, out of that harshness has grown a hospitable culture of hard-working and gregarious people.

In the 1980s, a boom in the assembly plant industry transformed the city profoundly and irretrievably. The demand for workers outstripped the local population and in the short span of two decades a wave of workers migrated from all over Mexico to work at the maquiladoras, as the assembly plants are called, and the city's population tripled to 1.3 million. In the 1980s and 1990s the city boasted near-full employment, though salaries were (and remain) meager. Juárez became one of the crown jewels of the Mexican economy.

Juárez natives will tell you that they grew up feeling safe in this city. It was always run down, full of desert dust, and architecturally lackluster, but the people were open and kind. In the summers, when the desert heat soared, people in the poorer neighborhoods (that is, much of Juárez), slept unafraid on their porches and rooftops and in makeshift arrangements out in the open air. In fact, in most of these homes, the only thing separating families from the world beyond in the summer was a screen door and a latch. Violence, to the extent that there was any, tended to be downtown where the bars stayed open, where prostitutes worked the streets or out of brothels, and where the shooting galleries and opium dens catered primarily to Americans. Most of that world was foreign to the average Juárez resident. Cartel-related violence was handled discreetly and the city was mostly shielded from its brutality even as most knew of its existence.

Downtown, in the old Zona Centro, one used to find the pharmacies, curio shops, restaurants, bars, and the doctors and dentists that once catered to the tourists who crossed the bridges from El Paso in a steady flow. The bullring and the bulk of the brothels were in this part of the city as well. The bullring remains, but most of the other businesses have closed, with the exception of the occasional shop that holds on to the hope that the Juárez of old will make a comeback after the current bloodletting ends. The violence has eviscerated the tourist sector just as it has ravaged everything else in this city.

■ ■ ■

At the time of his arrest, Saulo Reyes was already a well-known figure in Juárez. The son of a Protestant Evangelical minister, he was far from the stereotype of the gold-chained, western-attired, pickup truck–driving narco. Reyes dressed in Armani suits, wore Cartier watches, and drove sporty cars. Indeed, he had all the markers of a golden boy: he was a young, dynamic man of middle-class origins who had risen quickly up the city's economic and political rungs. At the age of thirty-five he was already a member of Coparmex Juárez, a powerful and influential business association similar to the American Chamber of Commerce, and he owned a string of Subway franchises, Kinsui Express franchises (specializing in Japanese takeout), and several Silver Steak restaurants. In short, in the eyes of those who knew him, or knew of him, Reyes was more likely to have been the subject of a *GQ* profile than a character around whom a *narcocorrido* might have been composed.

Saulo Reyes had reputedly come by his success partly under the tutelage of a man named Héctor "Teto" Murguía, who had preceded José Reyes Ferriz in the mayor's office, serving a three-year term between October 2004 and October 2007. It was Murguía who had appointed Saulo Reyes to be the director of operations of the Juárez municipal police in January of 2007, a job second in importance only to the police chief because it meant that Reyes was directing and supervising all police operations within the city.

By his own admission, Saulo Reyes had no preparation or background for such a position, but Murguía was apparently indifferent to that fact. The explanation that Murguía gave at the time of Reyes's appointment was that the city's business leaders wanted a civilian keeping close tabs on what went on within the police department in order to make the police more efficient and responsive. But everyone could see what lay behind that fig leaf. In fact, the day after the appointment was announced, the president of Coparmex publicly and vociferously distanced himself from it.

It was not the first time that Saulo Reyes and Héctor Murguía had been linked. Prior to his appointment as director of operations, Saulo Reyes had been the subject of an extensive exposé by *El Diario* that had revealed that in the first days of the Murguía administration Reyes had registered six companies with the state bureau of commerce in Chihuahua City, the state capital. The daily reported that in the fifteen months between October 2004, when Murguía had become mayor, and December 2005, fully a third of the city's purchases had gone to these companies, all of which were Sociedad Anónima (Anonymous Societies), which meant that the identities of the participating partners were protected behind a corporate shield. Three of these businesses shared the same physical address. When the *El Diario* reporter surprised the secretary occupying a desk at the location, she appeared bewildered and nonplussed, claiming that she did not know anything about the companies or what they did.

The exposé revealed that sometimes Reyes's companies had been awarded contracts outright, by "invitation" and without competition from other vendors. At other times, Reyes's companies had "bid" against one another, giving the false appearance that the city contracts had been subject to open, competitive bidding. It was a charade. The businesses were obviously mere shells through which Reyes and his silent partners were profiting nicely from the cozy arrangement with the city.

It was only a year after the publication of the *El Diario* exposé that Héctor Murguía appointed Saulo Reyes to be the police department's director of operations. At the time, José Reyes Ferriz was serving as the city's tax collector, and he remembers the day when Guillermo Prieto, the police chief, came to his office. Prieto and Reyes Ferriz had known one another for years because Prieto had taken law classes from Reyes Ferriz at the Autonomous University of Ciudad Juárez. They'd been friends ever since. "Prieto came to my office and said, 'Look, I don't like this Saulo Reyes situation,'" the mayor told me. The fact that Saulo Reyes knew nothing about police work troubled Prieto, but he also knew that Saulo Reyes was not trustworthy. Prieto told Reyes Ferriz that he'd made the decision to resign as chief if the appointment went through.

The next day, Saulo Reyes was sworn in as the director of operations as Guillermo Prieto looked on. The latter's grim expression said it all. Prieto waited a day or two before resigning, along with fourteen other commanders, administrators, and police department attorneys. Prieto would later allege that his resignation was prompted by Saulo Reyes pressing him to participate with the Juárez cartel, although at the time he told the local press that he was resigning "out of dignity," because he was "a professional" and it was evident that Saulo Reyes had no credentials for directing the operations of a law enforcement agency.

When Saulo Reyes became the number two man in the Juárez municipal police, many drew the inference that he was an operative of the Juárez cartel. He was leaving the world of business dealings and corporate franchises for a salary of eight hundred dollars a month. The word on the street was that he'd been placed there to be the cartel's moneyman: the Juárez cartel needed someone to manage the protection money that the municipal police picked up on their behalf, as well as to deliver payments to the police who were on the cartel payroll. But Juárez was a world where rumor and innuendo were commonplace, and those swirling about Saulo Reyes remained at the level of abstraction and gossip until his arrest in El Paso.

Saulo Reyes's arrest obviously posed problems for Héctor Murguía, who had his sights set on the Chihuahua governorship for 2010, when the term of the current governor, a man named José Reyes Baeza, was set to expire. In response, Murguía had done everything he could think of to distance himself from Saulo Reyes, blaming his appointment on pressures from Coparmex (despite the fact that from the start the organization had denounced the appointment); describing Saulo Reyes as a man with a compelling CV, "a successful business man who had a master's degree in finance" (suggesting, in other words, that he'd been appointed on the basis of his curriculum vitae, notwithstanding the fact that Saulo Reyes had no law enforcement credentials); or simply writing Saulo Reyes off as but "one of 8,000 employees in my city administration" (as if the man he had appointed second-in-command of the police department were as anonymous to him as an inspector in the sanitation department). In response to one journalist's questions, Murguía even sought to explain Saulo Reyes's behavior as an act of desperation that was perhaps due to his being a father: "Who knows what economic problems [he] might have? He's got a newborn daughter, that's what I know, and a little boy. Just look at this drama! This is a drama!" Murguía had exclaimed unconvincingly at a hastily convened press conference. But Murguía's attempts to distance himself from Saulo Reyes were disingenuous. Reyes had been anything but "one of 8,000 employees." Murguía and Saulo Reyes had had dealings with one another for several years, and there was no question that Murguía had taken a very personal role in imposing Reyes on the police department, prompting the resignation of fourteen officials, including the chief of police.

The precise unfolding of Saulo Reyes's relationship with the cartel remains unclear. There are those who claim that prior to his appointment to the police department Reyes had simply been a successful businessman. His insider deals with the city were easily rationalized. After all, such arrangements were the bread and butter of local, state, and federal politics in Mexico, where people traded favors, "lent" their names, and profited from family ties and social relationships as a matter of course. Everyone knew that reality. It was part of a business culture that, in the span of a single political term, could give some people world-class wealth at the expense of the good of the nation. For decades, if not for centuries, presidents, governors, mayors, and bureaucrats of every variety had used their moment in power for personal gain, ravaging the country in the process.

This kind of corruption has been hard for reformers to break. It is so deeply ingrained in the way institutions work and the expectations that people have of public service at all levels. New legislation requiring increased government transparency was just beginning to alter the ease with which such arrangements could be put into play. Indeed, that new transparency had helped *El Diario* put its story together (for example, a database of companies doing business with municipal and state agencies in Chihuahua was now accessible via Freedom of Information requests). But there was a long way to go before that culture of corruption could be changed.

The traditional structures of corruption had become a convenient and ready-made vehicle through which the cartels worked. They provided the indispensable mechanisms that gave the cartels free reign over ports and highways and airports as well as over broad regions that served as the cartels' staging areas. However, the narco-corruption that emerged from this culture was a different kind of creature—a creature engorged and emboldened by billions of dollars in drug profits, profits that surpassed by a large margin what any legitimate business could ever hope to bring to the timeless game of power and influence.

The people who wrote off Saulo Reyes's rise to economic success as part of the same old game argued that it was only after he took over as director of police operations that he became involved with the Juárez cartel. But the view that he was involved all along was much more plausible. Proponents of this second view argued that Reyes's extensive network of franchises and businesses were far from indications of the young man's entrepreneurial prowess. Rather, they suggested that behind Reyes's success lay the obvious hand of the Juárez cartel: that his businesses were part of the cartel's complex money-laundering network and that it was *that* relationship that "nominated" him for the job as the cartel's trusted moneyman within the police department.

Notwithstanding its size, Juárez is a small town. Mayor Reyes Ferriz knew who Saulo Reyes was and had interacted with him through business organizations such as Coparmex. Ferriz had always felt ill at ease around him. "I never trusted the man," Reyes Ferriz told me. Reyes Ferriz counted as one of his blessings that he had listened to his instincts when, as the newly elected mayor, he'd made the decision not to renew Saulo Reyes's contract. Instead, he reinstated Guillermo Prieto as police chief, the man who had resigned in January 2007 in protest over the Saulo Reyes appointment.

The Saulo Reyes affair exemplified the kind of corruption and insider arrangements that had historically pervaded Mexican government and politics. However, the age-old disease of corruption had gradually evolved, morphing into a more insidious phenomenon, a phenomenon that made drug cartel influence exponentially more powerful and corrosive than anything Mexico had ever known. There were those who would later accuse José Reyes Ferriz of the former vice, that is, of making insider deals, not so much as a matter of personal gain but as a matter of "honoring" the kinds of debts and obligations that come with working one's way to the top in politics. But Reyes Ferriz did not have the taint of the latter vice, the taint of this new creature, a creature so powerful and bold that it was on the verge of bringing a great country to its knees.

CHAPTER 3

A Meeting in Chihuahua

On January 17, 2008, the day following the arrest of Saulo Reyes in El Paso, a man named Patricio Patiño arrived in Chihuahua City, the state capital of Chihuahua, to confer with the governor and the state's attorney general. Patiño was one of García Luna's men; he was the undersecretary for police strategy and intelligence for the federal police.

Patiño's meeting with the state attorney general, a woman named Patricia González, was shrouded in secrecy and there had been considerable misinformation surrounding it, which only served to stir speculation. All morning, González's office had denied that the meeting was taking place at all. The governor, José Reyes Baeza, claimed that he had no knowledge as to where the meeting would take place, saying only that the state attorney general would announce it "at the opportune moment." Finally, reporters had been told that the meeting would take place in Juárez, 215 miles to the north, rather than in the capital city. It was all a ruse to minimize media coverage.

Patricia González and Patricio Patiño met in a private dining room at an upscale restaurant near the attorney general's office, which is where reporters tracked them down after they'd been tipped off about the location. As they left the restaurant following the two-hour meeting, the persistent journalists intercepted the officials. Patiño simply told them that he had no comment to make at the moment. González, visibly annoyed at the reporters' presence, offered only a terse statement wrapped in bureaucrat-speak to the effect that the two had discussed "strategy and intelligence issues." The Chihuahua attorney general did acknowledge that the state was experiencing "an upsurge" in violence between "two organized crime groups," but when specifically pressed as to whether or not El Chapo Guzmán had operatives in the state of Chihuahua, the attorney general flatly denied that possibility. The two officials were then spirited away by their security detail for a closed-door meeting with governor Reyes Baeza at the Palacio de Gobierno, the state government offices.

The heightened interest in the Patiño meeting had begun two days earlier, following a press conference in which governor Reyes Baeza had stated that federal intelligence had alerted him to the possibility of an impending eruption of violence between "two organized crime groups" (the phrase had obviously become the agreed-upon convention for referring to the Juárez and Sinaloa cartels). The impetus for that press release had been a dramatic shootout in Chihuahua City on January 13 in which a brand-new, silver-gray armored Audi, with tinted windows and no license plates, had been traveling at high speed on a freeway called Periférico de la Juventud, prompting a ministerial police patrol car to give chase. The passengers in the Audi had managed to put sufficient distance between themselves and the patrol car in pursuit that they were able to pull to a stop in the center lane and run across the freeway to a nearby upscale shopping mall, where a group of well-armed confederates were waiting. When two ministerial police officers exited their patrol car to give chase, they were cut down by a fusillade of gunfire, leaving them severely wounded.

Several things about the incident were perplexing. Chihuahua had long been a private reserve of the Juárez cartel, and a number of key cartel operatives lived in Chihuahua City. It was well known that the Perférico de la Juventud was patrolled by La Línea, the Juárez cartel's armed wing. This sometimes meant gunmen patrolling in SUVs, but just as often it meant the state ministerial police, who were controlled by the cartel. Inside the Audi the authorities found two AK-47s, hundreds of rounds of ammunition, and four cell phones. The scenario suggested that either there was a dispute within the cartel or, alternatively, that another cartel had entered Juárez cartel territory. It was at the press conference he'd called to address this incident that the governor had disclosed the federal intelligence reports in what became the first public statement in the state of Chihuahua about an impending cartel war. Thus, when rumors began circulating about the undersecretary's visit, many assumed that it had something to do with the governor's announcement.

Curiously, neither the governor nor the state attorney general had referred to either the Juárez cartel or the Sinaloa cartel by name in their remarks. José Reyes Ferriz, the mayor of the city most likely to bear the brunt of the prognosticated violence, was not notified of Patiño's visit, much less invited to participate. Neither was Reyes Ferriz later briefed about what had transpired during the meeting. The ordinary chain of command was that mayors did not typically deal directly with federal authorities (other than federal employees who might be stationed in their cities); those contacts were mediated through the offices of state governors. In addition, the Saulo Reyes affair had just broken the day prior to Patiño's visit, and it had already become a significant crisis in Juárez, one that was absorbing the mayor's attention.

Coincidentally, just a week prior to Patiño's arrival in Chihuahua and prior to the Saulo Reyes affair, Reyes Ferriz had formally requested that the governor send more state ministerial police to Juárez. Having ended 2007 with a record number of executions, the mayor was concerned about rising crime. It was obvious that Juárez needed reinforcements, and the normal recourse was for the mayor to request assistance from state authorities. However, the response to the mayor's request was anemic at best. He was told that the CIPOL (the crack state police "intelligence" group, which is charged with managing major law enforcement contingencies in the state of Chihuahua) was otherwise occupied in the Sierra Tarahumara, where cattle thefts were rampant. He was further told that "to the extent that it is possible" the state ministerial police would address his concerns. To Reyes Ferriz it was clear that he was getting the brush-off. Tensions were already becoming evident between the Juárez municipal government and the governor and the state attorney general, tensions that would only deepen as Juárez began to veer more definitively toward the abyss.

In an atmosphere defined by Patiño's silence and the equivocation of the state authorities, a lone voice appeared that seemed to have grasped the severity of the present circumstance from within the official posturing and half-statements. Juárez's *El Diario* published an editorial demanding immediate intervention by the federal government: "It is urgent that the words of the Federal Secretary for Public Security be made a reality," the editorial noted. "As Genaro García Luna said just yesterday: 'Where crime threatens citizens that is where the federal forces will be, protecting society and confronting the threat.'" *El Diario* went on to call upon federal and state authorities to "live up to their promises and responsibilities." There was something desperate in the tone of the editorial; it was an unmistakable plea for help.

■ ■ ■

Two weeks prior to Patiño's visit, Guillermo Prieto Quintana, the chief of the Juárez municipal police, arrived at the Juárez Police Academy. The academy is housed in a handsome, modern building whose gently curving, three-story entrance is constructed of Chihuahua-quarried, cream-colored cut stone. Tall brass letters and an imposing emblem identify the structure. The police chief was there to participate in a force-wide training due to new judicial reforms that were being instituted with great fanfare throughout the state. After almost a decade of wrangling and foot-dragging, the Mexican congress had finally passed a series of laws that ostensibly paved the way toward greater transparency in judicial proceedings, including oral arguments before judges, and brought to a halt the long-standing practice of corrupt behind-closed-door proceedings. The new guidelines were supposed to mark an end to the presumed-guilty-until-proven-innocent philosophy (a holdover from the days of the Holy Inquisition) that as often as not translated into abusive practices on the part of the police and innocent people languishing in over-crowded and stench-filled prisons.

The new judicial code ostensibly changed the role of the municipal police, who would now be responsible for securing and gathering evidence at crime scenes, activities that heretofore had been the exclusive responsibility of the district attorney's office, part of a byzantine and fractured law enforcement arrangement. Historically, the mission of the municipal police was merely "preventive"—they patrolled the streets and they could arrest people caught in flagrante delicto, but they were neither trained nor authorized to investigate crimes (that function was solely under the purview of the state police). The new role of the municipal police was characterized as "revolutionary"—it, along with new judicial processes, would result in more solved crimes and greater transparency in prosecutions as well as a positive impact on human rights, long a sore point when it came to Mexican law enforcement.

It was in this spirit of reform that Chief Prieto ceremoniously took a seat at a desk at the Juárez Police Academy as if he were just another fresh recruit. Later that day, Prieto's second and third in command, Director of Operations Juan Antonio Román and Supervisor of Field Operations Francisco Ledesma, respectively, would also come to the Academy to take part in the training. The police department's top brass were there to set an example, sending the rest of the force a message that the Juárez Municipal Police was making a fresh start and breaking with the old ways of doing things.

Francisco Ledesma was a young, snappy-looking thirty-four-year-old officer who, as the face of the municipal police in the community, was frequently out in the field. In fact, later that same day Ledesma attended a meeting involving some seventy angry and worried parents from working-class neighborhoods who were fed up with the local gangs that roamed the streets and tormented law-abiding residents at will. The gangs were partly a simple nuisance: neighborhood kids with nothing else to do but stand around on street corners drinking beer until all hours of the night, getting into minor mischief. But there was a more problematic and insidious side to the gangs. Some of them were responsible for the rash of burglaries, car thefts, and other crime that plagued the neighborhoods. The parents were also worried because they knew that these groups were often feeders for the city's more hardcore gangs. It was Ledesma's job to reassure the parents that the police department was on top of the problem and would be deploying their new gang task force, known as the Puma Group, into the neighborhoods to reduce gang-related crime and, specifically, gang violence.

The culture of neighborhood gangs was a widespread problem in Ciudad Juárez. Ledesma estimated that there were some eight hundred gangs operating in the city, whose active membership consisted of some fourteen thousand adolescents between the ages of thirteen and seventeen. The majority of these gangs, 521 of them according to Ledesma's Gang Taskforce, were operating in the eighty-six toughest *colonias*, where inter-gang violence and gang crime had become epidemic and a festering social problem. These neighborhood gangs were a fertile network whose ties and alliances formed the recruitment base for hardcore gangs like Los Aztecas, Los Mexicles, and Los Artistas Asesinos. The ubiquitous Juárez neighborhood gangs were thus the entry point for the gangs that, at the street level, ran the narco-show in Juárez.

For generations, neighborhood gangs had been a way of life in Ciudad Juárez, especially in the poorer *colonias*. Hanging out together night after night on the dusty, dreary corners of these enclaves, smoking cigarettes under the scraggly trees that grow in this desert climate while mangy, neglected dogs cast a weary gaze incubated life-long ties. One day, on our way back from a crime scene, Raymundo Ruiz and I drove through the *colonia* where he'd grown up. The streets here were mostly gravel, with an occasional ribbon of pavement bisecting the neighborhood here and there. Ruiz was a photographer for *El Norte*, one of the Juárez newspapers. "This hasn't changed since I was a kid," he volunteered as we made our way down a bone-dry arroyo that transformed into an engorged, angry flow when it rained. Houses sat up on the banks, their cinderblock walls raw and without so much as a trace of paint or decoration, surrounded by desert scrub brush and abandoned tires. A plume of dirt rose behind us until it was caught and fractured by the wind as we made our way down into the arroyo and up the other side.

Farther on, a man driving an old, battered truck spotted us and pulled to a stop midstreet. "*Que pasa*, Ray?" he shouted moments before he and Raymundo exchanged a knuckle-bump, slap-punch greeting through their respective windows. We were in Raymundo's gasping lime-green Toyota Tercel. The driver's-side mirror casing dangled against the door, barely attached by a single cable, the mirror itself long gone. The car's front grille was missing, too, exposing the black, dust-covered housing of the radiator fan. The front-right tire wobbled hideously any time our speed exceeded thirty miles per hour, which was frequently. The back seat was a pile of old newspapers, consumed water bottles, and a child's car seat (Raymundo has young children). A "Press" sign was taped to the inside of the car's windshield, giving Raymundo parking access at official events.

Raymundo's friend was indifferent to my presence. He told Raymundo that he'd been clean for a year and that he was going to church at a rehab center. "That's good," Raymundo said, right arm draped across the steering wheel as the Tercel sputtered, "that's real good."

After a few more minutes Raymundo said goodbye to his childhood friend and we pushed on through the wind-stirred dust along the streets of his old neighborhood. "That guy's been in and out of prison all his life,"

Raymundo volunteered once we were on our way. "He was a big-time user, doing petty chores for you know who," which I took to be a reference to the Juárez cartel. He never mentioned the cartel by name; that was part of his discipline. Raymundo paused. "He's never gotten his act together. I hope it sticks this time," he said.

Raymundo took advantage of the fact that we were in his old neighborhood to ring the doorbell of a woman who was his mother's best friend when he was growing up and whom he still visited on occasion. She was in her late seventies and lived in a small compound comprising several structures, one of which, like Raymundo's childhood home, was constructed from wood pallets lined with cardboard and tarpaper. The freestanding room was askew and appeared to be on the verge of collapse. The woman broke into a radiant grin the instant she saw that it was Raymundo at the door. She was wearing glasses with gray frames and had a matching shock of gray hair. Her ankle-length black dress gave the impression that she was a widow.

The three of us stood in the street in front of the house while Raymundo and the woman caught up on his brothers and sisters, the woman's children, and what had become of the neighborhood. "I'm sick of it," she volunteered. She told us that the gangs were out every night and that they had taken to pressing her to pay them $100 pesos a week (the so-called and increasingly ubiquitous *cuota*) in exchange for safe passage from the bus stop to her house. "It's extortion," she exclaimed. "I only make $300 pesos a week," she added. She told Raymundo that the neighborhood had gone to hell. The gangs were giving everyone the squeeze and there was no relief, she told us with a tone of resignation. It was an established fact that in Juárez the neighborhood and midlevel gangs now imitated the cartel strategies to increase their non-drug-related revenues. The difference was that the cartel gangs were extorting bigger businesses, while the neighborhood punks were extorting maquiladora workers, small shopkeepers, and street vendors.

Down the street we turned a corner and Raymundo pointed out graffiti marking a local gang's territory. "That gang's been here since I was a kid," he told me. At the time, there were gangs every two or three blocks—anywhere that there were ten or fifteen kids living in proximity. "We fought neighboring gangs, but it was fistfights, sometimes maybe sticks and rocks, that's the worst it ever got. We didn't kill each other," Raymundo volunteered. The gangs also didn't rob or terrorize the neighbors. On the contrary, the gangs were about the neighborhood; that was the source of their pride and identity. "Mostly we hung around and smoked cigarettes and drank beer and talked all night. Kid stuff." But some of Raymundo's friends had gone off in other directions, including some who ended up in "the business" and quite a few who ended up addicts, in jail, or dead.

■ ■ ■

Within the Juárez Municipal Police Department, Francisco Ledesma's charge, in part, was to address these facts of life given that gangs were a problem all over the city. Ledesma met with the group of parents on the morning of January 21, 2008, four days after Patiño's visit to Chihuahua. The meeting took place in a neighborhood that was indistinguishable from the one in which Raymundo had grown up. It was a neighborhood where parents worried about the gangs that were swarming all over the *colonia*, intimidating residents and acting as if they owned the territory. As the public face of the municipal police, Ledesma was the front man who did the meet and greets and told agitated parents and community leaders about the department's plan to rescue them from the grips of the gangs that were increasingly crushing them, threatening them even within their own homes. Ledesma talked as if he knew the ropes, as if he understood the game. He gave them facts and information about gangs and how they operated and what the Grupo Puma was going to do to take back the night in their communities—how it was going to put an end to the fear that had come to reign upon their lives.

But the next day Francisco Ledesma was dead. At 7:45 a.m., as he was leaving home on his way to his weekly Monday morning meeting at the Babícora police station, a commando team appeared out of nowhere and cut him down in a barrage of gun fire. Two men had waited patiently in a white Chevrolet Express van for Ledesma to leave his house. As Ledesma got into his car, the van pulled up and one of the men exited, briskly walking over to Ledesma before drawing a pistol from his coat pocket and assassinating the officer in full view of several witnesses, including a woman who was walking her children to the nearby elementary school. The van would be discovered a month later parked at a safe house; it had been stolen in El Paso almost four years earlier, in August of 2004.

Every morning, José Reyes Ferriz had a standing 7 a.m. phone appointment with his police chief in which Guillermo Prieto reported the events of the last twenty-four hours. The Ledesma assassination occurred after the daily report, so the mayor was not briefed on it. Instead, he was briefed on the murder of a police officer who had been hunted down and killed the day before. Later in the afternoon on the day of Ledesma's assassination, a third municipal police officer had been gunned down. His name was Julián Cháirez, and he came from a family with deep ties to the Juárez cartel. One of his brothers, also with the municipal police, had been assassinated a year earlier while traveling with a state ministerial police officer who was also executed (the then–director of operations, Saulo Reyes, had been unable to explain to reporters why it was that one of his agents had been traveling in a ministerial police vehicle, a fact that was highly irregular). In addition, acting on a tip from U.S. authorities, the federal police had apprehended another brother, Leonel Cháirez, in July of 2007. (American law enforcement had arrested an Immigration and Customs Enforcement agent named Margarita Crispín, whom they charged with accepting bribes from Leonel Cháirez, who was smuggling opium, cocaine, and marijuana across the border.)

The day's execution of police officers wasn't finished. That same afternoon yet another officer, this one with the state ministerial police, was gunned down in a hail of bullets that left fifty holes in him and in his vehicle. Almost concurrently, across town, there was an attempted assassination of a fifth law enforcement officer, a member of Agencia Estatal de Investigaciones, the state's investigative agency. He survived, but he was gravely wounded. In just two days, five law enforcement officers had been ambushed in Juárez and four of them assassinated. That tally nearly matched the total number of police killed over the course of the entire previous year.

■ ■ ■

At his offices at the Presidencia Municipal, José Reyes Ferriz was feeling in the grip of a process that would soon envelope and consume him. In the aftermath of the assassinations the tension was beginning to permeate the entire city. Some speculated that the wave of police executions was related to the arrest of Saulo Reyes in El Paso, suggesting that perhaps the Juárez cartel was executing those who had betrayed him. Alternatively, it was hypothesized that the cartel was executing anyone whom Saulo Reyes might have given up. A young man with a wife and family accustomed to upper-class comforts might easily be induced to talk under threat of years in prison now that he was in the hands of the DEA, so the thinking went. Perhaps the cartel was cutting its losses by executing people who might now be pressured into revealing more information about its operations, some speculated.

On January 23, two days after Ledesma's assassination, El Diario published the truth. It cited "unofficial sources" to the effect that "the criminal organization of El Chapo Guzmán" had authored the attacks against the police. The article further stated that the attacks were aimed at "destabilizing" the police force in order to wrest control of the plaza from the Juárez cartel. The El Diario article also revealed that a few days prior to the recent attacks on Ledesma and the others, El Chapo's people had contacted commanders in the ministerial and municipal police offering them an undetermined amount of money in return for their collaboration. Apparently, some them had not signed on.

It was evident that the police killings had not been arbitrary or random: someone had tracked these officers and taken them down one by one. The executions also appeared to be the work of professionals (they'd succeeded despite the fact that all of the assassinated police were experienced and armed). In fact, the executions were the beginning wave of a systematic, strategic plan to take over the Juárez cartel's territory by striking at the heart of its operational structure: La Línea, the cartel's enforcement wing, which was composed primarily of the Juárez municipal police and the state ministerial police. For Mayor José Reyes Ferriz, the waiting was over; the assault on Juárez by the Sinaloa cartel had begun in earnest.

CHAPTER 4

The Strategist

From the remove of Mexico City the developments in Juárez were being viewed with increasing alarm, drawing the attention of president Felipe Calderón's security cabinet, which met weekly at Los Pinos, the Mexican equivalent of the American White House. Guillermo Valdés Castellanos was one of the strategists charged with developing a policy for addressing what was taking place not only in Juárez (the violence was just beginning there) but also in the rest of the country. He was the director of Mexico's national security agency, the Centro de Investigación y Seguridad Nacional (or CISEN, its Spanish acronym). "There were three drug wars going on when this administration took office," Valdés observed the first time I interviewed him. He was referring to the violent battles and executions taking place between La Familia and Los Zetas in Morelia; between the Tijuana and Sinaloa cartels in Tijuana; and between Los Zetas/the Gulf cartel and the Sinaloa cartel in Nuevo Laredo. These battlegrounds had produced dramatic confrontations that were terrorizing communities and leaving many casualties all over Mexico, and not just in the most contested areas, because the cartels had extensive networks and operations in multiple states. Tijuana alone had claimed in excess of six hundred lives in 2007.

Valdés's office was deep inside a heavily fortified compound on the southern end of Mexico City—the exterior walls were twenty feet high, and there were checkpoints within the compound with heavily armed sentries guarding access to the building housing Valdés's office. My car was met at the gate and escorted to the compound by a CISEN vehicle. A tall man with a pale complexion, Valdés was in his shirtsleeves and not wearing a tie. He has a penchant for chain-smoking Delicados (filterless Mexican cigarettes that are more commonly smoked by factory workers and cab drivers than top government officials) down to a nub. In fact, Valdés seemed to eschew the bureaucrat's penchant for formalism. There was something disarming about his lack of pretension, given that he was one of the most influential men in President Felipe Calderón's administration.

Valdés mapped out the government's three-point strategy against the drug cartels: "Mexico has to recover lost territory," he told me. That required denying the narcos their current ability to operate at will. It was a telling point, for it acknowledged that significant cities and, in some instances, entire regions of Mexico, were effectively under the control of the *narcotraficantes*. The second part of the strategy against the cartels was to "break up their patterns and organizational structures." Finally, Valdés underscored the need to strengthen the country's institutions, especially law enforcement and the judiciary. Valdés concluded our first interview with a declaration that echoed what president Calderón was saying in his speeches to the Mexican public: "We're going to the root of the problem and there is no turning back."

The facts on the ground in Mexico made for enormous challenges in implementing the strategy that Valdés outlined that day at the CISEN headquarters. There were three basic tiers to Mexican law enforcement, though some of these had specialized units within them: the municipal police, the state ministerial police, and the federal police. Of these, the federal forces were considered the most reliable by far. For almost a decade, the Mexican government had been attempting to clean up the notoriously corrupt and infamous federal judicial police. Genaro García Luna had spearheaded those efforts during Vicente Fox's previous administration, which had created the Agencia Federal de Investigación, touted as the Mexican counterpart to the American Federal Bureau of Investigation. Cleaning up an institution that for decades had operated in collusion with organized crime when not operating as a criminal organization in its own right was a difficult and challenging task, and there had been several high-profile cases in which AFI agents were found to be working for the cartels. Nevertheless, García Luna moved forward with the implementation of a more professionalized federal law enforcement agency. Increasingly, AFI agents were required to have college degrees, they received better pay, and their careers in law enforcement were not dependent on the whims of new commanders who were changed out every six years with the election of a new president. All this created a more professional atmosphere within federal law enforcement, notwithstanding the intermittent successful efforts by the cartels to enlist the collusion of AFI personnel.

Felipe Calderón decided to focus on cleaning up the federal judicial police. They were consolidated under the Secretariat for Public Security and eventually renamed the federal police, with García Luna at the head, while the AFI remained the law enforcement wing within the federal attorney general's office. A major obstacle to the success of the federal police was the simple fact that there were so few of them: a mere sixty-five hundred officers throughout the country (perhaps ten thousand officers, if one included the agents temporarily assigned to the federal police from the army, CISEN, and other law enforcement agencies). García Luna set out to radically expand the force. By law, the federal police are only permitted to work criminal activity that falls within the federal purview, which includes things like organized crime, weapons, and explosives. Ordinary crime such as burglary, car theft, and murder (that is to say, the day-to-day work of local police forces), is outside the purview of the federal police except in cases where organized crime groups are committing these crimes. The federal government could send the federal police to do battle against the cartels, but one obvious problem was that their numbers were small, just 1 or 2 percent of the nation's law enforcement personnel. In addition, it was not always easy to differentiate organized crime from ordinary local criminal activity. If a man was executed in the streets of Juárez, for example, who was to say that it was the work of a cartel (thus bringing it under federal jurisdiction), as opposed to the work of a gang member assassinating a rival gang member in a territorial dispute or even simply a crime of passion (crimes falling under local police jurisdiction)? There were legal structures governing the activities of each of the three tiers of police work in Mexico, but, on a pragmatic level, these legal structures represented significant obstacles to effective law enforcement work given the character of what was taking place in the streets of Juárez, Tijuana, Nuevo Laredo, and many other Mexican cities where the cartels were creating significant challenges.

The restrictions on the state ministerial police and local municipal police forces posed similar but actually more grave problems. By law, municipal police, the police in Mexico's cities and towns, were not permitted to investigate crimes. That was considered outside of their area of operation. For this reason, municipal police forces were called "preventive" police, because their primary charge was just that: to prevent crime by patrolling the streets, to arrest people caught in flagrante delicto, and to respond when citizens called to report crimes. The state ministerial police forces were the law enforcement units charged with gathering evidence and collaborating with the district attorneys who oversaw the investigation of criminal cases. In other words, there were legal and structural impediments in place that ensured that police work in Mexico was arbitrary and profoundly inefficient, setting aside the matter of corruption. It was also the case that ministerial and, especially, municipal police were the lowest paid, the least trained, and the most susceptible to influence and corruption. Though the Juárez municipal police distinguished themselves when it came to corruption, corruption was a disease that had spread deeply into every facet of the country's municipal police forces. Even before the rise of the cartels, many of these police agencies had already been operating as criminal organizations.

One problem that the Mexican federal government faced, then, was that it simply lacked the law enforcement resources, in terms of both reliability and raw numbers, to take the now-declared war to the many states and regions where the drug cartels were operating. These were significant areas of the country where cartels functioned with impunity and where, typically, they were using municipal and state police forces as proxies and as a private reserve of foot soldiers to carry out myriad activities, from protection to transport to detaining and/or executing adversaries. From a strategic standpoint, in other words, the municipal and ministerial police forces in these areas were not only unreliable; they were, in essence, cartel troops. It was common knowledge that in the states where the drug cartels had the greatest presence, like Sonora, Sinaloa, Michoacán, Chihuahua, Durango, and Tamaulipas, among others, the cartels owned state and local law enforcement; in fact, over the years these police forces had become woven into the cartels' very organizational structures. From the standpoint of the stability and viability of the Mexican state, this arrangement had reached a critical point and there was no force in these areas to serve as a counterweight to the power and influence of the cartels. It was this circumstance that dictated another key strategic decision by Calderón's government: the use of the Mexican Army. The army was the only recourse available to the Mexican government, given that the federal police had insufficient numbers to assume what would have otherwise been its natural role. The army had the numbers (approximately 240,000 troops), and it was far less compromised (though not altogether untainted) by the corrosive influence of the drug cartels.

By 2007, the Mexican cartels had attained unprecedented power. They had emerged as the most important players in Latin American drug trafficking, and, as a function of the massive infusions of American drug profits that were pouring into their coffers, they had unprecedented resources at their disposal. Yet, at that very juncture, the Mexican government lacked the law enforcement resources to carry the fight to the cartels. As the federal government launched a massive effort to recruit and train an expanding federal police force, the army was thrown in as a stopgap, interim measure. Calderón and his security cabinet hoped that this would buy them time, giving them a chance to develop the federal police and begin cleaning up the ministerial and municipal police forces. The latter, as the Juárez experience was about to make clear, would prove to be a daunting challenge.

It has been suggested, both within Mexico and outside of Mexico, that a significant factor influencing Calderón's decision to declare war against the cartels was his narrow victory in the 2006 Mexican presidential election. Such a thesis fails to acknowledge the real problems facing Mexico in relation to the drug trade and the emergent power of the cartels and their control over significant portions of Mexico. The fact is that whomever succeeded president Vicente Fox in 2006 was going to have to address the newfound power of the cartels. They had been a force in Mexico for decades, but their strength and influence had entered a new era without parallel. This was, in part, Guillermo Valdés's message.

In the spring of 2008 the American private intelligence firm Stratfor Global Intelligence, issued a white paper titled "Mexico: On the Road to a Failed State?" Stratfor noted that federal police, from low-ranking agents to senior officials, were being assassinated in attacks both in Mexico City and in the countryside, "posing a strategic problem for the Mexican government." The intelligence group further observed that multiple well-armed organized groups had emerged in various parts of the country and that these groups were fighting among themselves as well as fighting the government. The Stratfor report estimated that the drug cartels were collecting approximately $40 billion a year (though they acknowledged that it was impossible to know with certainty how much money was coming into cartel coffers), enough money to increase competition, and therefore violence, amongst themselves, as well as plenty of money to bribe and coerce police and other government officials. In Stratfor's view, the picture amounted to a prescription for a "failed state," that is, a state where institutions are so dysfunctional, if not under the outright control of criminal elements, that the state could no longer function as a state. The Stratfor report also added this interesting bit of analysis in summing up the stakes: it noted that in 2007 Mexico had exported approximately $210 billion worth of legal goods to the United States. By this accounting, the estimated $40 billion in drug money coming back to Mexico represented more than 16 percent of all exports to the United States. Just as important, the article went on to note, was that while the $210 billion was divided among many businesses and individuals, the $40 billion was concentrated in the hands of just a few fairly tightly controlled cartels. The long-term implication of this state of affairs might well be that the cartels would become so powerful as to be beyond the government's ability to rein in or otherwise control. For Calderón and for Mexico, the time was now. By the spring of 2008 the crisis went beyond politics— except for the fact that within Mexico's budding democracy politics was as hard and unforgiving as the cartel wars themselves.

Everything that could be said about Mexico's national crisis in relation to the drug cartels applied to Ciudad Juárez by many orders of magnitude. As the Mexican government began to roll out its intervention in Juárez, it became clear that getting to "the root of the problem," as Guillermo Valdés, the head of the CISEN, had said, would prove to be much more difficult than anyone imagined. In Juárez the disease was so entrenched and insidious that even the federal government's top intelligence operatives had difficulty wrapping their minds around it.

CHAPTER 5

Public Relations

The Monument to Fallen Police in Ciudad Juárez sits on a small knoll where two thoroughfares, Juan Gabriel (named for a native son turned Mexican pop idol) and Avenida Sanders, intersect. Its centerpiece is a bronze statue of a larger-than-life police officer standing on a cone-shaped pedestal. The officer is rendered in über-exactitude: wearing a sharply pressed uniform with a policeman's day-to-day instruments of work—a gun and spare ammunition clips, a baton, a radio. The officer's eyes are closed as if in deep reflection and his head is oriented toward a police cap lying on its side at his feet—a symbol for all the fallen comrades whose names are recorded on plaques on a semicircular wall that frames the statue. Along the perimeter, facing the wall, are three metal benches, like those found in almost every town square in Mexico, where visitors can sit and reflect on the fate that has befallen these public servants. The first time I visited the monument my impression was that there was something excessively self-conscious about the setting's solemnity.

The monument had been a year in the making when, in 2002, it had fallen to José Reyes Ferriz to inaugurate it by placing a commemorative plaque to mark its completion. At the time, he was serving a nine-month stint as interim mayor, having been appointed by the Chihuahua state congress following a mayoral election that had been nullified because of irregularities.

The ceremony must have been infused with irony: grave and full of pomp as the police band played something formalized and fittingly reverential, yet tainted with the awareness that the police force was so full of corruption and prone to abuse of power that most citizens feared the police rather than revered them. At the time of the inauguration of the monument there were twenty-one names on the memorial wall, but in many cases it was impossible to know which officers had died in the line of duty, defending the citizens of Juárez, and which had died because of their involvement in illicit activity, including work on behalf of the Juárez cartel. In any event, the 2002 inauguration was likely but another of those de rigueur appearances that fill up a mayor's calendar, like so many ribbon-cuttings chock-full of formalisms and speechwriter-driven turns of phrase.

■ ■ ■

José Reyes Ferriz was born on July 23, 1961, in Chihuahua City, the state capital. His father, José Reyes Estrada Aguirre, was a judge in Camargo, a small, picturesque colonial town of less than forty thousand inhabitants in southeastern Chihuahua. There were no hospitals in Camargo, so the judge sent his pregnant wife to live with his mother in Chihuahua City until José's birth. The legendary General Práxedes Giner Durán, also from Camargo, was a close family friend. The general had fought in the Mexican Revolution as part of Pancho Villa's famous División del Norte (Northern Division, as Villa's army was called), and his exploits made him an icon, especially in his native Chihuahua. Partly riding on that fame, Práxedes Giner Durán had handily won the Chihuahua governor's race in 1962. The general then appointed José Reyes Ferriz's father to be his personal secretary, prompting the family to move to Chihuahua City before José had reached his second birthday.

The family took up residence on the second floor of José's paternal grand-mother's house, which was just two blocks from the Palacio de Gobierno. It was a large, rambling structure whose architecture was classic Mexican pro-vincial, with very high ceilings and an inner courtyard. José's grandmother was an avid gardener, and the house had lots of plants in pots and in the gardens. (The house still stands, but it has long since been converted into a school.)

When José got a little older, his father sometimes took him to the state capital building in the afternoons. His childhood memories include playing with his Hot Wheels cars on the parquet floors of the Palacio de Gobierno. When general Práxedes Giner Durán showed up, the *secretario general de gobierno*, who was also a good friend of José's father, would say, "Salute the general," and little José obliged. Then he'd say, "Sing the national anthem for him." José, who was not quite seven, already knew all twenty stanzas of the anthem, which he dutifully sang for the general under his father's proud gaze.

José Reyes Ferriz's father became a judge (he'd studied law in Mexico City) in Ciudad Juárez in 1968, when General Práxedes Giner Durán left the governorship. Reyes Ferriz was just beginning second grade. "My father always saw Juárez as a place of opportunity," he said. Along with the elder Reyes Estrada's real responsibilities, for a period he worked in his share of quickie divorces for American celebrities. (It has long been rumored that Elizabeth Taylor divorced Eddie Fisher in Juárez while she was making the movie *Giant* in Marfa, Texas. Although the evidence is sketchy, it was good PR for the city's tourism. Anthony Quinn did obtain a divorce there in December of 1964.)

The young José Reyes Ferriz was close to his father, whom he describes as a friendly, amiable man with a firm sense of duty. "He was a very serious person even though he was outgoing," the mayor recollected. From an early age, father appeared to be grooming son for politics. "I'd go out with him and he'd approach the city as if he were the mayor," Reyes Ferriz told me. His father would point out parks that needed to be redesigned, or repairs that streets required, or problems with how neighborhoods were going up. "He had that kind of an eye and he brought it to bear to everything he did," Reyes Ferriz remembered. His family was also prone to dinner conversation that spanned everything from local political skirmishes to issues of national and international importance. Both of his parents were very interested in politics and government affairs, and the family culture in their home was suffused with those topics.

Sundays the Reyes family ate together. "Once a month or so we'd go to a restaurant called Las Vacas," Reyes Ferriz remembered. The establishment specialized in tripe ("Delicious!" the mayor exclaimed) and the proprietor was a well-known butcher whose shop was next door to the restaurant. It was a very rustic, no-frills place with a concrete floor and wood chairs and tables. Each table had a small metal hibachi-type burner with glowing charcoal to keep the tripe warm. "It gets very greasy and it loses its flavor if it gets cold," Reyes Ferriz noted. The tripe was served with avocado, salsas, and fresh tortillas. "That was it. And we drank bottled Cokes." The manager of Las Vacas was none other than Rafael Muñoz, who, along with Rafael Aguilar and Gilberto Ontiveros, would soon found the Juárez cartel in the 1970s. "I saw him many times," Reyes Ferriz told me. "He was a normal guy, just the restaurant manager. None of us imagined anything." In the Juárez of the 1970s, with the Juárez cartel emerging as a powerful force, it was commonplace to see people like Rafael Muñoz, Rafael Aguilar, and Gilberto Ontiveros out and about even as people came to know who they were and what they did.

With the exception of a second-grade stint at Catholic school where he was taught by nuns, José Reyes Ferriz's education was in the city's public schools. He attended El Chamizal high school, which was on a parcel of land that Mexico had recovered from the United States amid great fanfare in the 1960s. The school was in a building that had once served as a U.S. immigration detention center prior to reverting to Mexico. El Chamizal was in the shadows of the El Paso skyline and the border was a short walk away. "There were almost no border guards in those days," Reyes Ferriz remembers. If he had a free period he and his friends would cross the bridge into El Paso to eat at McDonald's (there were no McDonald's restaurants in Mexico at the time), and after school they'd cross again to go bowling. "All you needed was your passport, there were no lines to speak of," he recalled, contrasting it with the present-day congestion at the international bridges.

The future mayor of Chihuahua's most important city spoke flawless

English. "My father forced us to watch English programs on television," the mayor recollected. "When the family moved to Juárez in 1968 we had a black-and-white Zenith television and my father wouldn't allow us to watch channels two and five, the Mexican channels, so that we'd only watch English-language TV." It wasn't until high school that he took his first English class, but by then he'd already learned the language. He later learned some French while attending college at the University of Texas at El Paso (UTEP) in 1982 and 1983.

After graduating from high school, José Reyes Ferriz went to aviation school at the renowned FlightSafety Academy in Vero Beach, Florida (the same flight school that the late John Kennedy Jr. attended), before going to work for Vitro (an enormous Mexican glass company) as a commercial pilot. While he was at aviation school, his father was elected mayor of Juárez (his term ran from 1980 to 1983).

José Reyes Ferriz would have been glad to make a career as a commercial pilot, but in 1982 Mexico suffered a profound economic crisis and Vitro downsized. Twenty-one-year-old José Reyes Ferriz returned home to Juárez to take some classes at UTEP and attend law school at the Universidad Autónoma de Ciudad Juárez, where his interest in politics was again rekindled. His father's successor as mayor was a man named Francisco Barrios Terrazas. Barrios's party, the Partido Acción Nacional, or PAN, had never before won office in Juárez. Chihuahua, like the rest of Mexico, belonged to the Partido Revolucionario Institucional, or PRI (in fact, the PRI had run Mexico since the end of the revolution, even though already in other northern states the PAN had begun to mount some successful challenges—the first signs of a budding democratic emergence in Mexico). Francisco Barrios was an engaging, charismatic man who later became the first member of the PAN to win the governorship of Chihuahua as well.

The PRI's hegemony had been so complete that Barrios's win shook the state. José Reyes Ferriz was a member of the PRI youth organization and as a project he set out to try to study how Barrios had won the mayorship by analyzing his campaign. "I came to realize that the Francisco Barrios campaign had followed the blueprint laid out in *The Making of the President*, step by step," Reyes Ferriz recalled, referring to the Pulitzer Prize–winning and hugely successful Theodore White book about the 1961 campaign to put John F. Kennedy in the White House. Reyes Ferriz then studied political marketing and began consulting on PRI election campaigns.

Reyes Ferriz's big break came in 2001, when irregularities led to the nullification of the Juárez mayoral election. It was the state congress's job to name an interim mayor until new elections could be held, and Reyes Ferriz not only had name recognition and party bona fides with the PRI (which still controlled the state congress), but he had also taught some of the PAN delegates when they were law students, so they knew him. The fact that he had a popular fifteen-minute radio talk show covering the financial markets and other topics of interest to the business community also broadened his support. Three candidates for the interim spot had been placed before the state congress and José Reyes Ferriz thought he was a long shot. "I called my mother and told her they'd put me in as a filler," Reyes Ferriz recalled. But the evening of the decision, as the clock neared midnight and he sat watching a movie in his pajamas, he received a call from the governor's representative in Juárez to tell him that he'd won the most votes. It was during that nine-month stint as interim mayor that Reyes Ferriz had inaugurated the Monument to Fallen Police.

■ ■ ■

For José Reyes Ferriz, the memory of the inauguration of the Monument to Fallen Police was just one among a blur of obligatory events that public office imposes on a mayor's schedule. He had neither been to the monument nor thought about it again for six years until early January 2008, when he'd come to lay a floral wreath as part of an annual event honoring the city's fallen police officers. Then, just a week later, a group of men exited a dark sedan in the dead of night and crept up to the monument, where they left a "narco-message" written on a white sheet of poster board. The message was simple, divided into two sections: at the top, in the smaller of the two sections, someone had written in neat if uneven Magic Marker calligraphy, "For those who did not believe." The word "not" was underscored several times with lines of decreasing length that reached a point below the word, forming an inverted triangle and giving the gesture the stylish flair that one might expect from a child in elementary school. Beneath this heading were the last names of five dead Juárez municipal police officers: Cháirez, Romo, Baca, Cháirez, and Ledesma. They were listed chronologically according to when they had been assassinated.

It had only been five days since Francisco Ledesma's execution. All of the men on the "For those who did not believe" list had been cut down in a hail of bullets save one, Romo, who had been *levantado* ("lifted") in June of 2007, never to be seen again. He had apparently been one of the early victims of the Sinaloa cartel's intelligence operation, in which they had been "lifting" key Juárez cartel operatives and torturing them for information at clandestine locations before killing them. The bodies of people who were lifted sometimes turned up in trash-filled vacant lots or in some dark corner of the city, but as often as not they simply disappeared altogether without a trace. If Romo's family had held out hope that he'd turn up alive, those hopes were dashed by his appearance on the "unbelievers" list.

Just below Francisco Ledesma's name, the heading "For those who still do not believe" marked the second section of the narco-message. Beneath that heading were the names of seventeen other Juárez municipal police officers, next to which were noted the precincts in which they worked and their code names. The name at the top of this second group was listed as "Román Z-1." The author of the poster had underlined Román's name in red and placed a red cross next to it. Román's was the only name highlighted in this fashion. Antonio Román was the operational director of the municipal police, the second in command, who just a few weeks earlier had sat next to Ledesma at the Police Academy when they'd participated in the course on the new judicial procedures.

In Chihuahua, the two law enforcement organizations most associated with the workings of the Juárez cartel were the state ministerial police and the Juárez municipal police, of which the latter was the more important. The officers working for the cartel within each of these agencies were known as La Línea, or "The Line." For days now, several state ministerial police commanders had been receiving anonymous calls to their private cell phones warning them "not to take sides." Whatever ambiguity there may have been regarding the meaning of those calls was resolved on that morning of January 27, when the narco-message left at the Monument to Fallen Police was discovered—all of the officers on the "For those who still do not believe" hit list belonged to the municipal police. It was apparent that Sinaloa cartel operatives were trying to create fissures within La Línea by going after the Juárez municipal police, the core of La Línea, and warning the state ministerial police to stand clear. The fact that the Sinaloa people had the personal cell phone numbers of the state ministerial police commanders was an indication of their effective intelligence work. What the narco-message made clear is that the five officers had been killed as part of a deliberate effort to neutralize La Línea. The narco-message was, in essence, a public declaration of war.

■ ■ ■

The problems within the Juárez police seemed to evolve with every day that passed, like a puzzle or a conundrum that takes on new dimensions of complexity the deeper one explores its contours. For generations in Mexico the idea of corruption within police forces has simply been a given, a fact so pervasive and universal that it was accepted as a matter of course, as a reality of life. But what was going on within the Juárez police force took the familiar paradigm to an entirely different level.

Reyes Ferriz first grasped the extent of the problem not long after he assumed office on October 6, 2007. At the time there were an estimated one thousand *picaderos* in the city, the so-called "shooting galleries" where addicts got their drugs and sometimes went to get high. They operated openly in many of Juárez's working-class neighborhoods. During Reyes Ferriz's campaign in the spring and summer of 2007 he had given speeches about attacking the *picaderos*. "I started getting messages saying, 'Don't even think about it,'" Reyes Ferriz told me one afternoon in his office. "The police would tell people close to me: 'Tell the candidate not to get involved in this.'"

Once elected, Reyes Ferriz instructed his newly appointed police chief to move on the *picaderos*, but the difficulty of the situation became immediately evident: "I was at home one night when Guillermo Prieto called. 'We have a problem,'" the police chief said. The police had arrested four suspects and were in the process of taking them to a nearby precinct when four Hummers had arrived. "They were brand new, and there were sixteen to eighteen guys with automatic weapons in them," Reyes Ferriz recalled. "They surrounded the patrol cars and demanded that we turn over the people we'd detained." "What do we do?" the police chief had asked the mayor. "Release them," was Reyes Ferriz's reply. "They're just going to kill the police."

What had most troubled Reyes Ferriz about the incident was the narcos' brazenness; he found the ease with which they displayed their power in public and their utter disregard for municipal authority to be revelatory. And there was something else: it was impossible to avoid the troubling suspicion that perhaps some of the police officers had themselves alerted the Juárez cartel to the operation as it was taking place.

"That's when we saw clearly the nature of the situation," Reyes Ferriz would later recollect. The police were in the hands of the drug traffickers. And the narcos had vehicles, automatic weapons, and the capacity to mobilize quickly and at will. "We'd only been in power one month . . . That's when the light went on in my head. . . . I'd known that the police were infiltrated, but the extent to which they had been delivered . . ." The mayor paused midsentence as if to transmit the full weight of his bafflement. He'd come to understand that the narcos controlled virtually everything within the force.

■ ■ ■

The "unbelievers" listed on the narco-message were municipal police who apparently had not accepted the fact that "La Gente Nueva" (The New People, as the Sinaloa operatives in Juárez sometimes referred to themselves) were now a force with which to be reckoned. The prevailing assumption was that the officers on the list were aligned with the Juárez cartel, but it was impossible to know with certainty that every officer on the list was a narco-cop; some may have been on the list because they had not acceded to the Sinaloa pressure.

It was clear that an operation was underway for control of the Juárez municipal police. For Reyes Ferriz, the post-Christmas meeting in his office with the federal intelligence officer, just a month earlier, was taking on a different meaning. Far from an abstract possibility, that war was now something irrefutable and concrete, a shift captured in the bullet-riddled bodies of the recently assassinated police turning up dead in the streets of the city.

The Sinaloa message targeted the shock troops of the Juárez cartel. La Línea served the cartel in myriad ways. Their most important function was that they were the cartel's muscle: they coerced and they threatened people, they lifted and they assassinated people as directed by the cartel. La Línea enforced discipline and settled scores, and in Juárez they were deeply feared by the citizenry because of their ruthlessness and brutality. At the time, the municipal police were the only force in the city. There were but a handful of state ministerial police or federal police, and although the army had a garrison in the city, they only patrolled the countryside. Thus, whoever controlled the police, controlled the city.

The Sinaloa cartel was targeting the Juárez police as a raw military move: attempting to defeat its enemy by eviscerating its forces. They viewed the municipal police both as an obstacle and as a strategic asset. If Sinaloa succeeded in taking over the police by "turning" its members (by force and intimidation or by offering sweeter deals), or if it could insert its own operatives into the force, the Juárez *plaza* would belong to them.

■ ■ ■

There was something haunting about the poster board left at the monument. The calligraphy, in particular, was evidence of its creator—obviously a person in some clandestine safe house who'd followed instructions like a schoolboy doing homework. It was somehow different from the tortured bodies and bullet-ridden corpses; the narco-message lying inertly at the monument, anchored by a large stone so as not to be blown away by the desert winds, bore the mark of something more personal. That morning, when Reyes Ferriz went to the monument to see the narco-message for himself, he found the experience unsettling. "We had never seen that kind of a communication from the cartels," the mayor would later tell me.

The narco-message turned out to be a public relations coup. The following day every newspaper in Juárez carried the story on its front page and it was the lead story on every television station. As a piece of public relations the narco-message was a stroke of genius: in one gesture the Sinaloa cartel had boldly announced its presence in the city.

The wreath that Reyes Ferriz had laid during the recent ceremony at the monument was still there, the flowers now withered and desiccated. One of the reporters covering the narco-message, apparently unaware of the recent wreath-laying, had written that detail into his story, suggesting that the narco-commando had left the dead flowers as some sort of a symbolic statement. That's how things went in Juárez. It was often impossible to tell facts from people's imaginings. Fantasy readily became entwined with reality.

Monument to Fallen Police, Ciudad Juárez. Photo copyright © Ricardo Ainslie.

■ ■ ■

Notwithstanding the sway that the Juárez cartel had over the city, I found no one over the course of countless interviews who suggested that José Reyes Ferriz had links to the cartel. The mayor claims to have never had one of those legendary *plata o plomo* (silver or lead) moments where he was offered money under the penalty of death if he did not accept what was being proposed. But early on there had been certain interactions that appeared to be cartel soundings. After Reyes Ferriz had won the mayoral election, but prior to his taking office, someone had come to him saying that there were "rumors" that he was going to sell the police. Reyes Ferriz took this to be a thinly disguised effort to feel him out. His response was to contact several attorneys who were known to represent the cartel's interests in the city and tell them that such rumors were mistaken. "The problem with organized crime," Reyes Ferriz would later tell me, "is when you accept money from them and then don't deliver." He wanted to set the record straight and prevent any "misunderstandings" from the outset.

When I subsequently asked the mayor why the Juárez cartel had permitted his election, his answer was simple: "They didn't need me. They thought I wouldn't be an issue for them because they already had control of the municipal police," he said. Later, I had the opportunity to interview a person who had worked with Amado Carrillo Fuentes, the man who had transformed the Juárez cartel into Mexico's most powerful cartel back in the 1990s. I asked him the same question. His response was different: "They thought he was going to be weak," he said. "They thought they'd either be able to control him or that he'd steer clear of them and give them free rein." Perhaps the incident with the Hummers had solidified that perception, given that the mayor had instructed the police chief to back off. If so, it was a premature reading; the mettle of José Reyes Ferriz had yet to really be tested.

■ ■ ■

By the end of January, with the assassination of several police officers, including Francisco Ledesma, the number-three man in the department, and with the narco-message at the Monument to Fallen Police, the extent of the problems within the Juárez municipal police took on new urgency for Mayor Reyes Ferriz. And they also took on new complexity. Having a corrupt police force was one kind of problem, but having two cartels vying for control of the force was a different problem. Mayor Reyes Ferriz trusted his police chief, Guillermo Prieto, whom he'd known for many years. But beyond Prieto, the ground fell away precipitously in terms of the mayor's confidence in the police. There was no way of knowing who could be trusted. It all came down to a matter of faith.

CHAPTER 6

Patiño

lthough federal intelligence was signaling a potential increase in violence in Juárez, in January of 2008 federal authorities were primarily preoccupied with what was going on in other parts of the Mexican republic. For example, over the course of the previous two years they had dispatched some three thousand federal police to the state of Tamaulipas, bordering southeastern Texas, to help quell the violence that had been taking place there as Sinaloa cartel operatives battled the Gulf cartel in Nuevo Laredo, Matamoros, and other communities. At the time there were only a few dozen federal police stationed in Ciudad Juárez. Neither were the governor of Chihuahua or the state attorney general doing much to respond to what was taking place in Juárez; notwithstanding the fact that the prior year had set a record for executions, there were only eighty state ministerial police assigned to the border city, and their presence was halfhearted—the officers were all from Chihuahua City, which meant that during the week they were housed in temporary quarters, mostly local hotels, and they went home on weekends.

The emerging crisis in Ciudad Juárez prompted Genaro García Luna to send Patricio Patiño, the undersecretary for police strategy and intelligence for the federal police, back to Chihuahua on February 8, a Friday, for a follow-up visit. Patiño landed in the state capital where he had met with Patricia González, the state attorney general. As if to welcome the federal officer, two men were executed in Chihuahua City on the morning of his arrival. Patiño also briefed members of the state's Chamber of Deputies, making a declaration linking what had become a national epidemic of burglaries and theft to drug trafficking: "Robberies are eating the nation up alive," he declared. "Organized crime is a school where a criminal begins robbing hubcaps but his aspiration is to become a drug trafficker," Patiño added. He also made another striking revelation: he reported that approximately twenty-seven hundred people had been executed in drug-related crimes during the first fourteen months of the Calderón administration. Of those, only 3 percent of the bodies had been claimed by the victim's families. Either they feared reprisals or they feared drawing the suspicion of law enforcement agencies, Patiño speculated.

Following his meetings in Chihuahua City, Patiño boarded his federal plane and made his way up to Ciudad Juárez. Because the recent assassinations of police officers and the Sinaloa cartel's open threats had created a pervasive sense of alarm throughout the city, a security meeting had been organized that included the city's key business, civic, and religious leaders, in addition to Mayor Reyes Ferriz and Governor José Reyes Baeza. The meeting took place later that same day, at a large, upscale venue called Cibeles, on Tomás Fernández Boulevard, which hosted everything from quinceañera parties and weddings to the annual Ciudad Juárez Press Association Awards Ceremony.

When he stepped up to the podium at the Cibeles meeting, Patiño outlined the federal government's security analysis and strategy for the region. Specifically, he said that in Mexico the emerging war between the drug factions was no longer exclusively to control the border access points to American drug markets, but rather it was increasingly for control of specific neighborhoods, schools, and streets. Patiño said that competition over retail markets was spawning the spiral of violence throughout the country. Patiño also told the civic and religious leaders something that most Mexicans did not understand at the time, namely that gradually, over the course of the last decade, the country had ceased being merely a transit point for drugs and had become a significant consumer of drugs as well. "The cocaine that isn't being sold over there is staying here with us," Patiño noted, making reference to the United States. He observed that for the first time in Mexican history, cocaine consumption had become a national problem, from large cities to small towns.

This new epidemic of domestic cocaine consumption was the centerpiece of the federal government's analysis of the national crisis. The violence that was emerging on a national scale had as much to do with seizing and controlling retail drug markets as with the traditional efforts to control the border cities that were key access points to the American drug market. Patiño concluded his comments at the Cibeles meeting with the sobering observation that violence had spread to virtually every corner of the country: "No one is exempt from this maelstrom, but you can be certain that it is not a problem that is unique to Chihuahua." Places where historically it had been rare to find evidence of retail drug sales and violence were now facing those very problems. Even states like Yucatán, Campeche, and Aguascalientes, which had long enjoyed reputations for being among the most peaceful regions of the country, were facing similar challenges. "People in every state are being victimized [by drug crime]," Patiño noted.

One other observation that the federal intelligence officer made at the Cibeles meeting may have gone unnoticed by most in attendance. It had to do with the drug cartels' growing media and public relations sophistication.

Patiño noted that the cartels were beginning to use production techniques to enhance video material that they were disseminating via the Internet, tactics similar to those being used by insurgents in Iraq. "These videos are being used to sow fear among citizens as well as among the police," Patiño stated. Although he made no specific reference to it, it is likely that he was thinking, among other incidents, about the Sinaloa cartel's calculated, media-savvy "For those who do not believe" message at the Monument to Fallen Police just two weeks earlier. Virtually every newspaper in the country had given the incident extensive coverage.

Still at the podium, toward the end of his talk, Patiño turned to mayor Reyes Ferriz to pointedly urge him to clean up the Juárez municipal police. Before the assembled audience, Patiño offered to have the federal police administer "Confidence Tests" to the entire force: "If the mayor is in agreement, we need to see how ill the patient is so that we can give him the necessary medicine," he said. Confidence Tests included drug and psychological testing, polygraphs, and other tests to evaluate the honesty and reliability of police force members.

As Patiño spoke at the podium before the city's business, civic, and religious leaders, it would have been difficult to miss the fact that he was putting pressure on the mayor. The two men did not know one another; Reyes Ferriz had not participated in the Chihuahua City meetings. The situation suggested that the federal authorities were not exactly sure where Reyes Ferriz stood, a circumstance that may have been further accentuated because Reyes Ferriz belonged to the PRI, whereas president Calderón's party was the PAN. There was no ambiguity, however, regarding the audience's response to Patiño's remarks about cleaning up the Juárez police: a thunderous applause erupted from those in attendance. The people of Juárez were fed up with the status quo, and Patiño had touched on something deeply pent-up and charged. Everyone in Juárez knew what was going on within the police force. It was at that precise moment that Patiño chose to invoke the already-infamous Saulo Reyes affair: "We all lived, at a national level, the case of the ex–director of operations who was detained across the river," Patiño said. "And how is it that we weren't aware? No? So, that's what it's about," he concluded, referencing the proposal to clean up the police once and for all.

When Patiño returned to the proscenium, he and mayor Reyes Ferriz exchanged some brief words. "I happened to be seated next to Patiño," the mayor later recalled, making the encounter appear serendipitous. "I asked Patiño to send me some support and he said, 'I'm going to send you two hundred federal police.'" The promised reinforcements were nearly a three-fold increase over the number of federal police presently in the troubled city, and to Reyes Ferriz the promise of two hundred crack federal police seemed like an entire army.

Patricio Patiño made many astute observations during his speech in Juárez, and he was effective in outlining the challenges the Mexican state faced in relation to the drug war, but one thing that Patiño did not do publicly, either in his address or in the subsequent press conference, was promise a massive infusion of federal forces. On the contrary, during the press conference following his Cibeles talk, Patiño said that at present he saw no need to increase the current force level of five hundred federal police deployed throughout the state, noting that these forces were primarily engaged in intelligence work to support the state ministerial police and underscoring the strong spirit of collaboration that existed between the federal and the state police forces. While Patiño did indicate that there was a contingency force of two hundred federal police available for mobilization, especially to Ciudad Juárez, for reasons that are unclear he chose not to share with the press the commitment he'd made minutes earlier in his private conversation with the mayor.

While Patiño's speech drew ovations inside the Cibeles hall, outside the apparent reluctance on the part of the federal government to send a meaningful force drew an angry response from the press. One *El Diario* editorial headlined the question: "Who are they trying to hoodwink?" The piece chastised the federal Secretariat for Public Security, and, by implication, its director, Genaro García Luna, for coming into Chihuahua (by sending his emissary, Patricio Patiño) intent on convincing the state's citizens that the appeal for federal help was due to overblown concerns. The editorial also took the federal authorities to task given that, by their own admission, the police forces in the state of Chihuahua were under-equipped, poorly trained, and underpaid, making them vulnerable to corruption. "It's more than established that organized crime has infiltrated the police rank and file as well as their commanders," the editorial observed, specifically referencing, as a way of underscoring the point, the still-fresh arrest of Saulo Reyes in El Paso. Given this state of affairs, the need for federal forces was obvious.

Patiño appeared to be walking a fine line. What could not be said or acknowledged by the federal representative was that at that moment there were insufficient federal forces to address the emerging crisis in Juárez. Too many other cities were already in the line of fire. It seemed that Patiño had been dispatched to reassure the people of Juárez but was not in a position to deliver substantive assistance beyond the two hundred officers he'd promised the mayor, a force that, technically, was not an increase given that they were already allocated as reserves in the event of a crisis.

One comment Patiño made during the press conference especially incensed *El Diario*. The federal intelligence officer volunteered at one juncture that the state's crime problem was "more perceptual than real," noting that several other states had higher indices of violence when compared to Chihuahua. It was clear that Patiño had gotten tangled up in his own words, and the farther he went to try to explain himself, the deeper he dug himself into a hole. Patiño noted that 73 percent of the crime in the state was robbery, while only 1 percent was assassinations, prompting *El Diario* to editorialize with a big dollop of sarcasm: "So watch out for the thieves, but never mind the *sicarios!*" (the common term for hit men). Since robberies were under the purview of the municipal and state police authorities while organized crime (and, hence, cartel-related executions) fell under the purview of federal authorities, the Patiño statements were taken to mean that the federal government was sidestepping its responsibilities. In the end, Patiño's visit to Juárez failed miserably in its mission to reassure, drawing instead a flood of media criticism.

The federal government appeared to be vacillating. On the one hand, they had taken the very significant step of informing Mayor Reyes Ferriz and, in a separate briefing, Governor Reyes Baeza, that according to their intelligence sources, there was a coming war. On the other hand, they were not mobilizing meaningfully to face the anticipated cartel violence, which was already at the city's doorstep. It appeared that the federal government had yet to fully grasp the full implication of its own warning.

The two hundred federal police started to arrive two days after Patiño left Juárez. For José Reyes Ferriz, that infusion represented a meaningful intervention. The state government, by contrast, continued to put the mayor off, remaining noncommittal and dragging its feet about increasing the number of state ministerial police units in Juárez. One detail from Patiño's press conference seemed stuck in the mayor's craw. He'd learned that on Patiño's second visit a meeting had taken place in Chihuahua City, where the federal intelligence officer had met with the governor, the state attorney general, the head of the state ministerial police, and key state legislators. This was the second time in as many weeks that the mayor had been excluded from key meetings concerning the fate of his city. That fact did not sit well with Reyes Ferriz.

■ ■ ■

The arrival of two hundred federal police in Juárez in mid-February of 2008 at first seemed to catch the cartels off guard. There was a short-lived dip in the number of executions, as the cartels appeared to be taking a wait-and-see attitude toward this new development. But the respite was brief. Within two weeks that lull had completely evaporated.

José Reyes Ferriz was an avid soccer fan. Sometimes when he had work commitments that overlapped with important matches, his wife called in periodic updates. He also used soccer metaphors when describing important events. For example, he'd once described the momentous election of Vicente Fox to the Mexican presidency in 2000 (the first time a non-PRI candidate had won, considered by most Mexicans as the juncture when Mexico began to emerge as a true democracy). "It was as if Mexico had won the World Cup," he said.

On the 23rd of February, a Saturday afternoon, the mayor was watching a soccer match on television when the broadcast was interrupted. "They cut to a firefight that was taking place on the street right outside of the television station," he recalled. What viewers saw on their TV screens was *sicarios* firing 50-caliber machine guns at one another in broad daylight on one of the city's main thoroughfares, which was lined with family restaurants chock-full of patrons. At the end of the skirmish, three of the establishments' walls were pocked with bullet holes but, miraculously, no civilians had been injured.

The incident betrayed a chilling indifference to the innocent people who might be caught in the crossfire. The cartels also evinced the kind of battlefield tactics typically associated with disciplined military units: "They left with their people, with their wounded and with their weapons," the mayor remembered. The cartels were acting as if they owned the city and feared no one. "They even took their wounded to Star Medical hospital," the mayor added with a tone of incredulity. Whatever the initial deterrence, it was obvious that the cartels were not the least bit intimidated by the newly arrived contingent of federal police.

CHAPTER 7

La Cima

On a cold winter night, I traveled through neighborhoods on the poor northwest side of town, toward the city center. My route took me through La Cima, Juárez's legendary drug quarter where for decades American soldiers were regular customers. No more. The city's violence had forced American military authorities to declare Juárez off-limits to military personnel. La Cima sits at the top of a rise on the western side of the city, a barrio in the hardcore Altavista neighborhood. Any given evening a slow drive through La Cima (meaning "the top" or "the crest") offered many an opportunity to buy hits of cocaine or heroin or any other drug. A green pickup truck just ahead of me pulled to an abrupt stop midstreet in front of a house, and a runner delivered a small packet to the car window, drive-in style. The two men in the front seat of a battered, white Dodge van had chosen to pull over. They parked, and a runner appeared at the driver's side window to take the order. Other people simply walked into one or another of the *picaderos*, where they could do their cocaine or heroin—syringes available for the asking—and hang out on the lumpy, moldy, stained mattresses scattered about until they came down enough to go home. No one would bother them. I spotted a young adolescent boy standing on the rooftop of a house on the corner; he was no older than twelve or thirteen. Kids like him were known as "falcons," or "whistlers," or "posts," and they patrolled from the rooftops or other points with panoramic views, where they scanned the streets that ran through the neighborhood and sounded the alert when the army or (non-complicit) police made a pass through the area.

This barrio had been the heart of the Juárez drug world for decades, but these days there were *picaderos* all over the city. Some were formal, that is, in houses and buildings, others informal—vendors, for example, who otherwise sold burritos or fruit or juices from small stands and mobile carts, or pushers who hung around parks and street corners. At least in Juárez, the thesis that Patricio Patiño had presented at the Cibeles security meeting that February in 2008, in which he'd argued that retail drug markets and domestic drug consumption were the new scourges of Mexico, was plainly in evidence. The *picaderos* were booming in Juárez, and the addicts were local. Juárez now had the highest concentration of drug addicts in all of Mexico.

There had been roughly one to two hundred *picaderos* in the city until 1994, when the U.S. government launched Operation Hold the Line in El Paso in an effort to more aggressively intercept undocumented workers attempting to enter the United States. Whether by design or not, the operation had a direct impact on drug smuggling; it became more difficult for the cartels to move product across the river. In the span of just a few months, the number of *picaderos* in Juárez doubled to four hundred. There was a clear-cut cause and effect: in response to Operation Hold the Line, the cartel had begun paying its lieutenants partially in product, which in turn had to be converted into cash. That was the force behind the sudden explosion of retail drug markets all over the city (indeed, the country). By 2007, there were approximately two thousand *picaderos* in Juárez, depending on what authority you asked. It was anyone's guess what the true number was, but they were everywhere. Juárez, a city that historically had catered to visiting customers from across the river, was now swimming in cocaine, heroin, and local addicts.

There were essentially four tiers to the Juárez cartel's operations. At the top were the capos and the lieutenants and their immediate people. A significant part of their work centered on the logistics of getting Colombian cocaine as well as Mexican-origin drugs across the border. Then there was La Línea, comprising the state ministerial police and the Juárez municipal police, who were the enforcement wing of the cartel. Beneath them were Los Aztecas, Juárez's most powerful street gang. And, finally, below Los Aztecas were the scores of lesser gangs that Los Aztecas controlled. The cartel outsourced the local distribution and retail sales to Los Aztecas. The people selling drugs on the streets were not cartel members, they were mostly poor, unemployed neighborhood people who occupied the very bottom of the hierarchy; they were utterly expendable.

Los Aztecas had their origins in American, especially Texan, prisons, where incarcerated Mexican and Mexican-ancestry inmates banded together to run prison rackets. Many gang members were from the Barrio Azteca in El Paso. Others were from Juárez and other parts of Mexico. The U.S. government had begun deporting many of the Mexican prisoners to Juárez, where they maintained their ties to their Barrio Azteca allies in El Paso. As Los Aztecas were again imprisoned in the enormous Juárez city prison (the Centro de Rehabilitación Social, or CERESO), they eventually took control of it, from which they managed a great deal of the criminal activity in the city. Mexican prisons are notoriously porous, and the Juárez CERESO was especially so. Between authorized conjugal visits and widespread corruption of guards and wardens, Los Aztecas had the run of the prison and ready access to what went on beyond it.

By early 2008 Los Aztecas had been identified as the gang that was running the local retail drug markets as well as bringing in a significant amount of weapons across the border from Texas. An exposé on the gang that appeared in *El Diario* at that time noted that Los Aztecas exerted such complete control in Juárez that 80 percent of the local gangs were working for them in some capacity, helping Los Aztecas manage the distribution and sale of drugs in the city.

Los Aztecas had structured their business in such a way that they could distribute thousands of doses a day, even when their workers were arrested or killed. The most important detail revealed by the *El Diario* article was that there were no longer any independent contractors in the Juárez retail drug world. Workers were paid 300 pesos a day plus commissions on sales (assembly plant workers in Juárez were making 500 pesos per week). The haphazard, incidental character of the prior independent contractor was replaced by a highly structured organizational scheme that included three eight-hour shifts per day. There were an estimated 120 distribution and retail centers in Juárez employing roughly twelve hundred people. Each of these, in turn, was in charge of several "runners," and for every runner there were, on average, five *puchadores* (a Mexicanization of the term "pusher"). This same system serviced the more traditional *picaderos* as well. Each center had security people, who were responsible for watching over the venues where drugs were sold and monitoring to ensure that people stayed within their prescribed territories. These retail centers were all over the city now, but the area of greatest sales was the Zona Centro, downtown. *El Diario*'s source noted that it was especially evident downtown that the municipal police were protecting the vendors. La Cima and the neighborhoods immediately surrounding it were also a high-volume area, notwithstanding the fact that the police had placed a substation just three blocks from La Cima.

A February 26, 2008, arrest of twenty-one Aztecas by the Mexican Army provided a snapshot into the workings of the local drug business. The Aztecas were working as operatives of La Línea and the Juárez cartel, and their duties included executions and lifting people, as well as protecting drug shipments that were distributed to the *picaderos* for retail drug sales. In other words, some of the jobs for which the cartel had traditionally used La Línea were now being subcontracted out to Los Aztecas. At the time of their arrest, gang members were found to have an arsenal that included ten AK-47s, a batch of federal police uniforms, police communications radios, twenty-three scales, thirteen thousand doses of cocaine, two kilos of cocaine base, as well as a "brick" of marijuana.

One of the universally reliable equations in drug culture is that where there is a high incidence of drug addiction, there is also a high incidence of ancillary crime. That equation held as true in Ciudad Juárez as it did in New York City or Houston or Detroit. The explosion in the number of people

Arrested Juárez gangbangers. Photo copyright © Raymundo Ruiz.

addicted to heroin and cocaine in Juárez translated into an explosion in crime, from burglaries and car thefts to assaults and holdups. By the spring of 2008, crime was beginning to reach epidemic proportions throughout the city.

■ ■ ■

A vast amount of cocaine and other drugs moved through Juárez into El Paso. The city was the most important transit point for the Juárez cartel's drugs, but it was also a vital point of passage for other cartels as well. Prior to the war, the latter had typically paid the Juárez cartel a fee to transit their product through the city, sometimes even under the protection of La Línea. One of the most telling details that betrayed the extent of police involvement in the Juárez drug trade was the fact that virtually no cocaine was ever confiscated in municipal police operations. Notwithstanding that Juárez was universally known to be one of the most important transit points for cocaine into the United States, a fact that should have translated into periodic interdictions of significant drug shipments, over the course of 2005 the police had only confiscated a paltry seventy-two kilos of cocaine. In 2006, the quantity had dropped to a mere sixty-one kilos; and in 2007 the amount of confiscated cocaine had dropped to a laughable three kilograms. Few of the cartel's midlevel operatives, the tier that moved modest quantities of cocaine across the border, would have bothered to waste a "mule" on a paltry run of three kilos. In a city that the Mexican federal attorney general's office had designated as having the third-largest retail cocaine market in the country, just behind Tijuana and Monterrey, one would certainly have expected commensurate cocaine seizures.

The Juárez cartel had created an efficient, lean organizational structure, one that would have been the envy of any corporation managing the marketing and sale of its products. However, the Sinaloa cartel had initiated an effort to alter this convenient arrangement. In attempting to take over the city, the Sinaloa people could not leave this part of the Juárez cartel's operations intact. Although media accounts of the ensuing violence would repeatedly characterize the conflict as between two cartels for control of access to the American drug market, this was only half of the picture. The other half was about the local retail business and the addicts it serviced. While net profits from the local Juárez drug trade were far less than those derived from shipping drugs across the border (the value of a kilo of cocaine doubled when it traveled from Juárez across the Rio Grande), Sinaloa could not ignore this segment of the Juárez cartel's business because the network was now intrinsic to the very structure of the Juárez cartel's operations. There was no way for Sinaloa to take Juárez without taking control of the retail drug markets as well—Sinaloa's flank would have been left exposed and vulnerable. Out of this imperative would come the thousands of dead, the wave of executions that was about to wash over the city as rival gangs assassinated one another's members as they vied for control of the city's *picaderos* and the addicts they served.

CHAPTER 8

The Mistress

Elena (a pseudonym) knew full well the extent to which the Juárez cartel owned the state and local police, controlling them and treating them like rank employees who did their bidding—from the mundane to the horrific. She came to know this world through Hernán, her lover and would-be common law husband (were it not for the fact that he was already married, with a family). Hernán had close dealings with many different police officers, some of whom he ran like a crew. He also had an associate who owned an auto-repair shop. Hernán sent his police in their cruisers over to the shop, where the associate's people siphoned the gas tanks until they were nearly empty. The municipality's gas was then sold, and Hernán and his associate divided the profits. Hernán was inventive in this way, but these were minor schemes, side deals. Running cocaine across the river was his real business.

Elena first met Hernán in her early twenties at a bar frequented by people involved in the Juárez drug world. The narcos had a reputation. They partied hard and were always flush with cash; the Juárez girls chased them around as if they were celebrities. The night they met, Elena spotted Hernán across the room and asked one of her friends to introduce them. Elena was aggressive that way. She was also strikingly attractive and had an edgy, oppositional streak that made her utterly disinterested in stable men with careers in accounting or sales or anything else that smacked of mainstream.

Elena's wildness surprised Hernán. He was accustomed to docile women whom he used and then discarded; he tended to have his way, and he was not used to being contradicted. Elena was different. She challenged him. If he pushed her she pushed back. And she was not afraid of his violent character—it was all-too- familiar to her as a personality trait in men, from her autocratic, abusive father to the men she'd been with from early on in her adolescence, when she'd discovered her sexuality. That discovery had given her a power she'd never before experienced. She grew confident in that terrain, as if something unknown and unanticipated had opened up within her. She'd felt no fear or apprehension that night at the bar when she'd walked across the room to meet Hernán, only a sense of opportunity.

The first time I met Elena was at a small gathering that had been organized to watch a Mexican league soccer match. The occasion was one of the first social events to which I was invited in Juárez, and I was aware of feeling a tension between the violence taking place out in the streets and the casualness of drinking beer, eating tacos, and watching a sporting event on television. I'd felt the contradiction before, say, observing a bike race at El Chamizal Park, with cyclists dressed in brightly colored garb, knowing that for a time the large park had been one of the cartels' preferred dumping sites for executed bodies. I'd also felt it at El Parque Central, where an old man ran a small Ferris wheel and laughing children flashed victory signs at me from colorful gondolas. Even in the midst of death, I thought to myself, life goes on.

We had gathered in a small, working-class home. At moments, the television's poor reception gave the match an otherworldly appearance, as distorted forms seemed to dance across the screen. Most of those who'd gathered to watch the soccer match were friends, although it was apparent that Elena did not know many of them. Like me, she was something of an outsider to the group. Elena said nothing about her past. It was only later, when one of those in attendance told me more about who Elena was, that I asked her to tell me her story, including her relationship with Hernán.

Elena and I subsequently met clandestinely in out-of-the-way locations— Ciudad Juárez's enormous city park; a Church's Chicken in a new strip mall on the outskirts of town; on a segment of El Camino Real (a boondoggle pet project of the previous mayor, Héctor Murguía); at an unfinished and therefore not-frequented overlook on the outskirts of Juárez—because she feared for her life were it discovered that she was speaking to me. Talking to anyone can be dangerous in Juárez, where it's difficult to avoid the small-town feeling that everyone knows everyone else and everything is watched, observed, noted.

The problem was not only Juárez's small-town feeling, it was that Juárez lived by a code of silence. It was very difficult to get anyone to talk about the world of the Juárez cartel. Some people even refused to mention it by name. There were people who would talk about the history of the cartel, recognized if unofficial experts to whom visiting journalists turned for briefings, for example. But to get someone who knew firsthand about the cartel to talk about it, someone who'd lived it from the inside—that took time, trust, and luck. The penalty for violating the code of silence—and this is no hyperbole—was death. That threat was something as present and real as the desert sands that blow through every neighborhood in the city. Everyone in Juárez knows that code as a truth.

Within the cartel culture, the code had a different configuration. Here there could be a great deal of performance. In a world where braggadocio is the lingua franca, and flash and pretense often mask substance, Elena figured out that Hernán was the real deal. For all his dime-a-dozen narco posturing—the abundance of cash, the ever-present gun, the gold jewelry, the western garb—there was plenty of evidence pointing to his status as a midlevel narco within the Juárez cartel. (And in the world from which Elena had come, midlevel might as well have been head capo—she was from a poor family in a poor neighborhood and, materially speaking, she'd never had a thing growing up.) As far as Elena was concerned, Hernán was a prime catch.

Elena saw one of the first signs that convinced her of Hernán's status during an encounter they had with the municipal police. One afternoon they were in his new pickup truck speeding down the Avenida de las Americas, one of Juárez's main boulevards. The windows were down and the sound system was blasting *narcocorridos*. Elena and Hernán were having a grand time. They'd been on a partying spree that had now lasted several days. Suddenly, a police patrol car was in pursuit behind them, lights flashing. Hernán cursed them, but pulled over. When the officer approached the truck and recognized Hernán behind the steering wheel, his entire demeanor changed. "I'm sorry, sir," Elena remembered the officer saying. "Can we escort you anywhere?" This incident told her that Hernán was the real thing.

As a child in Juárez, Elena had grown up in roiling poverty, but her personality was outgoing and spunky, and for a long time there was an inner optimism that transcended the reality of her family's economic circumstances. She accounted for it on the basis of the fact that she'd been a real daddy's girl (she was the only girl in the family). In elementary school she'd even imagined herself becoming an archaeologist or an astronaut, the latter following the death of Christa McAuliffe, the American schoolteacher astronaut who'd died in NASA's Challenger explosion when Elena was ten years old. The tragedy had captured the imaginations of schoolchildren in Juárez as much as it had children in the United States.

Whatever the source, those once bright and infinite dreams had long ago evaporated. The hard knocks of a woman's life, ground down in the underbelly of Juárez's lower social rungs, had taken their toll on her. The sparkle had long since disappeared from Elena's eyes by the time I met her.

Elena's father had been gruff with the children and abusive toward their mother. He drank and partied with his friends, and they never knew if he would come home at night. He barely provided for the family; Elena's older brothers helped support the household even though they were only adolescents and had to drop out of school to do so. Elena was spared such obligations. She was her father's favorite, and that gave her leeway even as it created continuous conflicts with her mother.

Elena's blossoming meant that she was always out and about. The boys and men who wanted her were legion. And she knew it. There were nights when Elena didn't return home, and she would walk in the door when she damned well felt like it the next day, unabashed, expecting to be fed. Her mother deemed her incorrigible and eventually resorted to the Catholic nuns in hopes that they could help tame her or put some sense into her, but after less than a month at the Catholic residential center for wayward adolescents Elena talked another girl into running away with her. For almost nine months her family did not know where she was. She slept at her girlfriends' houses or stayed with men in the cheap motel rooms where they happened to have spent the night. Elena felt no fear in this abandon; she was wild and fiery and full of that self-confidence that comes with commanding good looks.

By the time she was fifteen Elena was working as a waitress in a restaurant, visiting her family only sporadically. In her neighborhood, most kids her age were no longer in school and gangs were everywhere. Already her mind was full of the narco-culture that surrounded her. It was in the music they listened to, the way they dressed, and the social hierarchy within which they lived: the only people with power were narco-people. In Elena's world, everyone had friends and neighbors who made their living at least partly from the drug trade, helping to transport, warehouse, and package drugs, and sometimes running them across the river into El Paso. The only people with money that she knew were people with ties to the Juárez cartel.

On one of her rare visits home during this time, Elena caught her mother in a reflective mood. They sat down to drink a cup of coffee at the small, worn table in the barren room that served as both living room and kitchen in the family's cramped three-room house. The conversation turned to the family and how her brothers were doing and, eventually, to the depth of her mother's unhappiness, married to an at-times violent man whose disinterest in the family was all too evident. Elena could count on one hand the number of times she and her mother had talked like this. She'd never felt her mother's closeness; that mother-daughter bond was altogether foreign to her. As they sat at the table one of the things Elena's mother told her was that during her pregnancy she had considered aborting Elena, so spent was she by her husband's abusive treatment. The disclosure gave Elena a window into the lifelong strained feelings between them.

The conversation was a rare moment of candor between the two women, fostered by the serendipity of an unanticipated encounter in which each happened to be receptive to the other. As they sipped their coffee, Elena's mother told her that she hoped Elena would have a better life and find a better man than her father—a husband who was not a drunkard who beat his wife and children. In the atmosphere of frankness, Elena responded with something that she herself had not formulated before that moment but which, in the voicing, she immediately recognized as a truth: she told her mother that she had no interest in ever getting married. "I want to be an *amante*, not a wife," she said, using the Spanish word for a lover. What she meant, she later told me, was that she wanted to be a narco's mistress. There was greater honesty in that than in a conventional marriage, she thought. Such an arrangement would also give her the comfort of knowing that no one owned her, that she could leave any time she wished. At the end of their coffee, Elena asked her mother to forgive her for the years of back talk and sarcasm, for being stubborn and contrarian, and for adding to her mother's burden of woes by not coming home at night and running away. They hugged, and Elena walked out the door and into the dust of Juárez. It would be months before she would come back, and it was one of the few times ever that she felt a sense of calm in relation to home and family.

Elena discovered that she was pregnant after she and Hernán had been together for less than a year. His response was to buy her a house and put her up in it. The house was not in an ostentatious neighborhood; the neighborhood was working-class, and most of the people around her were employed at the nearby assembly plants. But in comparison to the other homes, hers stood out. It was two stories and had a wrought-iron fence with a postage-stamp yard in front, plus a large backyard with concertina wire all along the top of the fence that surrounded it. When their child was born, a boy whom they named Pedro, Hernán attended his baptism, which cemented for Elena the notion that while she was not Hernán's wife, she was important. If he had other girlfriends, which is what she suspected (because they all did), she believed herself to be first among equals.

"You have to come by every day to see your boy," Elena insisted to Hernán. "I don't care if it's for five minutes." And he did, Elena reported. In fact, many nights he stayed over. "I don't know how he did it in terms of his wife, but he knew how to have his way with her," Elena said.

■ ■ ■

Unbeknownst to them, Elena and Hernán were the unintended beneficiaries of the United States' anti-drug policies. In the 1970s, Colombian drug traffickers had little to fear from the U.S. Coast Guard. They were so bold that they took to stacking tons of marijuana on the decks of vessels, their loads in plain sight. These motherships would sail right up to American territorial waters, where they rendezvoused with ten to twenty go-fast boats. Still in international waters, the ships were beyond the reach of the American authorities. The illicit drugs were offloaded from the motherships onto the smaller vessels, which then made their runs to the Florida coast. Even if they were detected, the go-fast boats easily outran the coast guard vessels (the coast guard cutters had maximum speeds of twenty to twenty-five knots, while the go-fast could almost double that speed). At best, the coast guard might intercept one or two of the fast boats, while the rest eluded them and made successful runs to the coastline. Cocaine was even more difficult to interdict. If the coast guard caught one of the boats carrying cocaine shipments, the crews simply threw the cargo overboard.

By the 1980s, the United States was awash in Colombian cocaine and Miami was the cocaine capital of the world, followed closely by New York and Los Angeles. The cocaine was produced and controlled by the big Colombian cartels, such as the Medellín and Cali cartels, and 80 percent of it was coming into the U.S. via the Caribbean and the Gulf of Mexico to the Eastern Seaboard, especially Florida (most of the rest was arriving aboard commercial airline flights), as the Colombians continued to use the flotillas of small, medium, and large vessels to make the relatively short run from Colombia to the American markets. Mexican drug exports servicing the American drug culture were mostly marijuana, heroin, and modest amounts of prescription drugs; the amount of cocaine coming through Mexico was negligible.

Hamstrung, the Americans changed their tactics. Beginning in 1981, the U.S. Congress "clarified" statutory restrictions on the use of the military for law enforcement purposes. By 1984 and 1985 the coast guard was launching aggressive and complex operations, such as Operation Hat Trick I and Operation Hat Trick II, which involved the Customs Service, navy, air force, army, and marines, all participating in operations to interdict motherships as they transited the major Caribbean lanes. Prior to 1984, the highest cocaine seizure had been forty-six pounds. In 1984, cocaine seizures jumped to 1,967 pounds, and in 1985 they jumped to 6,500 pounds. Evidence of the success of the increased pressure on the Colombian cocaine smuggling operations was irrefutable: cocaine seizures were skyrocketing.

The next obstacle to interdicting drug-running ships was international law and the American Mansfield Amendment, which prohibited the coast guard and U.S. military forces from directly assisting foreign officials in the enforcement of their laws. This meant that if the coast guard discovered a Colombian vessel loaded with cocaine while it was still in Colombian waters, there was nothing it could do but report it to Colombian authorities and hope for the best. The U.S. had to rely on the Colombians to muster their navy, to apprehend, and to convict. The same held true for any other South American country that was a point of origin for drugs headed for the United States. It wasn't until 1985 that the Mansfield Amendment was changed to allow American officials to collaborate directly with foreign law enforcement.

International maritime law posed an even thornier problem. Every vessel flies under the flag of the country to which it belongs. Under international law, this means that any action against a foreign vessel is considered an action against the "flag country." As a matter of national sovereignty, most countries were not eager to have Americans boarding their ships at will in the open seas. Boarding foreign flag vessels created delicate situations with foreign governments, but the U.S. government found a way to work around this impediment. By 1986, when the coast guard boarded a foreign vessel on the high seas it could contact the flag country's government via the State Department for consent to seize the vessel. The process was exceedingly cumbersome, involving conference calls among the coast guard, the Department of State, and the Department of Justice every time the coast guard encountered a suspicious foreign vessel at sea. A request would then be made to the vessel's flag country to conduct a registry check and grant permission to board, search, and, if appropriate, seize the vessel. The coast guard's frustration with the procedures was more than evident when its commandant, Admiral Paul Yost, testified before Congress in 1986: "Response to such requests vary depending on the country and often on the day of the week or relation to a national holiday," Yost reported with evident frustration, adding that countries often had poor record systems for their vessel registries.

Eventually, the United States succeeded in cajoling the relevant countries into signing bilateral agreements permitting the coast guard and navy to interdict vessels flying their flags on the high seas. This resulted in the dramatic surge of cocaine seizures and was the final blow to the Caribbean as the preferred conduit of South American cocaine into the United States. The Colombian cartels turned to Mexico instead, and the cocaine that had been flowing into the U.S. through Florida and the Eastern Seaboard started flowing in through Mexican border crossings, creating an unprecedented boon for the Mexican cartels and paving the way for them to become the most important players in the cocaine smuggling business.

Almost all of the cocaine was entering Mexico via the West Coast, through the ports of Manzanillo, Lázaro Cárdenas, Acapulco, or Salina Cruz, in addition to dozens of smaller towns and fishing villages along the coast between Oaxaca and Sinaloa. Some of it also came overland through Guatemala. Once on Mexican soil, the cocaine made its way to Tijuana, Mexicali, Ciudad Juárez, Nuevo Laredo, and Matamoros, depending on the cartel that happened to own the shipment. The shipments might arrive in Mexico in quantities as large as a ton or more, but they were quickly broken down into more manageable quantities as they made their way to the key transit points into the American drug market. The shipments that arrived in Juárez varied in size as a function of how they'd been shipped up to the border. There, they were broken down further depending on the cartel operatives and how much weight they could move.

■ ■ ■

In the narco-world, having paramours and mistresses and leaving your women with children all over town was simply part of the culture. *Narcocorridos* often celebrated the fact that the big capos left so many women pregnant; such expressions of virility were a staple of the show-the-world-you're-a-macho narco-culture. Hernán's brothers and other relatives knew about Elena and Pedro. In fact, sometimes Hernán and Elena vacationed with his brothers and cousins or with his associates. Sometimes the men brought their wives and other times they brought their girlfriends. Even Hernán's mother knew about Elena. It was all loose, boundary-less, and dictated by the whims of macho men who felt entitled to have their way.

Hernán could be charming, effusive, and indulgent. He often catered to Elena's whims. Their son was never lacking in toys and Hernán constantly brought him gifts; keeping Pedro pampered and spoiled was one of his pleasures. He could be that way with others, as well. "He could be very noble," is the way Elena described it. One afternoon they had been out to eat and were driving home from the restaurant when they stopped at a light where a woman was begging, asking for money to feed her children. Hernán reached into his pocket and pulled out a twenty-dollar bill. Rolling down his window, he beckoned the woman over. "Here," he said. "Now go back to your house, *señora*, to be with your children." The woman started crying and thanked him.

Such gestures touched Elena. They made her trust Hernán, made her believe that he had a good heart. She saw those qualities, too, in the way he interacted with Pedro and with his family. He was very devoted to his parents, for example. At one of our meetings, as she reflected on Hernán's character, on the kind of man that he was, she summarized it all cogently: "As a son, friend, and father, he was very noble and good. As a man, he was a son of a bitch."

The latter was a reference to a darker side of Hernán, an abusive, authoritarian man that she characterized simply as being "a macho's macho." For all the ways he could be indulging, he was equally capable of being vicious, aggressive, and controlling. He could come home in an expansive, manic mood when things went well, but when they didn't, he blew in like the wrath of God, demanding, provoking, and attacking at the slightest perturbation. And Elena's nature was anything but submissive. When she felt that he was being unreasonable she stood her ground. She did not coddle him or engage in obsequious efforts to smooth his feathers. That was completely against her nature. She talked back. She shouted as loudly as he did. She told him to go fuck himself.

At these times Hernán often insulted her and sometimes beat her, which only served to mobilize Elena's fury all the more. She threw things at him or tried to hurt him. On one occasion she almost gouged his eye out, requiring a trip to the emergency room to save the eye. Hernán's abuse also took the form of a need to have Elena under his control. He had his police goons park on her block and in front of her house. He wanted to know where she was at all times. He did not like for her to leave the house even if it was to go grocery shopping. When she went out, he checked on her obsessively, insistently, by repeatedly calling her on her cell phone. But there was also a tender side to their relationship, and Hernán had the capacity to take her into his confidence and share parts of his business world with her. It was one of the features of their relationship that allowed Elena to know that she mattered to him.

Hernán and Elena lived lives of combustible desperation within the middle rungs of the Juárez cartel. Elena's restless instincts and combative nature played off of Hernán's macho disposition in ways that created unanticipated, and perhaps unacknowledged, balance between them. At the time, and within her frame of vision, there was little that Elena wished for beyond what she had. Her life already exceeded what most from her background could have hoped for.

CHAPTER 9

The General

In mid-March, as the 2008 Holy Week neared with its imagery of death and rebirth, there was an abundance of death in Ciudad Juárez but no sign of renewal. Executions had jumped to unprecedented levels. The tally of the dead was running at three, four, sometimes five executions per day and it was pressing hard upon the city and making daily headlines. The assassinations of police officers were having an especially unsettling and demoralizing effect within the force as well as upon the city as a whole. It was as if the veil behind which horror lurked had been torn away, unmasking something ever so raw and brutal.

In the aftermath of the discovery of the "unbelievers" list at the police monument, Guillermo Prieto, the chief of the Juárez municipal police, like all of his commanders, feared for his life every moment of his waking day. The police executions and the ever-present threats of more to come had brought Prieto to the breaking point. The chief had been an officer for nearly twenty years, but the pressure had become unbearable. "Let me go to El Paso to sleep on the weekends," he'd asked mayor Reyes Ferriz. It was the only way to get relief, even if temporarily, from the stress of knowing that he was being hunted.

Tension permeated the air at the police department's six command centers. The narco-list of "those who still do not believe" was weighing heavily on everyone. The threat could not be ignored, because it was a threat being made good. So unbearable was the anxiety that at one point there was a mutiny, with officers refusing to leave their command centers. "They were afraid that they were going to be killed if they left their stations," the mayor recalled. That meant that there was little police presence in the streets, a circumstance that could quickly deteriorate into all-out mayhem. In addition to the cartels, there was no shortage of garden-variety criminals in the city—the usual cast of scammers, thieves, carjackers, extortionists, and rapists. The city could not operate without a police force.

On the Thursday before Holy Week, Prieto called the mayor to tell him he was going to resign. "I can't do this, the risks have become too great," he said to Reyes Ferriz. The announcement hit the mayor hard. He had an ally in the chief, someone he trusted within a police department that he knew to be riddled with corruption and infested with cartel penetration. There were only a handful of people in the department in whom the mayor had confidence.

"What do you think about Antonio Román [the second in command] succeeding you?" the mayor asked Prieto, but the response he received only served to further unnerve him: "No," the police chief told him. "Román is going to resign before I do!"

The two key players in the department were walking out on him, and Francisco Ledesma, the third in command, had already been executed. "So who's going to take your place?" he asked Prieto. The police chief's response left the mayor cold: "There isn't anyone. All of the commanders are resigning." The Sinaloa cartel had succeeded in sowing panic within the ranks of the Juárez municipal police. The force was on the verge of implosion.

Despite the high levels of anxiety, the mayor succeeded in persuading his chief of police to stay on until he could find a replacement. Reyes Ferriz also promised that there would be more federal support. Prieto, in turn, helped calm nerves among the police commanders, at least temporarily averting their mass resignations. But the mayor knew the entire operation was hanging by a thread, a thread that could well be snapped by the next execution of a police officer, and there were plenty of names yet to go on the infamous Black List, as the "For those who still do not believe" list was now being called.

As the end of March neared, an atmosphere of dread saturated the entire city. The local media was brimming with stories related to the security crisis. Every conversation seemed to revolve around the dark fate that had overtaken Juárez. There was a collective sense of helplessness, frustration, and fear. At his Holy Week convocation, the Catholic bishop asked that everyone pray for their city.

■ ■ ■

There were other signs that the city was devolving into a state of anarchy, where the very structures that organize lives were yielding to something unspeakable, and where evil was sucking the life force out of Ciudad Juárez. At the end of January, just days after the Sinaloa narco-message had been left at the police monument, a tip to the federal police led officials to a house where the remains of nine people were found buried in pits in the back yard. Nearly a ton of marijuana was also seized at the location. Five complete bodies were exhumed from four separate pits, as well as the dismembered remains of at least four other victims. It was unclear if the latter victims had been dismembered as they were being tortured, or after their deaths. It was another "house of death," a macabre genre for which the Juárez cartel had become infamous.

The term "house of death" had been coined in Juárez back in 2004 by neighbors of a house in which a grisly discovery had been made. A dozen bodies had been found there, buried in the back yard of a modest house in a residential subdivision. Most showed signs of torture. Although it would become clear that there were many "houses of death," the 2004 case had attained special notoriety when an intrepid *Dallas Morning News* correspondent named Alfredo Corchado and Bill Conroy, an equally intrepid journalist who ran an electronic news site called Narco News, had written extensive stories about the horrors that had taken place at 3633 Calle Parcioneros. An informant for Immigration and Customs Enforcement, a man named Guillermo Eduardo Ramírez Peyro, who was a former Mexican Highway Patrol officer, had played an active role in the crime. It was later learned that Ramírez Peyro had infiltrated the Juárez cartel on behalf of American law enforcement. In fact, there was evidence to suggest that the Americans may have been aware of what was taking place at the house on Calle Parcioneros.

A month after the January 2008 discovery of the most recent house of death, a second site was found in a Juárez neighborhood called La Cuesta. Here, the federal police initially discovered a cache of weapons and drugs. Two men were also arrested at the house, which was located on Sierra del Pedregal Street and surrounded by a tall wall. The information provided by the two men prompted the federal police to bring two police dogs trained to detect human remains to the property. They also brought a backhoe. When they started digging in the backyard they immediately discovered three bodies interred in a six-foot grave. Over the course of the next two weeks, federal authorities eventually found thirty-six bodies buried in sixteen different pits in the backyard of the house in La Cuesta. Neighbors told the federal police that men driving late-model cars had been using the house for the last six months. Some neighbors pleaded for police protection for fear that the *sicarios* might return after the federal police left.

The houses of death were basically safe houses where the Juárez cartel did a great deal of its dirty work (the Sinaloa cartel operated its own death houses once it made its move on the city). The primary requirement for these houses was that cartel operatives could enter and leave covertly, which meant tall gates or garages with doors. This way, *sicarios* could come in and out and victims could be unloaded without being seen. The houses also required space. Rooms were needed to hold kidnap victims (who were being held to extort money from their families) as well as individuals who had been lifted—competitors, snitches, and people who were not following orders or who were otherwise uncooperative. Before killing them, the cartel often tortured those who had been lifted to extract information or simply to make them pay for their misdeeds. Some of the cruelty seemed to be inflicted for mere sport. The safe houses were also places where drugs were stored, weapons were stockpiled, and cars were secreted. Lastly, many of the safe houses had patches of ground where those whose agonies had come to an end could be secretly buried.

The safe houses were typically in working-class and lower-middle-class neighborhoods, where people went to work, where families lived in the shadows of what was taking place, and where sometimes the screams of the victims were insufficiently muffled. The late-night comings and goings of strangers in typical narco-vehicles—SUVs, pickup trucks, or stolen cars with no license plates—made what was taking place behind the walls all too transparent. Often, neighbors lived in fear that they might inadvertently see or come to know too much, a fear, in other words, that a misstep might turn them into victims as well. The people in these neighborhoods were completely defenseless; they had no recourse—there was no one to call and no one to whom they could turn. Everyone knew that the municipal police were complicit. It was also universally known that the city's 066 number, the so-called Anonymous Tip line, was anything but anonymous—officers in the pay of the cartel staffed it. Whenever a citizen called with information that the cartel might find inconvenient, a call was placed to cartel cell phones. Tip line callers with cartel-related information often ended up either brutalized or dead. There was no authority; the institutions that normally protect and serve the public welfare were all but nonexistent. The notion of law and order meant nothing in Juárez. That brutal fact made the residents of these neighborhoods hostages; they were unprotected and vulnerable. And all over the city the narcos had their safe houses from which they reigned their terror.

■ ■ ■

Everything in Mexico closes down for Holy Week. Next to Christmas, it's the biggest national holiday. José Reyes Ferriz took his family[1] to the El Conquistador hotel in Tuscon, Arizona, a five-star resort with world-class tennis courts, a golf course, and an expensive spa, among other amenities, nestled up against the Santa Catalina Mountains. Notwithstanding the sumptuous surroundings, Reyes Ferriz was completely distracted and preoccupied with his predicament. "I was trying to figure out what we were going to do," the mayor recalled. That Saturday morning the mayor received his customary call from his chief of police to report on the state of the city. "How are you, *mi Presidente?*" Prieto said, using the honorific for the mayor. "If you give me a number that's fewer than five, I'm fine," was the mayor's response (meaning that he hoped there had been less than five executions in the city over the prior twenty-four hours). There was something different in the police chief's tone. After a moment, the mayor asked the chief how he was doing. "Me, I'm fine," Prieto responded before dropping his bomb: "I'm here watching my ranch and feeding my pigs," he said. "I'm not coming back."

Prieto's words hit Reyes Ferriz hard. The burden of his position weighed heavily on him; he'd been worrying about saving the city from itself for months now. Even as he clicked off his cell phone, the chief of police's statement continued to reverberate in his head. "I was alone," the mayor noted. "There was no one who could fix this for me." The mayor returned home on Easter Sunday, immersed in worry.

At 10 a.m. on Monday morning, as he was meeting with his chief of staff, his personal secretary buzzed. "You have a call from General Juárez Loera," he said. Loera was the commander of the 11th Military Zone, a vast area of northern Mexico that included the important border states of Chihuahua and Coahuila. The general had a reputation as a tough, no-nonsense commander not given to niceties or trivial conversation. He also had a penchant for raising the hackles of civil libertarians by making such pronouncements as, "My search warrant is the sledgehammer." Loera was constantly at odds with human-rights activists seeking to make him accountable for army violations spawned by his iron-fist, tough-on-crime philosophy. At an opening ceremony to mark the initiation of a guns-for-food-vouchers exchange program that spring of 2008, the general had chided journalists who questioned him about army abuses in Juárez: "I'd prefer it if when journalists write of 'one more dead' they'd say 'one less delinquent,' instead," he suggested. The general was criticized for implying that the lives of narcos were worthless.

The mayor had already decided that he would ask the general to recommend someone to replace Guillermo Prieto. "*Señor Presidente,*" the general said, "Clear your agenda. I'll see you at 2 p.m. at the army garrison."

The mayor's calendar was already full. He was expected at an important meeting in El Paso at that same time. The Mexican foreign secretary, Patricia Espinosa (Mexico's counterpart to the American secretary of state), was coming to negotiate a new rail bridge across the Rio Grande west of Juárez so that trains would no longer have to come through the center of the city. The mayor of El Paso, the Mexican consul in El Paso, and the American consul in Juárez were all to be in attendance. "*Mi general,*" Reyes Ferriz responded, "I have something at 1 p.m. in El Paso with the *secretaría de relaciones exteriores.*" But the general was intransigent: "Clear your agenda," he repeated. "What I have to tell you will be of greater importance to you than anything madam secretary has to say."

Reyes Ferriz called the Mexican consul in El Paso and arranged to greet Patricia Espinosa prior to the scheduled lunch, and then headed across the river for the meeting, which took place in an elegant, Spanish colonial revival–style building from the 1920s called the Cortez Building. The Cortez, where a series of conquistador heads stared out from roundels above the first floor, had once been a hotel but was now an upscale office building.

During a break, the mayor stepped out into the hall and called governor Reyes Baeza to let him know that he was going to ask General Juárez Loera to give him a military person to serve as chief of police. An incredulous voice on the other end of the line simply said, "You're militarizing the police if you do that." Both men were attorneys who'd been steeped in the concept of the separation of civilian and military rule. "I did not see any other way out," the mayor would later tell me. He conveyed that sentiment to the governor, who ultimately endorsed the mayor's direction, albeit with considerable reluctance.

Following his meeting with the Mexican foreign secretary, Reyes Ferriz raced back across the river via the so-called Dedicated Commuter Lane, or the Express Line, which required drivers to be certified on the Secure Electronic Network for Travelers Rapid Inspection (SENTRI). This bridge obviated the lines that made crossing any of the other Juárez–El Paso bridges a time-consuming and tedious affair. The army garrison was a forty-minute drive from downtown Juárez to the south.

General Loera held his meetings in a spartan conference room with white tablecloth–covered tables arranged in a square. When the mayor arrived he left his bodyguards outside and entered the meeting room alone, taking a seat at the table toward which the general had gestured. General Juárez Loera was an old-school military man. He had an oval, jowly face and he combed his thinning hair straight back, a hairstyle that along with a moderately receding hairline gave his forehead prominence. The general wore bifocals and had the weathered look of a man who spent a great deal of time outdoors. Loera was gruff, direct, and spoke with a gravelly voice, but there was something reassuring about his solid, commanding style. His troops respected him. At sixty-two, he was nearing the end of his career but he was coming to the finish line at full stride: the 11th Military Zone was one of the most important of the army's sectors, given that the states within this territory, Chihuahua, Durango, and Coahuila, were key routes for the drug trade, where many cities and towns were controlled by one cartel or another—the entire region was awash in cartel operatives.

"We're coming to help, Señor Presidente," the general said. He told the mayor that president Calderón would shortly announce that he was sending twenty-five hundred troops to Juárez to help stabilize the situation in the city. It was big news indeed. For the beleaguered Reyes Ferriz the general might as well have been the Savior. The mayor's back was to the wall, and this news exceeded the mayor's expectations by a significant measure. It certainly lived up to the general's statement that what he had to say was more important than anything that might have happened in El Paso. But there was more; over the course of the meeting General Loera agreed to help the mayor find a current or former army officer to take over as chief of the Juárez municipal police.

On his way back into town, José Reyes Ferriz felt tremendous relief. For days his situation had seemed utterly hopeless, without remedy, and he'd felt a tremendous isolation in the face of his predicament. He was certain that the infusion of army troops would change the dynamics of what was taking place in Juárez. With some of his fifteen hundred officers refusing to leave their stations and the police department teetering on the brink of chaos, twenty-five hundred soldiers patrolling the streets seemed like a game changer. The fact that the general was disposed to help him find a replacement for Prieto was an added bonus. These were very promising developments in Reyes Ferriz's view. His immediate priority was to find a way of forestalling the mass resignations that Prieto had told him were imminent, a development that for all intents and purposes would leave the city without a police force. The mayor called Prieto in transit and asked to meet him at city hall. Reyes Ferriz hoped he could convince Prieto to stay on until his replacement was on board.

"It was a very candid and open conversation," the mayor recalled. The two men had known one another for many years; they liked and trusted each other. They spoke using the more personal "*tu*" rather than the more formal "*usted*." "We stood at the big window," Reyes Ferriz remembered. "I explained to Guillermo what the army was going to do and how they were going to intervene. And I asked him to stay on until they could find a replacement." The conversation had that look-you-in-the-eye character that comes to the fore in moments when the subject matter involves great risk and the stakes are absolute: life and death. Both men knew that the threats were real. It was no small thing what the mayor was asking when he urged Guillermo Prieto to stay on. In the end, out of a sense of loyalty and professional obligation, Prieto agreed.

At their meeting at the army command center, the general and the mayor had mapped out a course of action for the immediate days to come. Guillermo Prieto, assuming the mayor could convince him to stay on temporarily, would begin the long-planned cleanup of the police department while General Loera searched for his replacement and the identified army units were mobilized for their deployment to Juárez. The offer that Patiño had made at the Cibeles meeting to have the federal police oversee the administration of Confidence Tests to the entire police force had been more than an offer, it had been a precondition for the federal support that was now on its way to Juárez. The analysis remained the same: without a reliable police force overseeing the city, there could be no security in Juárez.

Note

1. The mayor is married and has two children. He was adamant that they not be portrayed in this book for fear that they might become victims of a reprisal against him.

CHAPTER 10

Twenty-Five Hundred Soldiers

The Juárez municipal police continued to be rife with tension. There had been more assassination attempts on the officers whose names had appeared on the "unbelievers" list. One of these, Casimiro Meléndez Ortega, a thirty-three-year-old officer who had been a close friend of the recently executed Francisco Ledesma, had spotted two suspicious cars as he was leaving for work one morning. Meléndez Ortega had drawn his service revolver just as *sicarios* jumped from one of the vehicles, spraying AK-47 fire as they ran toward him. The officer had returned fire and managed to repel the attack. Miraculously, he survived the attempt, shaken but otherwise unscathed, although the entrance to his house was pocked with bullet holes. Panicked neighbors had tried to call the city's emergency response number to no avail: despite repeated attempts, no one answered the line. Following the attempt on Meléndez Ortega, Guillermo Prieto placed the force on red alert, which meant that the police patrolled in teams of three and wore bulletproof vests, but it did little good: by the end of February the Sinaloa cartel had executed two more police commanders from the "unbelievers" list, and another had been lifted. The latter's whereabouts were still unknown, although part of his uniform had been found with blood stains in an empty lot, evidence that militated against a positive outcome to his abduction.

In addition to the violence directed against the municipal police, the announcement of the coming federal Confidence Tests, which would presumably ferret out those who were colluding with one or the other cartels or were otherwise engaged in criminal activity, was stirring unease. There was almost daily press coverage of the coming effort to clean up the department, and officers had begun deserting the force like rats jumping from a sinking ship. In the month of February alone forty-one police officers had tendered their resignations. "It's unprecedented in my years in law enforcement," Guillermo Prieto told *Proceso* magazine in reference to the resignations. Asked if the resignations were a symptom of police complicity with the cartels, Prieto would only venture to say that some had perhaps resigned for fear that their criminal activities would be revealed, while others had resigned because their families were pressing them to do so out of fear that they would be killed. The chief proffered an estimate of the number of corrupt officers on the force at 10 percent. It was an absurdly low figure; virtually everyone in Juárez would have scoffed at it.

For mayor Reyes Ferriz, the world seemed to be closing in. His police department was being decimated by assassinations, resignations, and work stoppages. The state police were hardly present in the city and the governor's responses to the mayor's petitions for additional support continued to fall on deaf ears. Reyes Ferriz increasingly found himself besieged from all sides and with few alternatives as the city descended into darkness and anarchy. The circumstance pointed toward a single, inevitable conclusion: the mayor had to put himself, and the fate of Juárez, into the hands of the federal government. Yet the costs to him of such a move were painfully clear. For one thing, it increased his personal risk significantly. There were also sure to be political costs, given that the decision to bring in the federal forces had already created tensions between himself and governor Reyes Baeza. There were many ways in which Juárez was at the mercy of the governor and the state legislature (which the governor controlled). The legislature was the source of funding that the city required to sustain services and projects whose budgets were already strained to the limit.

■ ■ ■

During the month of February 2008, while the mayor negotiated strategies for reinforcing local law enforcement and cleaning up his police, General Juárez Loera, whose 20th Militarized Cavalry Division was already garrisoned in the city, instructed his army units to take off the gloves. The five thousand troops in Juárez were part of the country's border defense, given that Mexico does not have either a Border Patrol or state National Guard–style militias. Officially, their primary duties involved the interdiction of smugglers moving people and drugs in the border zone, and, historically, the army's style had been low-key operations that did not receive a great deal of media attention. The military preferred it that way.

That had first changed on January 21, following the attempted assassination of a man named Fernando Lozano, who was a regional commander with the Agencia Estatal de Investigaciónes, the investigative division of the state police. Lozano had received extensive training with international police agencies. At around 8:40 on the evening of the twenty-first, Lozano left the state police command center in his armored Jeep Cherokee on his way to visit a relative at Juárez's Centro Médico de Especialidades, a respected local hospital. En route he realized that he was being followed by what appeared to be a cartel commando team. Lozano attempted to make his way back to the command center, but in his efforts to elude the *sicarios* he ran into another car and hit a bus-stop bench. The gunmen jumped out of their car and started raking Lozano's vehicle with automatic weapons fire. In the fury of the attack, Lozano exited his vehicle, pistol in hand, and shot back at his attackers. The assailants fled, leaving the severely wounded commander on the street. Lozano managed to flag down a passing motorist, who drove him to the nearby Centro Médico de Especialidades.

There is evidence to suggest that Lozano may have been collaborating with American law enforcement. His training had brought him into contact with many American law enforcement branches, including the FBI and the DEA. And as he received emergency surgery (a four-hour procedure to remove two bullets lodged in his thorax and lung), the Mexican Army maintained a perimeter of tight security around the hospital, including heavily armed guards posted at all entrances. This was highly unusual; it would have been typical for the municipal police to play this role, not the army. The police obviously could not be trusted to protect Lozano. Several days later, once Lozano's condition had stabilized, he was transferred to Thompson Hospital in El Paso under tight security. There were concerns that assassins might attempt to ambush Lozano's ambulance to finish the job, so a brand-new ambulance, one that presumably matched Lozano's social station, was used as a decoy. The empty ambulance left the hospital and headed for the international bridge under heavy army escort that included armored military vehicles with 50-caliber machine guns at the ready, while Lozano and a medical team, who were actually aboard an old junk-heap of an ambulance, trailed the convoy at a short distance. Authorization for the Mexican ambulance to cross the bridge into the United States is said to have come from high-level government authorities in Washington, DC. Once at the Thompson Hospital, Lozano remained under heavy guard by U.S. marshals and the El Paso Police Department. Lozano would never return to Mexico.

Within minutes of the Lozano assassination attempt, the army began patrolling the streets. The army set up intermittent roadblocks on main transit points hoping to catch people with weapons and drugs. Mexico's constitution prohibits citizens from owning weapons that are "for the exclusive use of the military," such as AK-47s, AR-15s and other assault-style weapons, as well as grenades, bazookas, and rocket launchers. Similarly, drug trafficking and organized crime are also federal offenses in Mexico. Thus, focusing on these specific crimes provided the legal cover (an inadequate basis, some would argue) that allowed the army to take to the streets and engage in what was, essentially, police work, even though the army was not involving itself with "ordinary" crime.

Almost immediately, the army's deployment produced successes. In the first week the military arrested Gabino Salas Valenciano, head of a Juárez cartel cell in the Valley of Juárez, when he was stopped at a military roadblock. In one raid in early February the army discovered a significant cache, including twenty-five automatic weapons and five handguns, seven frag-mentation grenades, fourteen bulletproof vests, communications equip-ment, and five vehicles. Although the Juárez media described the site as a Juárez cartel safe house, the fact that three of the five confiscated vehicles bore Sinaloa license plates suggested that perhaps it was the Sinaloa cartel occupying the safe house.

A few days later, the army, along with the Agencia Federal de Investig-ación (AFI), raided another building in which one of the cartels was pro-cessing cocaine and other drugs for retail sales. The army and the AFI appeared to have arrived just as something significant was about to take place, given that twenty-one individuals, some of them reputedly hit men, were found gathered in the building. Here, too, they found many weapons, but they also found 13,700 individual doses of rock cocaine and two kilos of "cocaine base," as well as 136 boxes of plastic sandwich bags and bicarbon-ate powder, which was used to cut the pure cocaine prior to packaging it in doses. The authorities also discovered both army and AFI uniforms in one of the rooms, presumably used for impersonating law enforcement. The twenty-one men were led from the building in blindfolds, Iraq War–style, and taken to the federal attorney general's compound for processing. Tell-ingly, all three of the vehicles seized at this second site also bore Sinaloa plates, although once again the authorities speculated that the site was a Juárez cartel operation.

These successes came on the heels of the army's seizure of nearly two tons of marijuana at the end of January. Near Juárez, the army had laid siege to the small town of Buenaventura, where they found a narco-armory with nine thousand bullets of different calibers, sixteen AK-47s and AR-15s as well as military-style sharpshooter rifles and tear gas grenades, thirty-one AK-47 silencers, thirteen handcuffs, Kevlar helmets, and, again, a stock of federal law enforcement uniforms.

Mayor Reyes Ferriz and other city officials were quick to applaud the army's successes. City council members who were part of the city's Public Security Commission praised the actions, lamenting only that the army had not been mobilized sooner. The fact that the army was receiving anony-mous tips, which they credited for leading them to the two safe houses, also suggested that the people of Juárez were responding to their presence, even as negotiations were underway to secure even more army troops for Juárez (the troops in the streets were those who had already been stationed at the garrison).

However, the army's activities immediately drew criticism from some quarters as well and, at times, misinformation. For example, *El Heraldo de Chihuahua*, a newspaper from the capital city, asserted that the army's seized narco-lab had actually been a facility run and protected by the army.

The federal attorney general's office immediately repudiated the allegation, noting that there had been armed people arrested and a cache of weapons and drugs seized. No other Chihuahua newspaper carried the *Heraldo's* version of this story, but it revealed the media crosscurrents in a state where newspapers were sometimes in the pay of the cartels.

The army also did little to endear itself to the press. One night shortly after the narco-lab bust, the army arrested two groups of people in a rural area along the U.S.-Mexico line. One group was in possession of 57 kilos of marijuana, while the second was carrying 107 kilos of marijuana. In all, ten men were detained in the two incidents, five of them carrying assault weapons. However, when reporters from *El Diario* arrived to cover the second action, there was a confrontation with the army. An armed man in civilian clothes wearing a ski mask flagged the journalists' car down and demanded to see the driver's press credentials. He told the driver that the "commander" wanted to speak to him. The situation appeared dangerous—the reporters were unarmed, it was the dead of night, and there were no witnesses. The driver refused, at which point the man tore the press identification from the reporter's hands and ran off with it. In a third incident involving the media, the army raided yet another safe house in Juárez, where numerous vehicles were stored. The army arrested three men inside the property, where they'd again found weapons and a modest amount of marijuana. As the cars were being impounded, a man walked up to a soldier and complained that one of the cars being impounded belonged to his brother. The man was taken into custody, but reporters covering the incident clearly thought he was innocent. They called out to him to give them his name, and in the published accounts he was described as someone who had merely happened upon the narco-house during the army's operation.

From the first days of its new role in Juárez, the army's overzealousness, and at times abuses, quickly created significant tensions between it and the press. Most of the coverage, especially by the Juárez newspapers, appeared fact-driven and fair. Unlike the false report in *El Heraldo de Chihuahua*, the local papers were covering the army's actions, good and bad, with professionalism, which meant that they not only covered the successes of the army and other federal law enforcement, but also the complaints against them. For example, a woman who lived next door to the first safe house had filed a complaint with the state Human Rights Commission claiming that the soldiers had not obtained a search warrant and had broken the lock on her front door and looted her home. Similarly, in a separate incident, a woman accused the army of breaking into her home at three o'clock in the morning and taking her father and husband away. Neither, she protested, was involved in the narcotics trade. In most instances, there was no way of determining the validity of either the accusations or the denials. But the discourse that defined those first months of 2008 was already enveloping the army's operations in controversy; the very legal basis for what was taking place was questioned, even as the army's actions were applauded in some quarters. "We all see ourselves as potential victims, that's why we want the heavy hand [of the federal forces]," one editorial read, citing, simultaneously, the need to guarantee civil rights. That was the double-edged reality of the situation in Juárez. People wanted protection from the drug cartels and their gangs and the wave of violence they had unleashed upon the city, yet they also wanted their civil rights safeguarded.

Patricia González, the state attorney general, told *Omnia*, a weekly Chihuahua magazine, that the use of the army to carry out policing functions was a violation of the Mexican Constitution. The governor took a similar stance. González voiced support for legislation pending in the Mexican congress that would enhance the municipal and ministerial police forces, allowing them to investigate organized crime, which at that time fell under the jurisdiction of federal forces. She further argued that seeing the army patrolling the streets "generated a climate of emotional instability among the citizenry."

The violence in Juárez, where there were daily executions, and elsewhere in the state of Chihuahua cast an ominous shadow over everything. González's call for judicial reform and improving municipal and state law enforcement turned a blind eye to the present crisis. In Mexico, there had been calls for such reforms for decades, but the Mexican congress was a body of quicksand that first slowed any proposal of substance down to a halt before extinguishing it altogether by sucking it under. Even forward-looking proposals that at first glance appeared innovative and transparent, like the new laws governing oral arguments at trials and the presentation of criminal evidence, were being perverted, perpetuating a system in which most criminals were simply walking free. The country was hopelessly mired, unable to move forward on this front. Substantive reform was indispensable to Mexico's future, but so was putting an end to the web of corruption and violence that had allowed criminal organizations to become power players in broad swaths of the country.

In Mexico City, the respected daily *Reforma* called for a recognition that within the emerging "Calderónista" war there had been "almost imperceptible" signs that the Mexican Army's role in the current political system was changing. The army was playing a new role in the realm of public security, the editorial noted, and this role "had no precedent" in Mexican history. The editorial further warned of the constitutional risks inherent in this strategy, as well as potential risks to the reputation of the Mexican military.

Reforma may have been correct in its analysis, but the problem was that Calderón had no good alternatives. Any objective appraisal of the national situation could not miss the conclusion that significant portions of the Mexican border states (states that were the economic dynamo to the country's financial well-being) were already under the control of one or another of the cartels. There was no municipal or state law enforcement agency in any of these states that could meaningfully counter the presence of the cartels. In fact, as was true in Juárez, most of these police forces were controlled by the cartels. In many places, the political structure in these states was also heavily influenced by the cartels. The same was true for a number of important states in the interior of Mexico, such as Michoacán, Durango, Guerrero, Quintana Roo, Oaxaca, and Sinaloa, among others, where powerful cartels operated. In many instances these cartels had been deeply entrenched for decades. The deployment of the Mexican Army raised a slew of important questions, but given the national crisis there were no viable alternatives.

■ ■ ■

The main body of the federal forces that had been promised after the mayor's meetings with Patricio Patiño and General Juárez Loera started making their way into the city on the twenty-eighth of March 2008. They came in long convoys arriving from Mexico City and other parts of the country. The olive-green trucks sparkled in the morning sun of the Chihuahuan desert, and the sight of twenty-five hundred troops in full gear, weapons at the ready, was impressive. The Mexican Army was sending its best forces into Juárez.

The army units immediately started patrolling the city and once again, right away they produced results. Everything that one might expect in a city that was an international hub for drug trafficking was suddenly happening: there were almost daily reports of army arrests and there were significant confiscations of drugs, cash, and weapons. The military had swagger and a sense of confidence and, most importantly, they did not appear to be intimidated by the cartels.

The army's successes translated into good publicity, too. One *El Diario* story noted that in its first ten days the army had already confiscated more cocaine than the combined law enforcement agencies in Chihuahua had managed to confiscate over the course of the preceding year. The army's successes gave further credence to the view that the Chihuahua police forces had been protecting drug shipments rather than interdicting them.

Some of the army's tactics were bold. When a drug trafficker named Gerardo Gallegos Rodelo was killed in a firefight with other narcos, the military surreptitiously tracked the funeral cortege to the cemetery. In a surreal scene, two helicopters suddenly appeared above the gravesite, landed, and disgorged troops who in short order forced the gathering of stunned mourners to the ground.

The army was looking for a well-known trafficker named Pedro Sánchez, an important Juárez cartel operative. They'd been given to believe that Sánchez and his crew would attend the funeral, because Rodelo had been one of his people. The soldiers proceeded to search the mourners, and to the shock and outrage of some, they even opened Rodelo's casket, either to ensure that he was indeed in it or to see if it contained something of interest. The army then searched the vehicles, where they reported finding eighty packets of marijuana and numerous handguns. Seven men were arrested, but Pedro Sánchez was not among them.

The out-of-the-box operation took the narcos by surprise. So accustomed were they to operating in the open and without fear that the stealth of such military operations caught them unaware. Many in Juárez applauded the army's actions (an opinion poll in *El Diario* found that 80 percent of the citizens favored the military's operations). There was no memory in the city of such aggressive tactics against the drug operators, and they brought a sense of hope that perhaps the city's agony might be relieved, that the oppressive weight of the cartels might at last be lifted.

However, not everyone was pleased by accounts of military helicopters descending on funeral processions, caskets being pried open, and mourners being treated roughly. While many citizens delighted in the creativity of the military's unprecedented tactics, others criticized the desecration of Rodelo's casket and the warrantless searches of cars and people who had gathered to pay their last respects to the deceased. Rodelo's mother complained to the media that the army had come to her home and torn it apart searching for drugs and weapons; she filed a human rights complaint. In fact, the army's operations brought a flood of such complaints, ranging from rough treatment during warrantless incursions into people's homes to the lifting of people who accused them of torture. Some families claimed that their loved ones had been killed while in army custody.

For the mayor of Juárez, there was the hope that the military's operations would finally bring a measure of stability to the city. One thing was clear: Reyes Ferriz had crossed the line as far as the Juárez cartel was concerned. "When I put in the army, they took that to mean that I was supporting El Chapo [the Sinaloa cartel]," the mayor observed. That could only mean one thing: the Juárez cartel would now be gunning for José Reyes Ferriz.

CHAPTER 11

La Línea

A Juárez business executive told me that as much as 50 percent of the city's economy was in some way linked to the vast American drug profits pouring back across the international bridges through El Paso into Juárez. The figure was impossible to verify or document, and it certainly suggested hyperbole (with 50 percent of the economy related to the maquiladora industry, that would have meant all other commerce in the city was drug-related, which was obviously not the case). But the statement spoke to a prevalent perception that no doubt contained a measure of truth: whatever the actual percentage, a meaningful portion of the economy was driven by narco-interests. Saulo Reyes, for example, owned multiple businesses, including fast-food franchises and restaurants, and was well positioned to launder narco-dollars. (Of course, these did not include the fronts that Reyes had purportedly used for his sweet insider-business dealings with the city during Héctor Murguía's tenure as mayor.) Saulo Reyes might have been first among equals, but there were lots of people in Juárez who, like him, benefited in one way or another from the narco-trade. "New money," they called it. Saulo Reyes and his ilk were the white-collar workers of the drug business, the people who lived in places like the upscale Campestre neighborhood, where they were members of the tony golf club and where beautifully manicured lawns surrounded mansions and gleaming SUVs of every make, including more than a few Hummers, were parked behind tall iron gates.

La Línea, the Juárez cartel's armed wing, represented the part of the Juárez cartel world where people got their hands dirty. There were no layers of distance between the players who were part of La Línea and the raw edge of the drug trade. They ensured that shipments of marijuana, cocaine, methamphetamine, or heroin got to where they needed to be and that cartel product was safeguarded until it was time to sell it or move it across the river. No one interfered with La Línea: they were the ones who lifted people and took them to the houses of death, where they met unspeakable fates; they were the ones paid to snuff other people out. Most of the members of La Línea were current or former state and municipal police who knew power in a way that few ever do. No rules applied to them, and they answered to no one except their cartel bosses. Many believe that it was this culture of malevolence that bred the infamous Juárez femicides of the 1990s: that La Línea was the central force in the killings of Juárez's young working women, and that they did it for sport and as an outlet for their sadism. Their violence knew only the bounds of their private whims. These cartel collaborators within the city's municipal police and the state's ministerial police were highly feared. An aura of evil hung over anything associated with La Línea, which operated like a secret society in Juárez.

Whenever a citizen of Juárez encountered someone in a police uniform, be it a state ministerial police officer or a city municipal police officer, there was ample reason for fear. The shadow of La Línea infused those perceptions. There was no way of knowing if the policeman was just another officer looking for a bribe or whether, instead, he was one of the truly evil ones. Those lines were never clear when it came to the police.

■ ■ ■

There were only fifteen hundred municipal police officers on the force, which, for a city of 1.3 million inhabitants, was paltry. Chicago, as a point of comparison, was almost twice the size of Juárez (2.8 million inhabitants), but had a police force that was more than ten times the size (approximately sixteen thousand officers). The size of the Juárez force had remained unchanged for almost three decades, even as the population had tripled over the same interval (the city was also far-flung, encompassing seventy-two square miles). The fact that the number of police had not kept apace with the city's growth was a testament to the general neglect of city services, but it was also not necessarily useful to La Línea and the Juárez cartel to have an expanded police force. That just meant more people who might get in their way or more people who needed to get paid for work that the cartel was already managing with the present "membership" levels. A smaller police force gave the Juárez cartel greater control.

The relationship between law enforcement and the Juárez cartel had evolved over time. Initially, in the mid-1990s, law enforcement was more powerful than the cartel, which had to negotiate with law enforcement officials for protection so that it could move its drugs through the city. The narcos controlled the pushers and the distributors, but they had to answer to the police. By 1998, however, the relationships between the cartel and the police had shifted dramatically, fueled, in part, by the cartel's enormous wealth, which also helped it gain more influence on state and federal politicians. That influence gave the cartel increased leverage when it came to the Juárez police. The cartel and the police came to occupy more equitable positions, with ex-police forming part of the cartel leadership, while the cartel continued to have outright control over pushers and distribution. But by

2004 the relative power differential had flipped altogether. The cartel had become so powerful and dominant that the police came to occupy a clearly subordinate role. The police now answered to the cartel bosses and had to carry out their directives as rank employees. "For the cartel, the police became 'disposable' players," is the way one source described it. Those who did not do as they were instructed were simply executed or lifted, and their replacements were then pressured via threats and inducements to do what the cartel wanted them to do.

Not all police were members of La Línea, but the cartel did not need to control every police officer in order to run its operations, it just had to be strategic. "My police budget was $60 million a year," mayor Reyes Ferriz observed, "but the cartel was able to completely neutralize the force with, say, $300,000 a year." The mayor was referring to the fact that the cartel only needed to buy off certain commanders and certain operations people to control the force. "For $50,000 pesos a month [less than $5,000 dollars] they could own a commander, and that person controlled what went on within his area. Operations people they could buy for anywhere from $20,000 to $50,000, depending on what they did." The mayor recalled a case in which the cartel had executed a policeman who had been working for La Línea but had run afoul of them for unknown reasons. The victim was one of three officers who had been working together and who were supposed to be passing information to the cartel regarding such things as which police were patrolling what areas of the city. Each of these officers was being paid $10,000 to $15,000 pesos per month. The execution of the first policeman had raised suspicions about the two other officers, prompting an internal investigation. "We shifted the two officers to other assignments while they were being investigated," the mayor continued. The reassignments meant that the officers no longer had access to the information for which they were being paid, but the cartel did not countenance excuses. If you accepted money, you were expected to deliver. Both of the reassigned officers were executed shortly thereafter, even though their failure to comply was obviously beyond their control.

La Línea also waged a war of terror upon the hapless beat cops and the ordinary riffraff within the department who weren't part of their mafia, not to mention the occasional honest officer. Bullying them for information or forcing them to collude and take part or look the other way was not difficult when they all knew the cost of not going along. The commanders had control of all assignments, schedules, and pay; they could also fire people at will. In addition, the threat of brute force or even execution was ever-present and very real. All of these elements made it relatively easy for the Juárez cartel to keep the police in line. Easy, that is, until the Sinaloa cartel had begun using the same tactics of intimidation and coercion to win over the very police officers who for years had been part of the Juárez cartel organization.

■ ■ ■

By the 1990s the Juárez cartel had become the most important cartel in Mexico, moving tons of Colombian cocaine, in addition to Mexican marijuana and heroin, from Juárez into El Paso, Texas, and points beyond (until relatively recently, methamphetamine was primarily a Sinaloa cartel product, although that's no longer the case). The cartel arranged to get bulk cocaine shipments delivered to Juárez, where they were broken down into lots of various sizes depending on where they were going and to whom they were allocated. These drugs had one of two destinations. One was El Paso and beyond, the other was the Juárez retail market. The profits were obviously significantly higher for the product that made it across the river, but so were the risks. Local distribution generated fewer profits, but was a cakewalk by comparison.

Hernán, Elena's paramour, was one of many in the chain of operators who helped the Juárez cartel move product across the border. He was something of an entrepreneur who ran his own crew, recruited his own mules, and sometimes invested his own money in his deals. He operated as a franchise of sorts, although he was under the control of the Juárez cartel and took orders from them. Once the Juárez cartel got the product to the city, operators big and small, people like Hernán, got it across the river.

Hernán moved fifty to seventy kilo loads every week or two. The cartel people above him knew how much he handled and delivered product to him accordingly. "When he had a shipment, they allowed him to buy two or three kilos with his own money," Elena said. The cocaine that Hernán paid for outright bumped up his profits. Because he was a known, reliable quantity, Elena said that most of the product he received was fronted. Elena mentioned this as a point of pride; the Juárez cartel didn't front that much cocaine unless they trusted you. According to the Mexican federal police and the DEA, a kilo of cocaine could be purchased in Colombia for approximately $2,780. By the time that kilo arrived in Mexico it was worth $12,750. That same kilo was worth at least twice that once it crossed into El Paso, and three times that by the time it arrived in Chicago, say, or New York. At those prices, Hernán was moving tens of thousands of dollars of product into the United States on a regular basis.

A constant preoccupation for Hernán was lining up his mules to move his cocaine across the river. Once he received a shipment, he had to get it into the U.S. in short order. Delays meant that he didn't pay in a timely manner, and it did not take long for that circumstance to generate tensions between him and the cartel people above him. They did not take well to being owed tens of thousands if not hundreds of thousands of dollars.

That kind of tension got people killed. Hernán's favored way of smuggling product across was to find young women with SENTRI passes. These passes were originally created for the Juárez elite and the managers of the maquiladoras who lived in El Paso but crossed into Juárez daily to work in the assembly plants. The premise was that passholders received a security pre-screening that allowed them to cross back and forth with minimal inspections. There was even a special bridge for these vehicles, thus obviating the ever-lengthy wait to cross the other bridges into El Paso, which could be hours, depending on the time of day. The SENTRI passes were popular and, more and more people had them.

Hernán met these young women at bars and nightclubs where, after chatting them up with a few drinks, he proposed his deal: $200 ("In other words, almost nothing," is how Elena characterized it) to cross a small load of five to seven kilos. He promised to take care of them if they encountered problems, and he assured them that first-time busts of relatively small amounts of drugs would just get them bounced back to Juárez after a short interval in American detention, during which they'd be photographed and finger-printed, which was true.

Hernán was persuasive and seductive. He had a way with words and he was charismatic. More often than not, he was successful in enlisting their collaboration. The typical run involved strapping the kilo packets of cocaine to the mule: one kilo on each of the inner thighs, one on the small of the back, two around the stomach and one in the crotch area. The size of the mules sometimes dictated the quantities they could carry and how easily loose-fitting clothing could cover the packets. SENTRI passes helped but they were not a prerequisite: sometimes a single mule hit all three bridges in a single day. These young women were the bread and butter of Hernán's operation, but he used others as well, and, in a pinch, he ran loads himself. "He'd get crazed about it," Elena said, likening it to a game of Russian roulette. He'd strap himself up with a load (although he never carried more than three kilos) and hit a bridge, make his drop, and head back to Juárez, where he'd strap on another load and hit another bridge, until he'd hit all three bridges. He never got stopped, but it wasn't because he'd paid off an ICE agent, it was because he was lucky, according to Elena.

The mules were unreliable. They flaked out on him; they got cold feet. Some moved away. Some got boyfriends who didn't like their girlfriends working for Hernán, risking themselves for him. It threatened them. For any number of reasons, Hernán was constantly on the mule search. It was the lifeblood of his business; if he couldn't get product across he was dead in the water. More than once in her description of this process Elena likened him to a pimp. "He was a narco-pimp," she said derisively.

Hernán never kept anything related to his business in Elena's house. He had safe houses for that. But there were ways in which he allowed Elena into his world. At times he shared his escapades with her and periodically he asked her to come to a safe house to help clean and repackage cocaine freshly arrived from Colombia. The kilo packets were often greasy and soiled and Hernán was extremely meticulous about how he managed his merchandise. He claimed it was for security reasons so that the ICE dogs could not pick up the scent, but no doubt it was also his way of assuring that no one had tried to pull something over on him by slipping a dud or two into the stack. Hernán paid Elena $400 for that service. He could get it done for less, but there was the bonus that he could trust Elena.

The narco-business kept Hernán flush with cash. When he walked in the door after a good run, he had a gleam in his eye. "What do you want to do?" he'd say. They'd have carne asada barbecues in the back yard and invite family and friends over for what sometimes turned into a running, multiday party. He'd take Elena and her brothers and their families to the movies. "We'd fill up two entire rows," she remembered. He loved to be the big spender. At times he took her family on vacation, as well, driving down to Parral, or over to Monterrey for the weekend, or even as far as Mazatlán. Her family liked him, and every one of them knew exactly what he did. This was simply life in Juárez's narco-world, where for many the comings and goings of the Juárez cartel members were just part of the accepted order of things. If there was any opprobrium, they kept it to themselves.

This was also the life of the Juárez cartel away from Club Campestre and Saulo Reyes's Subway franchises. It was full of people like Hernán and Elena, people who had grown up with nothing in Juárez's desolate neighborhoods, which often lacked even basic utilities and resources. In these neighborhoods the buses ran irregularly, the streets were unlit at night, and the desert dust covered everything with a fine coat, despite the occasional rain that turned it all to mud. The people in these neighborhoods rarely had more than an elementary school or middle school education, and they lived in areas full of despair even as, paradoxically, they were also full of life and neighborhood conviviality. Most of all these were people with few prospects who could not imagine themselves locked into the life of assembly plant work (and, in any event, the maquiladoras mostly hired women). The Juárez cartel gave people like Hernán and Elena access to what felt like real money. The Juárez assembly plants were paying full-time employees $200 to $300 a month. Twelve-year-old kids were making close to that just sitting on the rooftops of La Cima and calling an alert every time the army or the police came into view. Elena made more than that every time she unpacked, washed, and carefully repacked the shipments of cocaine that had made it all the way from Colombia to Mexico's Pacific Coast and overland to Juárez in anticipation of their passage into the United States.

CHAPTER 12

The Human Rights Activist

Gustavo de la Rosa was one of those who were not amused by the Mexican Army's tactics in Juárez. De la Rosa was the Ciudad Juárez representative for the Human Rights Commission of the State of Chihuahua. He took his job seriously. A corpulent man in his midsixties with a striking white beard and a matching mane of long hair, Gustavo de la Rosa was long accustomed to being called Santa Claus. His wire-rimmed glasses completed the portrait. However, de la Rosa's kind face and velvety voice belied a harder core. A veteran of the region's 1960s leftist movements, de la Rosa was an attorney with a long history as a defender of human rights, labor unions, and other causes that many would characterize as left of center. From the start of Operación Conjunto Chihuahua, as the federal government's campaign in the state was called, de la Rosa became a thorn in the side of the army as well as of Mayor José Reyes Ferriz. "He likes to stir things up," Reyes Ferriz told me at one point. "He panders to the rabble." De la Rosa was no more complimentary of the mayor, whom he did not view as corrupt but as someone whose privilege and class position translated into interests and a worldview that differed radically from his own in almost every respect. De la Rosa saw Reyes Ferriz as a man who catered to the city's elite business interests, one more attuned to the moneyed classes than to the city's working men and women.

From the start, the army's tactics produced accusations of human rights violations, all of which eventually ended up on Gustavo de la Rosa's desk. This set de la Rosa on a collision course with the mayor, the federal forces in the city, and the apparatus of Operación Conjunto Chihuahua itself. One evening, on his way home from a meeting, de la Rosa was idling at a stoplight when a red Honda carrying two men pulled up next to him. "A man got out and came over to my car," de la Rosa would later tell me. The man had a sinister look as he stood outside de la Rosa's window. De la Rosa feared that he was about to be assassinated. "You need to tone things down or we're going to kill you," the man said, making his hand into the shape of a gun and pointing it at the activist's head. The exchange was unnerving; de la Rosa knew that he was on someone's hit list. Before long, in addition to receiving a steady flow of human-rights complaints against federal forces, de la Rosa was also receiving constant death threats.

■ ■ ■

Gustavo de la Rosa and Teto Murguía, the former mayor, had attended high school together at the Federal #1 College Preparatory School in Juárez. At the time, the two had been school chums of a man named Rafael Aguilar, who would subsequently become one of the founders of the Juárez cartel. In small-town Juárez, those early relationships often became lifelong acquaintances, if not friendships. Aguilar's father had brought his family to Juárez from Mexico City when he'd obtained a customs position at the international port of entry—a lucrative post given the enviable opportunities it offered for collecting bribes. According to de la Rosa, fellow students had nicknamed Rafael Aguilar "El Chilango," typically a term of derision for people from the nation's capital, though de la Rosa insisted that, in Aguilar's case, "it wasn't with malice." The family had subsequently returned to Mexico City after Aguilar graduated from high school; Gustavo de la Rosa went off to Chihuahua City to study law at the Universidad Autónoma de Chihuahua.

Gustavo de la Rosa was nostalgic about the 1960s; the era had been life-defining for him. Like the United States, Mexico during the sixties was awash in revolutionary fervor and the emerging counterculture. De la Rosa found himself immersed in it, listening to the Sonora Matancera, the Beatles, and the Rolling Stones, and engaging the work of Andy Warhol. De la Rosa and his fellow students periodically drove up to Juárez to protest the Vietnam War at the international bridge. "There was a storm of change," he remembered.

For many in Mexico's youth movement there was a single moment that defined the emergence of their political consciousness: the October 2, 1968, massacre of student protesters in Mexico City's La Plaza de las Tres Culturas in Tlatelolco, in which hundreds were killed and many more wounded. That event became seared in the consciousness of the entire country, and the Mexican Army and the Mexican secret police—an organization known as the Federal Directorate for Security, or the DFS by its Spanish acronym—each played a central role in the massacre. It would take decades for the army to regain a reputation as a disciplined force worthy of respect.

"Sixty-eight surprised us in Chihuahua," de la Rosa recalled one afternoon as we sat across from one another at an Italian restaurant. The dead and wounded in Tlatelolco became martyrs, and their memory radicalized de la Rosa along with tens of thousands of other Mexicans. The student movement was strong in Chihuahua and it shaped de la Rosa's imagination. "As student activists we read Marx, Engels, and a few of us even read Bakunin," de la Rosa recalled. He became an avowed Marxist. "My inspiration was Che Guevara. It was very strong for all of us. He'd only been dead eighteen months," de la Rosa told me.

At the time, guerrilla movements intent on revolution were sprouting all over Mexico, and the state of Chihuahua became particularly fertile soil. By 1969 there were two major factions within the leftist movements, with different strategies for pressuring the government. One group was urging armed struggle, starting in rural areas and then converging on cities, much like Mao in China and Fidel Castro in Cuba. The other group wanted to organize workers and *campesinos* as a long-term strategy toward revolutionizing workers. The factions split, and the groups advocating armed guerrilla actions became known as La Liga Comunista 23 de Septiembre (September 23rd Communist League), taking its name from an unsuccessful assault on the army garrison at Ciudad Madera in Chihuahua on September 23, 1965. The Liga was in fact a national collective of revolutionary organizations across all of Mexico, not only in Chihuahua. In addition to other guerrilla activity, by 1970–1971 La Liga had begun robbing banks in what it termed "expropriations" and kidnapping the wealthy in order to underwrite its efforts to rid the Mexican state of corrupt politicians who it argued were enriching themselves unfairly while keeping the poor from participating in the political system. La Liga sought to eradicate the existent Mexican state.

De la Rosa allied himself with the group that sought to organize workers, which brought him into conflict with La Liga, who came to view him as a counterrevolutionary who was working within the system. That status earned de la Rosa his first death threat, which appeared in the official La Liga organ, called *Madera*.

At the apex of the guerrilla movements, Luis Echeverría, Mexico's president between 1970 and 1976, authorized the formation of what came to be called the White Brigades. The White Brigades, under the direction of the DFS, set out to find and exterminate the leftist revolutionary groups throughout Mexico. Over the ensuing six years, government agents would abduct, torture, and murder hundreds if not thousands of citizens in what became known as Mexico's "Dirty War."

Rafael Aguilar had been gone for ten years when he reappeared in the streets of Juárez as head of the DFS efforts in Chihuahua. The DFS was deeply feared throughout Mexico. It had a reputation for acting ruthlessly, and it was essentially above the law; it had no one to answer to except for the country's top leadership. The DFS lifted people who were considered enemies of the state or who were simply inconvenient to some of its powerful functionaries. Many of these hapless individuals simply disappeared, never to be heard from again. The DFS was also adept at the dark art of torture, which was its preferred investigative tool. Juárez had an especially active nucleus of leftist activity at the time, and Rafael Aguilar's people began torturing and assassinating leftist sympathizers. Others whom they considered "high value" targets were shipped to Mexico City, where they met similar fates.

Gustavo de la Rosa considered himself to be a Marxist activist, with strong political convictions. However, his life may have been spared because he'd decided to use his legal skills to represent workers, students, leftists, and people whom he considered victims of the system's powerful elite, rather than throwing his lot in with the armed factions that were advocating the overthrow of the Mexican state. He set up his "People's Law Office," where he represented dissidents who were being arrested, including members of La Liga Comunista 23 de Septiembre. De la Rosa had not seen Aguilar since high school, but after his return to Juárez there were times when he personally interceded with Rafael Aguilar in an effort to secure the release of people who had been picked up by the DFS—people, that is, who otherwise were quite likely never to see the light of day again.

"I remember one case in 1975," de la Rosa told me. A woman and her nephew, a young man named Raúl, both from Los Angeles and of Mexican ancestry, were in Juárez ostensibly "visiting family" when Raúl was picked up by the DFS and accused of subversive activity. The woman sought de la Rosa's help.

"I started making calls looking for Rafa Aguilar," de la Rosa said, using one of the nicknames that school chums had used for the DFS commander. De la Rosa finally tracked down information indicating that Raúl had been taken to Calle Oro, where the DFS had its command center. "I rang the doorbell, and one of Aguilar's men came to the door," de la Rosa said. When he asked to speak with Rafael Aguilar, the man said, "The *jefe* can't speak to you at the moment."

De la Rosa demanded Raúl's release. "He may be a sympathizer, but he hasn't committed any actions that violate the law," de la Rosa told the DFS agent. The man who'd answered the door left, but returned a few minutes later to inform de la Rosa that of the five individuals who had been apprehended two had confessed to being guerrillas. "We're still looking into the rest," the man said, which de la Rosa took to mean that they were being tortured. An agitated de la Rosa instructed the DFS agent that they had better not "lose" or kill Raúl, to which the agent simply responded, "Let me mention that to the *jefe.*"

Later that evening de la Rosa received a call from the DFS at his law office. "You can pick him up. He's at the Café la Nueva Central." Raúl's aunt returned shortly to de la Rosa's office with the young man. "He'd been beaten severely," de la Rosa recalled. "He was terribly frightened and he was crying." Raúl told de la Rosa that there were three others still in custody, but de la Rosa said there was nothing he could do for them. Raúl's retort stunned him: "You people who are working within the system are strengthening it, and that's why we haven't been successful," he said, referring to the revolutionary aims of the group. "He was convinced of his ideas," de la Rosa said philosophically. De la Rosa also succeeded in interceding with Rafael Aguilar on behalf of several other would-be revolutionaries like Raúl. "They were usually lesser players," de la Rosa told me. "The government never turned people over to me whom they considered important." After a rueful pause, de la Rosa added, "There were some eight hundred people who disappeared during that time."

Mexico's Dirty War drew to a close in the late 1970s and early 1980s, and La Liga Comunista 23 de Septiembre was dissolved. Rafael Aguilar was left as the most powerful man in the state. For years, as head of the DFS in Chihuahua, Aguilar had controlled the state's highways, airports, and international bridges. He and his agents knew the names of every significant smuggler, their areas of operation, and the products they worked. Aguilar now put his position to work in the service of the drug business. "The apparatus that Aguilar controlled remained intact," de la Rosa noted. "They just became narcos and they were no threat to the Mexican state," he said, implying that that fact had allowed them to operate without interference. It was then that Aguilar brought together the most important smuggling groups, forging an alliance that became the Juárez cartel. Along the way he put his DFS experience to work, exterminating everyone who resisted or otherwise posed obstacles to his vision.

Rafael Aguilar thus became one of the founding members of the Juárez cartel, along with two associates: a man named Gilberto Ontiveros, who went by the nickname "El Greñas" (the shaggy-haired one); and Rafael Muñoz, the man who'd been the manager at the Las Vacas restaurant where, as a child, the mayor and his family had periodically lunched on Sundays. It was one of those strange ironies that the founding of the Juárez cartel would be so closely linked to the forces of repression that gripped the country in the 1970s as part of Mexico's Dirty War. In 2008, when Calderón dispatched the army and the federal police to Juárez to attempt to take down the cartels, the political left severely criticized these actions, and Gustavo de la Rosa's voice of opposition was one of the strongest. Many perceived a parallel between the government's current intervention and the earlier intervention against the leftist guerrilla movements, even though the parallel was far from apt. While there was truth to the accusation that the government's tactics were creating significant human rights abuses, the cartels themselves could hardly be seen as victims. Their violence was terrorizing entire communities, and the dysfunctional judicial system that had long resulted in the arbitrary detentions of innocent people was the same system that was now permitting cartel operatives and their gangs to execute people at will in the streets and to lift and torture rivals as well as the citizens who reported on their activities, all without fear of prosecution.

The Mexico of 2008 was far-removed from the one-party, autocratic oligarchy that had governed the country with an iron fist for decades until the democratic opening that led to the 2000 elections. And the leftist movements whose idealism had driven their 1960s activism were not analogous in any way to the drug cartels and their gangs. One could legitimately take issue with the Calderón government's tactics and strategy, but only the most naïve, or the most cynical, could fail to see that the Mexican drug cartels posed a real threat to the future viability of the country.

CHAPTER 13

Román

José Reyes Ferriz went to Mexico City at the end of February 2008 to meet with federal authorities and found their response heartening: they were eager to help. But they had one precondition: the Juárez municipal police had to be cleaned up. In order to accomplish this, the entire force would have to submit to Confidence Tests administered by the federal police. It was a key plank in the federal government's national strategy: the municipal and state police forces were the most corrupt; they were the nexus that would unravel any effort to confront the cartels. For this reason, the government was pressuring the most critical municipalities, where cartel infiltration and violence were strongest, to submit their police forces to the Confidence Tests. Given that the police functioned as the Juárez cartel's enforcement wing, this meant depriving the cartel of a vital tool, an essential component of their business. While the Juárez cartel was still thought to be the main player within the local police, there was widespread suspicion that in recent months the Sinaloa cartel had made significant inroads into the force. Cleaning up the police was going to be a difficult, contested process. The cartels would resist it tooth and nail.

Toward the end of March, Mayor José Reyes Ferriz announced at a press conference that Guillermo Prieto and Antonio Román, the chief and the director of operations of the Juárez municipal police, respectively, would be going to Mexico City, where they would be administered the Confidence Tests at the Secretariat for Public Security, the agency headed by Genaro García Luna. Prieto would leave on April 2, while Román and four district commanders would be given appointments soon thereafter. The federal police would come to Juárez to administer the tests to the rest of the force. "We're going to rid the police of the corruption that this administration inherited," the mayor vowed. As part of its strategy to combat corruption within the national police forces, the federal police were developing a national database of fingerprints, iris images, and voice recordings for everyone associated with law enforcement at the municipal, state, and federal levels. The federal government was using federal funding for security needs as leverage to force the municipalities into compliance: Juárez, for example, would only receive its allotted 104 million pesos ($8.4 million dollars) in security funding upon completion of the tests.

Testing the currently active members of the Juárez municipal police would be no small undertaking. The mayor leased an old empty warehouse on Lerdo Street that had previously been home to the AC Nielsen Company. Thirty-six specialists from the federal police arrived at the end of April and beginning of May to begin administering the tests. They estimated that they would be able to process up to fifty-eight municipal police agents a day and that the entire process would take them approximately six weeks. It was decided that it would be less disruptive for the results to be announced at the end of the process rather than piecemeal.

■ ■ ■

Felipe Calderón's security cabinet came to Juárez on May 8 to assess the status of Operación Conjunto Chihuahua. It was the third time in as many months that they had visited the city, and an orchestrated wave of bad news welcomed them. The bloodletting of the police was starting anew. There had already been seventeen police executions since the start of the year, but now, after a lull, the pace again quickened. In the forty-eight hours prior to the official visit, five municipal police and one commander had been ambushed and wounded in two separate incidents. In a third incident, José Roberto Ortiz, recently named to head the Babícora sector, had gone on the police radio to exhort his troops to do good work on behalf of the force. Moments later, a cavernous voice jumped on the same police frequency to berate the "kiss ass" cops, shouting this threat in reference to Ortiz: "Let's see how long this son of a bitch lasts you!" The answer was not long in coming; Ortiz and his two bodyguards were executed within hours of the threat.

It was impossible to miss the conclusion that the rash of assassinations and attempted assassinations were related to the announced start of the Confidence Tests and the fact that Calderón's national security cabinet was meeting in Juárez. Nevertheless, the governor of Chihuahua, José Reyes Baeza, attempted to dampen such speculation. "They don't have the [security cabinet's] agenda," the governor said in reference to the cartels. "The killings take place whether or not the authorities are having meetings." But the newspaper headlines that greeted president Calderón's security cabinet upon its arrival in Juárez said it all: "Six More Yesterday," "Six Assassinated: So Far 29 in 9 Days." It was only early May and already, at 291, the year's tally of the dead was about to break the city's record-setting 301 executions for 2007.

The press conference following the security cabinet's meeting was a somber affair. It included the head of the Secretariat for Public Security, Genaro García Luna; the heads of the army and navy; the federal attorney general, Eduardo Medina-Mora; and the secretary of the interior, Camilo

Mouriño. It fell to the secretary of defense, Guillermo Galván Galván, to summarize the facts that would hopefully reassure the populace that the federal government's efforts were producing results. The general ticked off the numbers: hundreds arrested, tons of marijuana and kilos of cocaine seized, and tens of thousands of dollars recovered. It was then left to Camilo Mouriño, the secretary of the interior, to try to explain that the city was witnessing a full-blown war between cartels for control of the Juárez *plaza*. What Mouriño could not explain was what was in most need of explanation: the temerity of the assassins, the rising tally of the dead, and the failure to generate the most important, indispensable metric of all, a sense of stability and hope among the people of Juárez.

Following the Juárez meetings, the security cabinet returned to Mexico City. The president had sent the cabinet to Juárez in part as an effort to reassure and to convey the high priority and importance that he gave to turning back the tide of violence in Juárez. Timing the arrival of his key cabinet members with the initiation of the Confidence Tests and the police cleanup was part of the same message: that the federal government was in Juárez to take care of business. But the cartels were media-savvy. They understood the president's intended message all too well, and they were more adept at conveying their own message. The cartels had no need for press conferences; they created events that of necessity drew the media and became front-page copy.

The challenge that Calderón and the men in his security cabinet faced, the problem that all of Mexican society faced, had been in the making for years. The dysfunctional institutions were so tightly entwined with the social fabric that an anthropologist might have concluded that they'd become part of the culture itself. Mexicans had lived with overt, daily corruption on the part of the police forces for generations. It was not new and it was not a surprise; it was a thoroughly familiar fact of life. Mexican society had permitted PEMEX, the national oil company, to operate with unbridled graft and corruption. It had allowed the teachers union to destroy the country's once-proud educational system. And it had permitted generations of politicians to plunder the public coffers without restraint and without fear of consequence. The president had labeled the cartels "a cancer," but *this* was the medium that bred that cancer. The cartels were merely exploiting an extant disease that had well-near broken the spirit of the country and spawned the pervasive cynicism that undermined even well-intentioned efforts to reset the great nation's course. This is what the men of the president's security cabinet, heads of the most influential government institutions in the country, were really facing. It was a challenge that was bigger than their collective powers combined, and all the more elusive because the problem was interwoven and burrowed deep within the core of the society itself. Even for people with the best intentions, the conundrum was too complex, appearing to defy solutions.

■ ■ ■

On the day of the security cabinet's arrival, Guillermo Prieto officially started the cleanup of the police force. One of the first things Prieto did was transfer control of the city's emergency response number, 066, to the army. The intent was to send a signal to citizens that it was now safe to call and report suspicious activity. There was consensus between the mayor, Guillermo Prieto, and the federal authorities that a key to winning the city back was to regain the trust of the public so that actionable information could flow into the system. The city's security team considered the transfer of the Emergency Response Center to the army to be an important step toward creating a safer city.

Later that afternoon, Guillermo Prieto and Juan Antonio Román, the department's chief of operations, met in Prieto's office. The chief, in a celebratory mood, pulled out a bottle of tequila. The two heads of the Juárez municipal police marked the day's accomplishments with a shot. One shot then led to another. Prieto and Román started reminiscing and reflecting on the hard road they had been traversing. The recent death of their friend and colleague Francisco Ledesma was still fresh and weighing heavily on their minds. Ledesma had been gunned down in late January, just days before his name had appeared on the Sinaloa cartel's "For those who did not believe" list. Both men were acutely aware of the fact that Román's name topped the "For those who still do not believe" list. Many on this second list were now dead.

That evening Román told Prieto how much he missed the simple things, such as going to restaurants with his family or hanging out with his friends. The marked man now traveled with a heavy security detail at all times. Later that night, Román decided to call one of his *compadres*: "Let's go play dominoes. Get some friends together," Román told him.

Perhaps Román felt assured that he had not been followed. Perhaps he felt safe in the hands of the friends who he'd be joining at the domino table. Or perhaps he was simply exhausted and the tequila had lulled him into dropping his guard. Whatever the reason, once Román arrived at his friend's house, he dismissed his bodyguards. "I'm going to be here late," he told them.

Román and his friends played dominoes, drank, and talked until nearly three in the morning before Román decided it was time to head home. He left his friend's house alone. Somehow, through the network of informants and collaborators, the would-be assassins had learned that Román had released his security team, which meant that he was defenseless. Someone recognized the unusual opportunity to execute the police's second in command, and by the time Román arrived at his house, a cartel commando unit lay in wait for him. When Román pulled up to his house, he was killed in a hail of gunfire.

At home in bed, Reyes Ferriz received a call from Guillermo Prieto. The police chief was breathless, running to Román's house. "He was extremely agitated," the mayor would later remember. "They've just attacked Román!" Prieto screamed into the phone, and when he was close enough to verify the report, he seemed to break down: "It's him! Damn it! Why him? Why him?"

At a hastily assembled press conference later that day, a shaken Reyes Ferriz attempted to put a brave face on it all. "This administration will not waver in the face of these attacks by organized criminals who want to destabilize the [police] department," he said. But behind the public pronouncements lay a more desperate reality: the cartels were continuing to decimate his police force, tearing it apart and systematically eliminating its leadership. Back in Mexico City, the morning after their visit to Juárez, the members of Calderón's security cabinet awoke to the news of Román's assassination. It was the cartels' response to the government's plans for saving Juárez.

■ ■ ■

The day of Antonio Román's funeral the words he'd spoken four months earlier at the funeral services for Francisco Ledesma seemed hauntingly prescient: "When you die in battle, confronting a criminal, that's nice," Román had said at Ledesma's graveside. "That's how police want to die," he'd continued.

"He always said: 'If they're going to kill me I want to go down shooting,'" the mayor would later tell me. "And he did. He fired six shots from his pistol that night."

When asked if he was going to resign from the police force after his name had appeared on the "For those who still do not believe" list, Román had replied in the negative. "This is a real bitch," he'd said, "but I'm continuing here. When it's your time to die you're going to die." At the time of his death, Román was the last one on the infamous list who was still on the force. The remaining sixteen individuals were either dead or had resigned. Román's loyalty to Guillermo Prieto was the reason most often cited for the fact that he'd stayed on. Just a month earlier, Prieto had talked Román into remaining on the force after the mayor had convinced Prieto himself to stay on until the army could launch Operación Conjunto Chihuahua.

José Reyes Ferriz felt this assassination more personally than most, because he'd had considerable contact with Román. "He was a strong, brave guy who wasn't afraid to get into things," the mayor said. He recalled one of the last times he'd seen Román, not long before his assassination. At the time, the police were feeling the pressure of the threats and the reality of so many executed comrades, and, as everyone was all too aware, Román's

Evidence marker at execution scene. Photo copyright © Raymundo Ruiz.

name topped the "unbelievers" list. "He came into the *presidencia* and he was wearing his bulletproof vest," the mayor recalled. With inch-and-a-half-thick steel plates, the vest reputedly could withstand the impact from an AK-47 round. "I could see it in his eyes," the mayor recalled. "The fear. He was afraid of being killed." The mayor continued after a moment, "I thought he was an admirable man," he said. "It was tough, hard, very tough emotionally. They say that JL personally came to kill him," the mayor added. "JL" was the man running the Juárez *plaza* for Vicente Carrillo Fuentes and the Juárez cartel. Although the Sinaloa cartel had been behind the "unbelievers" list, Reyes Ferriz believed that the Juárez cartel also wanted Román killed because he had been cooperating with the federal government's Confidence Tests. Being hunted by both cartels had reduced Román's likelihood of survival to zero.

■ ■ ■

One detail about Antonio Román's funeral caught the attention of nearly every observer: Guillermo Prieto, the police chief, was not present. Nor was he present at the subsequent news conference in which José Reyes Ferriz addressed Román's execution. This immediately set off a flurry of speculation as to his whereabouts and whether he had resigned.

Román had been assassinated in the early hours of Saturday morning. Later that afternoon, Prieto himself had received death threats. The police department was already decimated. With Román dead, all of the section heads had either been killed or left the force. Prieto put in a call to Reyes Ferriz. "I'm going to resign," he told the mayor. Reyes Ferriz went directly to police headquarters where the chief was holed up to talk with Prieto in person. The chief told him he was going to El Paso. It took some convincing, but the mayor and Prieto reached an agreement: Prieto would take refuge in El Paso, but he would not formally resign. Instead, he would continue running the department over the phone while Reyes Ferriz looked for his replacement. It was a desperate measure to preserve the illusion that the police department was not in utter shambles. Prieto issued a press release saying that because of the threats against him he would remain at an undisclosed location for security reasons, but that he continued as chief of the Juárez municipal police.

Later that day, as Mayor Reyes Ferriz headed home, a convoy of Suburbans driving at an exceedingly high speed blew by his security detail. "We were frightened," the mayor recalled. They had momentarily taken the convoy to be a cartel hit team, but it turned out to be the police chief and his security team heading for the international bridge and the sanctuary of El Paso, Texas. Press releases notwithstanding, Guillermo Prieto's tenure at the helm of the Juárez municipal police was finished.

CHAPTER 14

The Pajama Chief

Within a day of Guillermo Prieto's departure for El Paso, General Juárez Loera presented mayor José Reyes Ferriz with a recommendation for a new police chief. The mayor immediately flew to Mexico City to interview the candidate, whose name was Roberto Orduña. Orduña was a retired army major with some law enforcement experience; Reyes Ferriz offered Orduña the position on the spot and, to his surprise, Orduña accepted. "I didn't think anyone would take the job," the mayor later recalled, noting his relief. The one condition that Orduña placed was this: he wanted to have nothing to do with the media. "I'm allergic to them," the soon-to-be-chief told Reyes Ferriz.

Orduña was sixty-four years of age and had a serious air about him that complemented the bearing of a career military man. He sported a salt-and-pepper moustache and slicked-back hair with a receding hairline. Orduña's sagging eyelids gave his brown eyes a hooded look, and thick lines marked the man's face. He was crusty and no-nonsense, but then only a man with a steeled outlook toward life would have accepted the offer to be chief of the Juárez municipal police. There wasn't a corner of the Mexican republic where people had not heard about what was taking place there.

At 7:30 on the morning of Monday, May 19, 2008, Mayor José Reyes Ferriz swore in his new chief of police. The dysfunctional state of the force was obvious, the challenges facing the mayor and the police chief enormous. "To those who thought that the municipal police had been defeated, and that we had capitulated in the face of the cowardly attacks perpetrated by organized crime," the mayor told the assembled press and dignitaries, "today we are here before society to say to those voices that they are mistaken." He acknowledged that there were "bad elements" collaborating with organized crime within the police force. "We will fight all of those black grains in the rice," he said, noting that the police cleanup would continue. The mayor promised that the episodes of terror that had engulfed the city and generated a climate "of psychosis" would come to a stop. "There are more of us who wish to live in peace than there are of them," the mayor said.

The press learned from a short biographical sketch circulated at the swearing-in ceremony that Orduña had retired from the military after twenty-five years of service in 1983. He appeared to have had an illustrious career, serving with the 4th Artillery Regiment within Mexico's prestigious Heroico Colegio Militar. He'd had a smattering of law enforcement positions thereafter, including antinarcotics courses taught by the DEA and antikidnapping courses taught by the FBI. The curriculum vitae disseminated to the press had omitted the fact that Orduña had faced "labor problems" during a short five-month stint as chief of police in the city of Gómez Palacio, Durango, but some journalists had tracked this information down and raised it during the Q and A following the ceremony. Orduña played the episode down, saying only that it was a "disciplinary" matter that had been resolved within twenty-four hours through the intervention of the city's mayor. It was evident that he resented the questions. This was the initial salvo in what would become an ongoing battle between Orduña and the Juárez press.

The new police chief appeared intent on isolating himself. With the exception of his interactions with the mayor and his staff, the military, and the requisite contacts with state law enforcement, Orduña's interactions were mostly limited to his commanders within the municipal police. While it was typical for new chiefs to bring in their own trusted people and place them in the department's top positions, Orduña had negotiated no such arrangements when he'd met with the mayor in Mexico City. He seemed not to care about such details. When Orduña arrived in Juárez, he came by himself. No one knew if he even had a family.

The mayor had offered the services of his staff to help Orduña find a house to lease, but the former military man was uninterested. Instead, he asked Reyes Ferriz to construct living quarters for him at the headquarters. It was an odd request, to be sure, but the mayor complied with Orduña's wishes and an apartment was created for him inside the Babícora precinct compound. The existing police chief's office had been an ample room on the second floor with a large conference table on one side, across from a work area where the chief's desk sat. The office already had a bathroom, but no shower. The mayor had a partition built dividing the room in half, and the conference table area became Orduña's bedroom. A closet was converted into a shower.

Roberto Orduña was eccentric and, toward the outside world, misanthropic. He took to living like a monk. His entire life seemed to center around the challenges of wresting the police force from the clutches of the cartels. He brokered no fools and he eschewed niceties or even rudimentary comforts. Orduña announced that henceforth the media would not be permitted on the grounds of the Babícora station (headquarters) "for security reasons." He claimed that with all the threats against the police it would be too easy for assailants to infiltrate the building. The chief said he would host a weekly press conference on Monday mornings, but that would be the extent of the media's access to him.

Not surprisingly, the local media did not take well to the new arrangement. "The media lives off of police reports," the mayor noted, not unsympathetically. It seemed that Orduña was hell-bent on creating as much enmity as possible between himself and the press. The media was so incensed at Orduña's unavailability that they took to calling him, with obvious derision, "the pajama chief." But Orduña was hard as nails, and the thought of making enemies discomforted him not in the least. He worked from his second-floor bunker surrounded by his police officers, most of whom he knew disliked him and most of whom he knew he could not trust. Orduña was at war with his own force and thus alone and unprotected; he was living in the very jaws of the beast. That took nerves of steel. But Orduña had faith in his instincts and the judgments he formed, and on this basis he selected the people from within the municipal police that he believed he could bring into his inner circle to help him carry out the difficult work that lay ahead.

Within days of Orduña's assuming the position of chief, the cartels made their discontent with his selection known in three separate incidents: ten people were found shot execution-style, three of them beheaded. Then a narco-message was left on a bridge with a new list of police officers to be executed. Finally, a police officer's head was found in a plastic bag with a note signed "La Línea"—the officer was apparently one of the ones who had crossed over to the Sinaloa side.

Roberto Orduña's approach to his police was that of a tough drill sergeant. He announced at his first department meeting that he planned to "bring discipline" to the force. "*Señores*," he told them, "if you don't like the work you have here, the door will be open for whoever does not want to follow the new procedures." He seemed intent on running the department like a military unit. The "procedures" included an edict that the police shifts would be thirty-six hours on and twelve hours off. It was not well received. It was one thing to give such orders to a group of army conscripts; it was something else to give them to officers who had families. Orduña's order immediately set off protests within the force. A crack tactical group called the Delta Group led the protests, refusing to go on patrol or leave the station until Orduña met with them. The chief refused.

Historically, police officers had eight-hour shifts, but six months earlier, shortly after Guillermo Prieto had become chief, these had been increased to twelve-hour shifts. The proposed thirty-six-hour shift, the officers complained, was unacceptable (it was an effort to extend police coverage in the city). Orduña finally relented after extensive negotiations that included Mayor Reyes Ferriz, who said that there had been a "misunderstanding." The twelve-hour shift was reinstated, but officers would be required to work six days a week. Orduña also issued a stern warning to the malcontents on the force: "I won't tolerate insubordination," the former army major declared.

Another confrontation between Orduña and his force occurred shortly thereafter when Orduña instructed that officers would no longer be permitted to take their weapons home. Instead, they would have to be turned into the armory at the end of every shift. The practice of allowing police to keep their weapons and bulletproof vests was recent. It had been instituted earlier in the spring when the "For those who do not believe" list had been left at the monument and when a rash of police executions had led the mayor and Chief Prieto to put the police on red alert. The new edict made the police feel vulnerable, given that police executions were still epidemic.

Orduña's weapons edict activated another mini-insurrection within the police department. This time, however, Reyes Ferriz backed Orduña. The rationale given was that the military and federal police were now patrolling the streets and feared an "accidental" armed confrontation between the police and the military. According to the mayor, the agreement he had signed with the federal government stipulated that police would only carry their weapons during the hours they were in service. "The military doesn't want a situation in which they are confronted by people in civilian dress who are carrying weapons," the mayor explained.

There may have been another agenda at work as well. The so-called Technical Preventive Group, or Delta Group (its name had changed, but its functions and responsibilities remained the same), had been created during the administration of Héctor Murguía, during a time when the former mayor had vowed to "militarize" the police force. The elite, specialized force was deployed in a variety of ways. They were permitted to set up roadblocks when they felt the need, and they oversaw neighborhoods that had been identified as high-crime areas. One of their most important assignments, however, was investigating the city's retail drug markets, which presumably brought them into direct contact with the cartels and the gangs that were working for them, such as Los Aztecas. It was in the performance of these duties that the specialized force was most at risk for cartel corruption and coercion. The new chief suspected the Technical Preventive Group of collusion with the Juárez cartel. Those suspicions were reinforced when a narco-message was left outside of the Technical Preventive Group's administrative offices at 7 a.m. on the morning of May 30. The message listed the names of a dozen members of the group, under the heading "For the ones that are still left."

Although the names on the new narco-list were all members of the Technical Preventive Group, the message sent waves of terror throughout the entire force. The audacity of the act (someone had walked right up to the building to leave the message) was itself shocking. It also suggested that perhaps it was an inside job. Such evidence tended to stir a great deal of paranoia within the police force, given that no one knew whom they could trust.

The entire circumstance further fueled tensions over the directive that police would no longer be allowed to carry their service weapons at the end of their day's tour. Incensed officers called on Orduña to take into account the present level of danger in the city; they asked him to back them up. Some police claimed that the decision was a reprisal for their protests over the thirty-six-hour shift. "We aren't going to disarm ourselves," a police officer told one of the Juárez newspapers. "There are threats against us and we refuse to relinquish our weapons. . . . No one [on the force] is in agreement with this." But the only concession the protesting officers garnered was that they would be permitted to wear their bulletproof vests home.

Once again, there was massive unrest within the Juárez municipal police. At all six of the city's command centers officers threatened to strike, and there were work stoppages and slowdowns. Officers reported to the stations but were not going out on patrol; they stopped patrolling the northwest side of the city altogether. Neighborhoods with a disproportionate number of *picaderos* and where a disproportionate number of executions were taking place had no police presence. Some officers took to the police radio frequency to shout, "Strike!" "Strike!" "Strike!" The entire force was threatening to walk out.

But Roberto Orduña stood his ground in the face of the widespread unrest, reiterating his earlier "the door is open for those who wish to leave" statement. The police were on the brink of striking on three different occasions, but each time the protests were cancelled at the last moment. In the end, the officers caved. Orduña won the game of chicken, and the officers went out on patrol, although still "under protest."

From his bunker, Roberto Orduña set out to clean up the Juárez municipal police and rid it of the corrupt cops. The federal police continued running Orduña's officers through the Confidence Tests, and Orduña was counting on them to help him separate the good cops from the bad.

The army and the federal police were patrolling the city as well, but their distrust of the municipal police was so great that they refused to patrol jointly with them. All the while, the city of Juárez continued tumbling into the abyss. It was an anarchic war zone, and its institutions and social structures, many already taxed and deficient, were fraying rapidly. For the citizenry, ordinary crime had become as demoralizing as the daily tally of cartel executions. Bank robberies hit an all-time high and kidnappings, extortions, and car thefts were rampant. With the police force imploding, it was the army and a small contingent of federal police whose convoys were patrolling the city, while the municipal police presence in the streets was reluctant and sputtering at best. But the army knew little about law enforcement; they were trained for armed confrontation and direct engagements, not criminal investigations. The federal forces were also outsiders; they often had a difficult time negotiating the city, whose ad hoc *colonias* and ever-changing street names formed a disorienting urban labyrinth.

Despite their criminal activity, when the police were under the sole control of the Juárez cartel, they had also done real police work, at least the "preventive" police work that was the mandate of the national municipal police forces. There were units that were less compromised, for example, and even those units whose commanders were in the pay of the cartel still carried out functions that were not in conflict with the cartel's needs and desires. In other words, the police still had informants, patrolled, and arrested people. Even at the height of the narco-police, the police had managed to keep something of a lid on garden-variety criminals and day-to-day crime. But with the police now in shambles, there were no controls on criminal activity. This gave urgency to the planned Confidence Tests; they would be the foundation for building a new police force.

The federal police started processing municipal police agents through the Confidence Tests in May. Groups of forty to fifty officers were ordered to present themselves at the large warehouse that the city government had leased for the purpose and converted into the assessment center. It was hoped that the tests would prove effective in ferreting out untrustworthy officers.

■ ■ ■

In late summer of 2008 the federal police informed the mayor that the results of the Confidence Tests were ready. The mayor and Orduña rounded up the police in each of the six precincts, checked their weapons in, and waited for the federal people, but, according to the mayor, they didn't show. The city's entire force had been mustered amid a great deal of tension and apprehension, but it was all for naught.

In my subsequent conversations with them, the federal police blamed the mayor, suggesting that he had balked, fearing he would be assassinated. Notwithstanding the reality of those fears, they continued, it should have been his duty to fire the officers who were found to be questionable. However, Mayor Reyes Ferriz was unapologetic about leaning on the federal government to do the dirty work. He had every reason to believe that any of his personnel associated with the Confidence Tests would be executed: in an unmistakable signal early in the summer, as the assessments were starting up, the police department's head of personnel, a woman who scheduled officers for their testing dates, had been executed in a brutal assault. Her assassination had shaken the mayor profoundly. It made clear that as far as the Juárez cartel was concerned, every step to clean up the police would be taken as a direct attack. Cartel operatives also repeatedly jumped on the police radio frequency, shouting that the mayor would be executed if he fired any police.

From that point on, the mayor made every effort to position the police cleanup in the hands of the federal police, hoping to reduce the likelihood of more assassinations. He flew to Mexico City to meet with Genaro García Luna's people at the Secretariat for Public Safety. "I need you to fire them. I can't put my people in because they will kill them," he told them. The federal police were equally adamant that firing local police was outside of their jurisdiction. Reyes Ferriz would not budge: "I decided that no one on my staff or within the Juárez municipal police would so much as touch a single piece of paper [related to the Confidence Tests]," Reyes Ferriz later told me. Reyes Ferriz and the federal police were at an impasse.

The tug-of-war between the mayor and the federal police continued for several weeks, with the mayor insistent that the federal police handle the firings and the federal police equally insistent that under federal law they had no jurisdiction over municipal workers and hence could not legally fire them. In the end, Reyes Ferriz broke the impasse by hiring a Mexico City law firm to handle the firings as official representatives of the municipality. In Mexico City, the federal police gave the legal team the test results for the entire Juárez police force, and on October 16, 2008, the team flew to Juárez, where they spent a nervous night at a La Quinta hotel. The next morning, city staff delivered severance packages for every single officer on the force to the attorneys. The intent was to underscore the fact that only the Mexico City people knew the test results indicating who was to be fired and who was to be kept on. The police were simultaneously mustered at each of the city's six precincts, with the team of attorneys distributed accordingly, announcing who had passed the test and giving severance packages to those who had failed. The process was sloppy, tense, and unwieldy, but at the end of that day 334 police officers had been dismissed for not having passed the federal government's Confidence Test. Another 227 police had left the force since January out of fear of being executed or having their cartel alliances discovered, and a score had been assassinated.

Since spring, the police radio frequency had been in constant use by the narcos. These were analog radios, and anyone could purchase the requisite technology at a Radio Shack for a few hundred dollars. Thus, in addition to the police, the narcos and Juárez journalists could listen to the police frequency, and the narcos themselves also sometimes communicated on the frequency. At first, every time a police officer was assassinated, the narcos would play a *narcocorrido* on the frequency, all the while mocking the victim and threatening others. The Sinaloa and Juárez cartels had their respective *narcocorridos*, making it easy to know which cartel had carried out the execution. Into the summer, the cartels had taken to playing their *narcocorridos* prior to executions, sowing panic within the police force. There had been many threats against José Reyes Ferriz on the police frequency that spring, but the Confidence Tests took them to a new level. "You'd better watch your boss!" the narcos would shout onto the radio waves, referring to the mayor. "Throughout the day I fired the police I kept asking my bodyguards, 'How are the radios doing?'" Reyes Ferriz would later tell me. There had been a flurry of threats all day. "It was no game," the mayor said. "We knew it was dangerous."

That night was the first that José Reyes Ferriz slept with a loaded AR-15 assault rifle under his bed. He also started posting a municipal police patrol car outside the gates to his residential community (he'd already been sleeping with guards posted at the door to his house for months). One night an ominous-looking Hummer parked nearby. The police suspected that the occupants were waiting for another resident to pull up so they could tailgate behind them and gain entry into the gated community. The police managed to drive them off, but the next day the officers came to the mayor with a proposal: "Let us park inside the gate, otherwise they're going to kill us," they said. From then on, the patrol car stood vigil all night just inside the tall iron gate. The mayor had been driving in a "Level 4 Plus" armored vehicle. These could withstand an AK-47 assault but not that of an AR-15, which was increasingly the weapon of choice for the narcos. So the city purchased three "Level 5" armored vehicles: one for the mayor, another for the chief of police, and the third for the new director of operations. Not long thereafter, the army apprehended a *sicario* in the town of Villa Ahumada, seventy-five miles south of Juárez, a known Juárez cartel stronghold. The man was in possession of a copy of the floor plan for Reyes Ferriz's house, which he had obtained from the public registry.

■ ■ ■

Not long after the conclusion of the Confidence Tests I had the opportunity to meet an ex–police captain who had been fired from the force because he'd failed the test. He was presently working in a small, dilapidated office next door to a down-at-the-heels restaurant that had a daily *comida corrida* lunch for a fixed price (that day it was beef in *ranchera* sauce, rice, and beans, along with a mountain of still-hot tortillas wrapped tightly in a cloth towel like a swaddled baby). Iced fruit juices ladled from large glass jars, sodas, and beer were available for an additional charge. We sat at a flimsy metal Corona table, and I was struck by the fact that the man across from me did not seem quite as hardened or malevolent as I expected given the infamous reputation of the Juárez municipal police. I'd come primed to find a dark edginess in the former officer, who was in his early forties and balding, but he showed few signs of it.

The ex-captain described a police force that for the last year had been living in a state of panic. The executions of fellow officers had created a pervasive disquiet that permeated everything that went on, he said. He claimed not to have had direct involvement with La Línea, "but we all knew who the players were," he told me. He acknowledged that everyone on the force knew what was taking place although none dared speak out about it. In his telling, less than half of his fellow police officers were actively involved in La Línea activities. "They were the ones with the fancy watches, the ones with cash in their pockets," he said with a trace of envy. "The rest of us just watched and kept our mouths shut." Officers worried about their assignments. If you were placed in an area that was of use to the cartel you would be pressed into collaboration. "If they pushed you, you had to comply, you had to say yes, there was no alternative, no way out." Of course, there were also those who sought out such "opportunities."

He had worked in the gang unit, tracking neighborhood graffiti and complaints from people in the *colonias*, but he stuck to the minor-league stuff. He did not touch the big gangs, the ones allied with the cartels, the ones that had a stranglehold on the city. Those were off limits. No one needed to tell him to steer clear, he said. "You just knew not to tread on that ground. You might get a warning if you strayed into their things, but you might not" (meaning you might simply be executed). It depended on what you knew and what you did with the knowledge.

He'd worked closely with Francisco Ledesma, the third in command who'd been assassinated in January of 2008. He liked him, he told me. When I asked who it was that had killed Ledesma, the ex-captain grew visibly stiff, claiming not to know. He also refused to speculate. "All of that is too dangerous," he said, looking at me intently across the table. "They must have had their reasons. Whether its that he got in with the wrong people or that he wouldn't go along with what someone wanted, I can't say." It was obvious that he did not want to delve further into this line of inquiry. He looked me in the eyes as if to say, "What do you want?" He brought this thread of the conversation to a close by describing life in the police department for those who were not involved with the cartel as something akin to battered children living in terror of their abusive parents. "Being silent, feigning ignorance—that was the only way to stay alive," he said grimly. It was clear that he was still living that code of silence.

The former municipal police officer told me that he had presented himself to take the Confidence Test in a cavernous room at the old maquiladora plant, where both federal police and military people were running the operation. The Juárez officers were informed that they were in a federal building and were thus required to obey orders from federal personnel. There was an adversarial tone to the process, he told me; "They treated us arrogantly," he complained. After completing some paper-and-pencil tests, one by one the men were called to a series of cubicles where federal agents were performing the assessments. At the first station, he was asked to say a series of words like "town" and "lake" into a microphone. He was told that, like a vocal fingerprint, voice-recognition software would be able to identify him were he intercepted making calls to cartel operatives, negotiating with kidnap victims' families, or attempting to extort someone over the phone.

"They made us 'play the piano' at the second station," he said, adding, "That's our vulgar term for taking fingerprints." In addition to fingerprints, the federal police also took the officers' palm prints. At yet another station, a social worker asked him about his interests and hobbies, how much he earned, his wife's salary, the family budget—things of that nature. Next came the lie detector. "They asked me if I'd committed any crimes, if I'd been unfaithful to my wife, and if I'd ever taken drugs, among other questions," he remembered. Lastly his urine was tested for the presence of drugs, and he was given a vision test and a general physical. He was least happy about the physical, claiming that the physician had "handled him excessively," adding that he suspected the physician was gay.

The ex-captain complained that he'd received no explanation as to why he had failed the test, and he asserted that the entire process was a sham, an "inside deal" to find sacrificial lambs to take the fall so the department would look like it was doing what it was supposed to be doing. He knew for a fact, he said, that some of the officers with known cartel ties had not been dismissed from the force.

As we talked in the restaurant, he seemed tense. He kept looking up, glancing behind me toward the entrance as if someone might show up. I found it unnerving. That kind of paranoia is infectious. I also found it difficult to bracket out the awareness that he had been a member of the infamous Juárez municipal police, and throughout I kept thinking that there was no way for me to assess the truth of the ex-captain's statements. As the interview drew to a close he volunteered that it was good to be out. His time with the municipal police had taken a toll on him. He'd developed ulcers, he told me, but he was feeling much better now that he didn't have to live under those pressures. The number of sliced raw chilies that he'd heaped on his lunch was evidence that his ulcers were, indeed, no longer bothering him.

■ ■ ■

In the aftermath of the Confidence Tests, the executions, and the resignations, more than a third of the police force was gone. Almost immediately, a new crime wave broke out in the city; kidnappings, extortions, car thefts, bank robberies, and assaults surged. The theories were many. Some argued that the arrival of the army had so disrupted cartel activities that they had turned to other income-producing strategies. But the prevailing thesis was that it was the fired police who had gone on a crime spree. There were accusations that in dismissing so many police, Mayor José Reyes Ferriz had left the city defenseless.

CHAPTER 15

The Journos

I t was an unseasonably warm fall afternoon, and the streets of Juárez felt worn and heavy. Cars, buses, and trucks were up and down the boulevards: horns honking, music blaring, brakes groaning, gears grinding. The smell of exhaust and oil was in the air. I was with Raymundo Ruiz, the *El Norte* photographer, who was unusually quiet. Ruiz traveled at all times with two cell phones: a Nextel two-way phone[1] and a police scanner. The scanner's chatter was an ever-present backdrop to his life; he turned it off only when he went to bed for the night.

This day the police scanner had been squawking incessantly. Even knowing many of the codes (Ruiz had given them to me and I'd written them down), I missed half of what was being said over the scanner because voices were garbled and static-filled, and the people communicating on the police frequency continuously stepped on each other's lines, talking over and through one another. Ruiz had a sixth sense for the scanner. He could be in conversation, or talking on one of his phones, but the scanner world was always with him. Most of what was coming through this afternoon was the drudgery of day-to-day police work: "*Motivo* fifty," the scanner barked (an officer was pulling someone over for speeding); "*Motivo* one" (traffic accident). There were even codes to describe the gender of the offenders or victims. In the current scheme, "ninety-one" meant that the subject was male, "ninety-two," female.

When a "*Motivo* fifty-nine" came through the scanner, everything else came to a stop for Ruiz: it was police code for an execution. The dispatcher had given the location as an intersection in southeastern Juárez, and Ruiz started tracking it down. He called his crew, the fellow journalists with whom he was in constant contact, making sure they, too, had heard the "*Motivo* fifty-nine" and that they knew how to reach the location—no one knew this city better than Raymundo Ruiz.

Ruiz drove through the city as if he were racing in a rally; he was indifferent to speed bumps, stop signs, or stoplights. The car's gears were grinding and the brakes fumed and protested. Over and over again the bottom of his worn-out Toyota Tercel scraped the ever-present speed bumps as we made our way through the back streets of dusty neighborhoods to the execution. I worried that he was going to hit an unsuspecting pedestrian or that someone with the right-of-way coming from a side street would ram us, but Ruiz seemed impervious: his driving was governed mainly by intuition and instinct.

The payoff for this bit of insanity was that we were among the first to arrive at the crime scene—a gas station at a busy intersection. The army and federal police units had cordoned off the area, but even from behind the yellow crime-scene tape the body was clearly visible through the partly ajar car door of a recent-model Ford Explorer. A printed sign at the fuel pumps read: "By disposition of the management, we do not accept $1000 peso bills." The black SUV looked glossy, obviously recently washed and waxed. The thud-thud of a hail of bullets had activated the driver's airbag, which, now deflated, had fallen to the ground through the space between the door and the car, its snow-white end resting almost casually on the oily pavement. The victim had apparently just pulled up to the pump when a *sicario* had approached and emptied his pistol into him. The bullets that burst through the tinted glass had left a tight pattern with but a few wayward rounds falling beyond the perimeter of the fist-sized hole created by the volley: the hit was clearly the work of a professional. Inside the vehicle, a man's body could be seen still slumped between the steering wheel and the console, his sky-blue, short-sleeved police uniform multiply perforated with bloody holes.

The victim was a captain with the Juárez municipal police from the Delicias station. "He's from the old guard," I overheard one of the other journalists at the scene say in hushed tones to one of his buddies. Someone else said, "That's three [executions] in the last hour and a half." The blood was flowing freely in Ciudad Juárez today.

■ ■ ■

Later that evening, I was with a family gathered to say a rosary in memory of one of the Juárez dead. This was the fifth night that the family had come together like this; there were four more to go to complete the *novena*, the nine-night ritual of Catholic mourning.

There were eighteen of us in the modest working-class home where living room, dining room, and kitchen were pressed together into a single space. Most were family members of the deceased, including school-aged children and elderly relatives. Those that could were sitting in the dining table chairs that had been placed around the room and on a sofa. The rest of us stood. Our number filled the entire space and our bodies were close together; the room was hot, the air heavy. A family friend, a woman in her fifties, led the prayers, holding a rosary in her hands with the casualness of someone for whom this ritual was all too familiar.

The woman made the sign of the cross, and at the first bead she led the assembled in an Our Father prayer. "Forgive us our sins . . . ," the words floating in the collective murmur. The Hail Marys followed, ten for every Our Father. "Holy Mary, Mother of God, pray for us sinners, now and at the hour of our death." That came to five Our Fathers and fifty Hail Marys. A sense of mystery pervaded the space.

Bead after bead, the prayers slid into the room, one after another, becoming an all-enveloping chant. "Holy Mary, Mother of God . . ." Voices wrapped themselves around each other and echoed across the room . . . "now and at the hour of our death" . . . bead after bead moving nimbly from finger to finger, keeping track of place lest the chants became perpetual and infinite. Her hands moved through the beads slowly. Children and adults chanted in unison, and the woman's voice was like a drone within which we had become enveloped. The prayers bounced from the walls across the room and back in an invisible wave until our voices dissolved into one another: "Pray for us now . . . pray . . . pray for us . . . now . . . and at the hour . . . the hour of our death . . ."

Every night at the end of the rosary there was a reflection on one of the five Glorious Mysteries. Tonight it was the Resurrection: "The risen Jesus has proved that man, together with Him, can have power over sin and therefore death . . ." The woman read; we listened. The reflection changed the tone in the room as it became silent save for her reading. But the silence was broken by restless children and by barking dogs out in the street as well as people shifting in their chairs, all of which brought relief from the lingering hypnotic echoes of the chanted rosary. I found it to be an intense experience.

My mind drifted from the reading of the reflection. If for every execution in Juárez a family did a novena, I thought to myself, that would mean that already thousands of rosaries had been chanted in rooms like this one all over the city. And the cartel war was little more than a year old.

■ ■ ■

The Juárez journalists were an embattled group. They suffered the typical professional rivalries and jealousies, but conflicting pressures also tore at them. On the one hand they had their journalistic ideals and commitments, on the other the brutal reality of intimidation and possible assassination. All knew that there was a line they could not cross in their work, but its location shifted on the whims of the cartels, making it an unreliable reference point. The federal authorities were not enamored of the media, either. Antagonizing them could mean confiscation of equipment, a beating, or arrest. Adding to the volatile mix was the fact that some of the local journalists worked for newspapers that were said to receive subsidies from the Juárez cartel.

As a photographer, Raymundo Ruiz was constantly factoring in details about crime scenes, assessing what was fair game and what was not. He

Raymundo Ruiz, Juárez photojournalist. Photo copyright © Ricardo Ainslie.

knew, for example, that he had to be especially careful when photographing individuals on the periphery of an execution: they might well be the people who had carried out the killing or their allies. Ruiz had received death threats when cartel operatives had inadvertently appeared in the background at crime scenes that Ruiz had photographed. The rule of thumb for journalists was simple enough: the cartels allowed you to report the facts on the ground, what was in plain view for all to see. However, the cartels did not tolerate journalists naming them or their people, much less doing anything that smacked of investigative journalism. "What's on the street is fair game, but anytime you venture beyond that you run great risks," one Juárez journalist told me. "It's suicide." Some newspapers just used the byline "Staff" for drug-war related stories as an added measure of protection. Failing to take such precautions was a recipe for assassination, and there were plenty of Mexican journalists (almost thirty in the prior three years) who were now dead because they had not toed that line, or because they had been unsure as to just where the line was.

There was a new problem complicating Raymundo Ruiz's efforts to earn his livelihood: the *sicarios* had taken to circling back to crime scenes to make sure that their victims were dead. In the process, they were shooting witnesses they encountered and had even taken to killing ambulance workers who arrived while the *sicarios* were still there. Ruiz had been forced to factor this variable into his work habits. He now feared that if he arrived at a crime scene too soon, he might be added to the tally of the dead. If he delayed too long, however, he'd be unable to get the images that sold.

■ ■ ■

Armando Rodríguez was one of the Juárez journalists who were always thinking about that line, about what was fair game versus what the cartels might deem to be excessive coverage of their activities. Rodríguez was a crime-beat writer for *El Diario*, arguably the city's best newspaper (he'd authored the piece that had appeared on January 1, 2008, noting the record-breaking tally of the dead for 2007). Rodríguez was a prominent member of the Juárez Journalists Association who over the prior fifteen years had earned numerous awards for his coverage, which had included hard-hitting articles about the 1990s femicides. That fact may have had Rodríguez in a higher-than-usual state of alert. In early November, one of the cartels had decapitated a man (he was yet to be identified) and hung his headless body from the Rotary Club Bridge such that morning commuters, including parents driving their children to school, were terrorized by the ghoulish image. A few hours later, someone placed the victim's severed head in a black plastic bag and left it at a statue of a newspaper boy in Juárez's Plaza of the Reporter, across the street from a hull of a building that had once been home to a movie theater. The inescapable conclusion was that the incident was a message to the local press corps, but the precise meaning of the message had been the subject of much speculation in the days since the gruesome discovery. Armando Rodríguez, who went by the nickname "El Choco" (as in "the chocolate," because of his dark complexion), covered the story for *El Diario*.

A week later, on the morning of November 13, Rodríguez and his eight-year-old daughter left their house in a middle-class Juárez neighborhood. Rodríguez was taking her to school in the family's white Nissan, a perk from his job at the newspaper, before heading to work at *El Diario*. Just as he was about to turn the ignition key, a man walked up to his car and pumped a hail of bullets into him, killing him on the spot. Though physically unscathed, Rodríguez's daughter was left with the horror of seeing her dead father's bullet-ridden body slumped over the steering wheel. Armando Rodríguez died instantly, and in the time it took for his wife to make it out the door and to the car, the gunman had already slipped into a waiting vehicle and left the scene.

Like virtually all of the killers in this city, Armando Rodríguez's executioner would most likely never be brought to justice. To further ensure their impunity and perhaps also to make a point, Rodríguez's killers subsequently assassinated the special prosecutor sent to Juárez to investigate his murder. Not long thereafter, when a new prosecutor was sent to replace the first prosecutor, he, too, was assassinated in short order. If a society requires functioning courts and judicial processes to operate, in Juárez and the state of Chihuahua, as in much of the rest of Mexico, the system was completely dysfunctional, rendered inert and ineffective sometimes because of fear and intimidation and other times by a mix of corruption and contorted, incoherent practices that rendered the judiciary a useless, pathetic shell. As evidenced by the fate of the two prosecutors, the cartels were much more efficient than the authorities when it came to meting out their perverse justice. Unlike Mexico's judicial system, almost everyone who crossed the cartels' line was executed.

■ ■ ■

Like most people in public office, José Reyes Ferriz had an ambivalent relationship with the media, but there was also a warm place in his heart for them. He knew well the challenges they faced because his paternal grandfather had been the owner and editor of *La Voz de Chihuahua*, one of the state's most important newspapers at the time of the Mexican Revolution. Because the newspaper supported Pancho Villa, Porfirio Díaz, the dictator who ruled Mexico at the time, had persecuted Reyes Ferriz's grandfather, who was forced to flee to exile in San Antonio, Texas. When he returned he became a state deputy and later the mayor of the small town of Aldama, Chihuahua.

When the young José's family visited Chihuahua City from Juárez, he enjoyed walking into the room at his grandparents' home where the old issues of *La Voz de Chihuahua* were archived. There, he especially delighted in the accounts of all that was taking place at the time of the Revolution, and he followed closely the events that had led to his grandfather's exile, stories that had also become family lore. There was no way for the young José to know, of course, that his own life would eventually be enveloped in a similar spasm of violence, a spasm that could destabilize not just Juárez and Chihuahua, but the whole nation.

■ ■ ■

Such was the level of fear among the Juárez journalists that in the aftermath of the Armando Rodríguez murder, Raymundo Ruiz had taken to wearing a bulletproof vest whenever he was out on assignment. But that did not last long—it was impractical for a photographer trying to manage multiple cameras and a backpack full of lenses and his laptop. After a few weeks, the bulletproof vest ended up a permanent fixture in the trunk of his car, its presence still reassuring.

Raymundo Ruiz and I sometimes spent a great deal of time together; when I didn't have interviews scheduled, I liked to tag along on whatever assignment he was working. It gave me a window into the life of the city, as we covered everything from flood-control strategies, to children's theme park renovations, to school problems, to unpaved streets, and, of course, executions. Ruiz's natural inclination was to be a bit taciturn. I had learned not to ask him anything about La Línea or the Juárez cartel, for example. This was our unspoken agreement, as if to say, "Ask me anything about the city, but don't ask me about La Línea because I prefer to stay alive." I understood Ruiz's position and I respected it.

"It's dangerous to know too much," he would tell me. It was part simple statement of fact, part warning. In this city, that axiom was a survival strategy. I didn't make a visit to Juárez without Ruiz giving me some version of the survival axiom, quaint Spanish sayings that translate, roughly, to the following: "Flies don't enter a closed mouth." Or, "Playing stupid is better than playing dead." I had to go elsewhere to learn about the parts of the city's life that were off-limits with Ruiz.

■ ■ ■

Around the time of the Armando Rodríguez assassination, a tragic event in Mexico City dealt a blow to the federal government's efforts against the drug cartels. A small jet had fallen from the sky, jerking and corkscrewing like a lightning-struck bird. The aircraft plunged into the Mexico City commuter traffic that was jammed and tangled all along Paseo de la Reforma and then exploded into a brilliant ball of flames. Aboard the Lear 45 on that November evening in 2008 were two of Mexico's most important men. Juan Camilo Mouriño was only thirty-seven, but his star was already shining bright: he was the secretary of the interior, one of the central players in President Felipe Calderón's government. Mouriño had made numerous trips to Ciudad Juárez to meet with Mayor Reyes Ferriz and to help strategize the government's response to the Juárez violence. Santiago Vasconcelos was also aboard the jet. Vasconcelos was the head of the division of the Procuraduría General de la República, the federal attorney general's office, whose job it was to bring down the drug cartels. Like Mouriño, Vasconcelos was one of Calderón's most important strategists. Both men had also worked closely with Genaro García Luna, the director of the Secretariat for Public Security. In a matter of seconds, two key players in Mexico's war against the cartels had been incinerated beyond recognition in a molten pyre of metal, glass, and rubber, along with four aides and the plane's crew.

There was immediate and widespread speculation that the crash was no accident, as the authorities asserted, but rather retaliation by one or another of the cartels for the role that these two men were playing in the government's war against organized crime. The Mexican government was forced to take the unusual step of bringing in American aeronautical specialists to investigate the crash, hoping that such a step would quell the rumors, but the conspiracy theories continued unabated.

■ ■ ■

As Christmas of 2008 approached, crime in Juárez continued to metastasize. It was no longer possible to know what criminal act was tied to the cartels and their gangs and what acts were simply a function of the fact that criminals throughout the city were seizing targets of opportunity in a context in which the police department, whose recruitment of new officers was going slowly, remained broken and fractured. Every week there was a new wrinkle. In late November and early December, schools became the targets. In Mexico the tradition is to pay employees an *aguinaldo*, or an end-of-year holiday bonus. Criminals had begun threatening to execute teachers or their students and families if the teachers did not hand over their bonuses. At one school, seven bodies were dumped on a soccer field before dawn. The victims had been beaten, choked, and shot. The threats and resultant anxieties reached such a pitch that the city ordered schools to close days before the scheduled break. Juárez was living in the grip of terror.

As the one-year anniversary of his Christmas warning of an impending cartel war neared, José Reyes Ferriz could not help but be struck by the cards he'd been dealt. There were no models from which to draw to understand what he was facing. The city was slipping from his fingers; he could feel it. His police department was an intractable problem. There had been work stoppages, massive firings, and fifty of his officers had been killed over the course of the year. Crime was out of control, and the number of cartel-related assassinations had risen from 301 victims in 2007 to almost 1,500 (Juárez would end 2008 with a staggering 1,623 executions). There were other significant problems as well. The city's tax base was rapidly evaporating. The violence was causing record business closures, with owners and employees alike fleeing across the border into El Paso or to other cities in Mexico; tourism, once an integral part of the city's economy, was now nonexistent. Reyes Ferriz had long championed the North American Free Trade Agreement, believing that expanding the assembly plants was vital to creating needed jobs and that the future of the city and the solution to its problems lay there. But the American recession, the worst economic crisis since the Great Depression, was already having a profound impact on the Juárez economy. Half of the assembly plant jobs in the city were tied to the U.S. auto industry, an industry on the verge of bankruptcy. Reyes Ferriz also worried that the violence would lead parent companies to move their assembly plants elsewhere. The plants represented a relatively small investment on the part of the companies in terms of equipment and infrastructure. Any of them could pull up stakes and move to China or elsewhere at a moment's notice. Between the cartel war, the crime wave, and the economic crisis, the mayor's back was to the wall. "This was like a perfect storm," Reyes Ferriz would later tell me. Every one of these problems was deep and consequential and none of them had obvious, much less easy, solutions.

José Reyes Ferriz approached his second Christmas in office with a sense of dread. The only lighthearted news he'd had in months had been the arrest of Laura Zúñiga just a couple of days before Christmas. Zúñiga, a twenty-three-year-old beauty queen, was Miss Sinaloa and had recently won the national pageant, which meant that she would represent Mexico in the 2009 Miss International pageant. Zúñiga had been traveling in an entourage of two SUVs, in the company of a man named Ángel Orlando García Urquiza and six bodyguards, when they were stopped at an army checkpoint near Guadalajara. Urquiza was a top operative in the Juárez cartel. The army found a large stash of weapons and $53,300 dollars in cash. Miss Sinaloa's defense (she was subsequently dethroned) was that she was under the impression that they were on their way to Colombia "to shop." In the city where the Sinaloa and Juárez cartels were in a fight to the death, the idea that a Juárez capo was having his way with Miss Sinaloa inspired much holiday humor.

Note

1. These phones are ubiquitous in Juárez. The "push to talk" feature changes frequencies every time, which makes it nearly impossible to trace or monitor calls made on a Nextel phone (which can only be made to other Nextel phones). Colombia had banned the use of these phones because they were key tools of the drug cartels.

CHAPTER 16

Forty-Eight Hours

By the spring of 2009, Roberto Orduña, the "Pajama Chief," had been at the head of the Juárez police for almost a year. The mayor had relied on him to oversee numerous efforts to clean up the force, including the Confidence Tests and the firing of over a third of the force. The mayor trusted him. Through these actions, Orduña had incurred the wrath of many in the department, all the while knowing that the cartels had put crosshairs on his back.

The army's operations continued to garner arrests and seizures of drugs, money, and weapons, but such victories were having no effect on the violence; the tally of the dead continued its steady, disquieting rise. The fact that Orduña was a former military man backed by the commander of the region's military forces, General Juárez Loera,[1] facilitated coordination between the police and the military. Such coordination was particularly delicate given that there were ongoing confrontations and skirmishes between the army and elements of the municipal police, some of whom were clearly still in the service of the cartels. Notwithstanding the Confidence Tests, the efforts to clean up the police had not solved the problems within the force; police corruption was proving to be as intractable as an antibiotics-resistant strain of bacteria.

It was all a matter of strategy. Somewhere, from the safety of their protected enclaves and safe houses, the leadership of the cartels had made the calculus that control of the municipal police remained indispensable to their operations in Juárez. The cartels continued to use their time-tested techniques of violent coercion, abduction, and inducement in order to infiltrate and control the force. José Reyes Ferriz and the federal government strategists had made their own calculus and arrived at the same conclusion, which is why they had devoted so many resources to cleaning up the force. Whoever controlled the police controlled the city.

Reyes Ferriz's agreements with the federal government were being reevaluated and renegotiated every six months. The mayor knew that the army and the federal police were not going to stay in Juárez indefinitely. Eventually he was going to have to have a police force that he could trust; the alternative was either a city besieged by continuing cartel violence or a city in the hands of the last cartel left standing. The police, in other words, remained a strategic objective, the key to future viability for the city.

One of Orduña's most trusted aides was a man named Sacramento Pérez Serrano, a former army captain who'd graduated from Mexico's most prestigious military college. Orduña had handpicked Pérez the prior July to oversee the police cleanup effort. Pérez was forty-nine years old, an energetic man with a decidedly military bearing. He was part of a thinly veiled or at least not formally acknowledged strategy to recruit ex-military to the ranks of the Juárez police, in the hope that they would be more disciplined and less susceptible to cartel corruption. Orduña and Pérez had gone as far as the southern-most Mexican states in search of recruits. On one Sunday afternoon, February 17, 2009, Pérez and his bodyguards were traveling in one of the police department's large Ford F-150 big-cab pickups, just blocks from the U.S. consulate, when they were blocked in on three sides and attacked by *sicarios* in multiple vehicles. Pérez's pickup was not armored; the fire from the assailants' assault weapons penetrated the truck with ease, killing everyone on board. The fusillade left the windshield and driver's-side windows pocked with holes that gleamed like snowflakes gathered on the shattered glass.

Sacramento Pérez typically traveled in an armored vehicle with an accompanying "wing" car in a blocking position to prevent just this kind of an ambush. However, the woman who ran the city prison had received numerous death threats, prompting Pérez to let her use his armored pickup temporarily until her security was reinforced. Reyes Ferriz and Orduña were convinced that someone inside the police department had tipped off the Juárez cartel to the fact that Pérez was now driving an unarmored vehicle, making him an easy target.

Pérez became the third director of operations to be assassinated in less than a year. For José Reyes Ferriz the assassination of one of Orduña's key people was an enormous setback. There were few people he could trust, and the mayor counted Pérez as one of the good guys. The boldness of the attack (in broad daylight, just blocks from the U.S. consulate—a tony area that was constantly patrolled by municipal, state, and federal police) once again served to remind that the fight for control of the police was far from resolved.

Reyes Ferriz felt trapped, like Sisyphus. No matter the effort, no matter the strategy, the result always appeared to be variations on the same: terrifying executions of police personnel. Within hours of the killing of Sacramento Pérez, a series of coordinated narco-messages surfaced throughout the city giving Orduña forty-eight hours to resign. The messages, left at a car dealership, a cell phone store, and a Kentucky Fried Chicken, among other locations, threatened to assassinate a police officer every forty-eight hours until the police chief complied.

At a news conference, José Reyes Ferriz told the press that he and Orduña were standing firm in the face of the new attacks. "We will not be terrorized by these criminals," he declared. But forty-eight hours later, a municipal police officer named César Iván Portillo heard a knock on his front door. When he opened it, a lone gunman emptied his 9-millimeter pistol into Portillo, killing him instantly. A handwritten narco-message left next to Portillo's crumpled body said, "The [forty-eight] hours have passed and the director of public security, Roberto Orduña Cruz, has not resigned."

A prison guard was killed a few hours after Portillo's assassination. These two deaths, and the assassinations of Pérez and his bodyguards, brought to six the number of law enforcement officers killed in just two days. Reyes Ferriz was again facing a crisis. "Orduña told me he was going to resign," the mayor recalled. This would again leave the police force with no leadership. Reyes Ferriz did what he could to talk Orduña out of it, first appealing to his military pride: "We can't allow the criminals to dictate to us," Reyes Ferriz told him. But the entreaties were futile; Orduña had already made up his mind. The police chief responded in kind with a military analogy: "When someone retreats in the battlefield it does not necessarily mean the battle is lost, sometimes it's simply a strategic retreat," Orduña told the mayor.

At a hastily arranged press conference, Reyes Ferriz and the chief of police appeared together to make the announcement. Reyes Ferriz spoke first, stating that Orduña had tendered his resignation and praising him as a dedicated officer. Orduña then stepped up to the microphone. "I can't put my professional pride above the lives of my men," he said. "Respect for the lives that these brave officers risk every day on the streets for the residents of Juárez obliges me to offer my permanent resignation." Mustering profound indignation, Orduña added: "To the enemies of Mexico I say, don't misunderstand the action I am taking. Notwithstanding your initial reluctance [the chief gestured toward Reyes Ferriz, who was standing next to him], this is an intelligent step for life, not for death," Orduña said.

Immediately following his resignation, Orduña left Juárez, seeking refuge across the border in El Paso just as his predecessor, Guillermo Prieto, had done almost a year earlier. For good measure, the Juárez cartel left another narco-message for the mayor: "It's good that you have gotten rid of Orduña, but if you put in another asshole working for El Chapo we're going to kill you."

It was Friday, February 20, and José Reyes Ferriz found himself once again staring out his office window onto the streets of Juárez that lay below. Almost exactly a year earlier, Patricio Patiño had visited Juárez and the mayor had met with federal authorities for the first time. They'd sent two hundred federal police, they'd sent the army, they'd given his entire police force Confidence Tests and he'd overseen the firing of hundreds of officers, yet here he was again without a chief of police and with Sacramento Pérez, the second in command, executed. Scores of police had been killed over the course of the year, and the city was enveloped in a crime wave of such proportions that Juárez seemed to be devolving into anarchy. Sisyphus, the mayor thought as he stood alone in his office staring out the window: Sisyphus.

■ ■ ■

The cartels are strategic. They plan, they observe, and their actions have a clear and definite logic. The execution of Sacramento Pérez and the decision to oust Roberto Orduña were calculated moves, but the cartel wasn't finished. They appeared to have received inside information about a federal plan to reinforce Ciudad Juárez. José Reyes Ferriz and the governor of Chihuahua, José Reyes Baeza, were to travel together to Mexico City on Sunday, February 22, to meet with Genaro García Luna, Guillermo Valdés, and the other key members of President Calderón's security cabinet to seal the deal.

The Mexico City meeting was scheduled for Sunday evening. That morning, while waiting to catch a flight to Chihuahua City, where he was to rendezvous with the governor (they would fly to Mexico City together aboard a state plane), the mayor received a call from his communications director, Sergio Belmonte, informing him that there were narco-messages all over the city threatening to decapitate him and kill his family.

The Juárez cartel was raising the stakes for Reyes Ferriz on the eve of his meeting with the federal authorities. "It was the first time that they had threatened me so publicly and it was the first time that they had threatened my family," Reyes Ferriz told me. The mayor had already moved his wife and children to El Paso as a security precaution. The narco-message made specific reference to that, indicating that there was no safe haven for them. Reyes Ferriz cancelled his flight in order to set in place the necessary security measures, calling the governor to say that he would catch a commercial flight and meet him in Mexico City later that evening. The governor informed him that there was no rush; the meeting had been rescheduled for Monday morning at the offices of the secretary of the interior.

Sunday night Reyes Ferriz arrived at the Marriott Hotel in the fashionable Polanco neighborhood in Mexico City. The plan was that he and the governor, also at the hotel, would convene to discuss their approach to the meeting with the federal people. Moments after checking in the mayor received a call from Governor Reyes Baeza's personal secretary; the governor's convoy had been ambushed in Chihuahua City and one of his bodyguards killed. Two other bodyguards had also been wounded in the attack. The Juárez cartel had obviously decided to send the governor a message as well. Though the governor was unscathed, Reyes Ferriz was informed that he had cancelled his trip to Mexico City. That meant that responsibility for decisions regarding federal involvement in Juárez would be the mayor's, and the cartel had made clear how they felt about it. Once again, José Reyes Ferriz was alone.

The next morning, José Reyes Ferriz made his way to the Interior Ministry at Avenida Bucareli 99, near the city's Centro Histórico. The ministry occupied an ornate nineteenth-century building surrounded by a lush garden, but its beauty belied the fact that within its walls some of Mexico's most powerful men had shaped the destiny of the nation. Fernando Gómez Mont, the secretary of the interior, was of that mold; he played host to the members of Calderón's security cabinet and Reyes Ferriz in the ministry's richly appointed library, which had an exquisite antique conference table that could comfortably seat forty people. The cabinet members were aware of the death threats that the mayor had received and the prior day's ambush on the governor's convoy. Gómez Mont went straight to the question at hand: "Are you going to resign?" he asked Reyes Ferriz. The mayor's response was equally direct: "Absolutely not," he said, adding that while this was the first public threat, he had received numerous death threats since the outbreak of the narco-war in Juárez. Reyes Ferriz assured the security cabinet members that he planned to stay the course until the end of his term of office in October 2010. The federal people presented their plan to Reyes Ferriz: They would send five thousand more troops into Juárez, and the army would take over all policing functions in the city, in addition to other measures to shore up security.

Almost a year earlier, the governor had voiced his opposition to what he'd called the "militarization" of the police. That comment, and the fact that the governor had chosen not to be present for the meeting, left Reyes Ferriz on his own, but just as in the spring of 2008, he now saw no other alternative. The cartels had succeeded in thwarting every initiative that had been tried with the Juárez municipal police. The security cabinet had not failed to see the obvious: there was little to show for the Confidence Tests and the firings of hundreds of Juárez's police officers and commanders. They were going to have to start from scratch with the police force, and the added military presence would buy them time.

Before the meeting broke up Gómez Mont looked at the mayor and added something unexpected: "We need you to be the face, the front man for Operación Conjunto Chihuahua," he said. Reyes Ferriz argued for appointing a spokesperson, but the federal people would not have it. In the end, the mayor agreed, knowing that in doing so he was increasing his personal risk exponentially. He'd been cast in the role of savior.

José Reyes Ferriz left the meeting at the Secretaría de Gobernación and headed back up the historic Paseo de la Reforma to his hotel. He knew he'd made a fateful decision, a decision from which there could be no turning back. There was a Starbucks across the street from the Marriott, and he ordered himself a cappuccino (a creature of habit, Reyes Ferriz always ordered the same). He called his two most trusted advisors, Sergio Belmonte, his director of communications, and Guillermo Dowell, his chief of staff, and laid it all out for them. The consensus was that his options were to try to keep a low profile, as he'd done with prior death threats, or, as the mayor put it, "enter the threat terrain." In the past, the first strategy had lowered the level of threats against him, but those threats had not been public. They decided on the second course of action, to speak to the threats publicly. It was a calculation aimed at pressuring the federal forces into keeping his back. "Our thinking was that if I increased my public profile, it increased the costs to the federal government should something happen to me. They would have to make sure that I was protected," Reyes Ferriz recalled.

In the aftermath of the death threats, Belmonte had been receiving many requests from national and international media for interviews with the mayor, but had not granted a single one. Now he opened the floodgates. From his table at the Starbucks, while sipping his cappuccino, Reyes Ferriz spent the afternoon giving interviews to the best-known nationally syndicated journalists in Mexico, including Denise Maerker, Joaquín López Dórgia, Carmen Aristegui, and CNN (Spanish), among others. "I sat in that Starbucks alone, without any bodyguards, wondering about every car that drove by," he later told me. The mayor tried to position himself carefully in these and other interviews. "I did not personally go on the attack against the cartels, but I said I would collaborate fully with the federal government and that it was their responsibility to take care of this threat in Ciudad Juárez."

Following the Mexico City meeting it became evident that something had changed in the relationship between the mayor and the federal officials. It was unspoken, unacknowledged, but the federal people henceforth moved closer to José Reyes Ferriz, treating him more as a partner. In equal measure, they appeared to distance themselves from the governor, who was clearly lukewarm to the whole enterprise for reasons that no one could know with certainty but which lent themselves to innuendo and suspicion. After all, he'd made the decision not to appear in Mexico City.

Note

1. In apparent retaliation for his campaigns against the drug cartels, General Jorge Juárez Loera was assassinated near his home in Mexico City on May 22, 2011, just weeks after he'd retired from the Mexican Army. He was sixty-five years old.

CHAPTER 17

Martial Law Undeclared

few days after the Mexico City summit, the key members of President Felipe Calderón's security cabinet arrived at the Camino Real hotel in Juárez under tight security. The team included the head of the Secretariat for Public Security, Genaro García Luna; the federal attorney general, Eduardo Medina-Mora; the interior minister, Fernando Gómez Mont; and the national defense minister, Guillermo Galván Galván, among others. Two dozen armored assault vehicles with 50-caliber machine guns were in position around the perimeter of the hotel as military Black Hawk helicopters hovered above. The Juárez airport received bomb threats and was temporarily shut down. There was no mistaking the fact that Juárez was a war zone.

The president had sent his emissaries to present his plan to save Juárez before an increasingly skeptical national public. Though the country had responded favorably to Calderón's declaration of war against the cartels a year earlier, the president's poll numbers were now falling precipitously. Calderón's policies were being assailed as shortsighted, overly militarized, and failing to reduce the violence that was spiraling out of control not only in Juárez but also in many of the country's narco-zones.

In Juárez, February 2009 ended with a record tally of 230 executions. Just a year earlier, the city had been shocked at the 301 assassinations registered for the entire year of 2007. Now, the city had almost reached that mark in a single month. On any given day an average of seven or eight bodies were turning up all over the city. José Reyes Ferriz had the additional twenty-five hundred army and a few hundred federal police personnel to manage the city, but that support was not having an appreciable impact on the violence. The police, those who had not been fired or resigned, were still on the payroll, but they were essentially useless. The mayor counted the days until the ides of March when the five thousand additional federal forces were due to arrive en masse.

■ ■ ■

On the morning of March 14, 2009, the anonymous tip line for the Juárez municipal police received a call reporting that there were bodies at a location southeast of the city. The area is open desert where sparse clusters of creosote, acacia, ocotillo, and mesquite dot a landscape populated by giant centipedes, scorpions, snakes, and the occasional Mexican prairie dog.

Protected by police escort, a forensic team arrived at the site, clad in white protective suits, rubber gloves, and surgical masks (the latter a futile attempt to dilute the stench of decomposing bodies). The team immediately went to work and soon found the first of the remains. In a smooth drift of sand that rose like a gentle swell in a grainy ocean, a single, tennis-shoe-clad foot protruded from the ground, its untied shoelace dangling gently in the wind. Not far away another body lay half out of the sand. Before their work was finished the forensic team would find five shallow graves, or *narcofosas*, as they were called in Mexico, containing nine bodies, some with telltale signs of torture (burn marks, cuts, limbs whose unnatural orientation indicated broken bones). At least one of the victims was handcuffed, his arms behind his back. Two appeared to be women, and one a child. Like archeologists searching for rare artifacts, the forensic team used a screen to carefully sift the sand around the remains. One shovelful yielded a telling piece of evidence: a police badge.

There was something haunting about the Fraccionamiento Villa de Alcalá, the terrain where the *narcofosas* had been discovered. The area was a well-known dumping ground for those whose lives had been extinguished by one criminal element or another. Over the course of the last decade, hundreds of young women were murdered in Juárez (most of them maquiladora employees), their remains left in the desert, many near this very spot. The femicides brought ill fame to Ciudad Juárez, attracting news organizations and human-rights groups from all over the world. There had been countless newspaper accounts, documentary films, books, and television programs covering the femicide story, from *Geraldo* to CNN. Every major American newspaper, including the *New York Times*, the *Los Angeles Times*, and the *Washington Post* had been down here as well. There had even been scholarly articles written about the femicides, in which the authors expounded about the complexities of gender, class, and power. What there hadn't been were answers. Few if any of the more than four hundred cases had been solved. But then, that didn't surprise anyone in Juárez, where arrests were the exception and impunity the norm, no matter if the crime was a street corner holdup or a brutal murder. Most crimes went unsolved and therefore unpunished in Mexico. That was the defining characteristic of the Mexican judiciary system.

Now that the cartels were also dumping many of their victims out here in the desert, there was no expectation that the authorities would solve these crimes, either, although that didn't stop people from engaging in the sport of speculation, assembling a picture, no matter how flawed, from the available puzzle pieces. In fact, Juárez was abuzz with theories as to the identities of the bodies discovered in the *narcofosas*. The police badge lent itself to the view that among the victims were one or more of the municipal police officers who'd been lifted and disappeared without a trace over the last year. Jesús Enrique Solís Luévano, an agent assigned to the Babícora district, had never arrived home after completing his tour the morning of February 3, 2008. There was also Juan Hernández Sánchez, who'd been with the force over ten years before three vehicles intercepted him in Barrio Alto, a well-known narco stronghold. Hernández's bloodstained uniform had been found in the street days later, but there was no other trace of the officer. There were also other officers who had similarly disappeared over the last year.

The day after the discovery of the shallow graves, I met with a news director in Juárez, a man of strong opinions who told me right off that this was one of those crimes that would never be solved. The city morgue was overrun with bodies, he told me: "They don't even know where to put them." In addition, the victims' bodies were going unclaimed because families feared that the authorities would link them to the activities of the deceased. "It creates problems for them," the news director noted. Many of the victims were also found without identification. Finally, with a knowing look, the news director added this detail: "And then there's the problem of the police," he said quietly, fearing that someone in an adjacent office might be listening.

Opinions were easily had in Juárez as to the fate of the officers who'd been lifted, and the motives that lay behind their disappearances. There were countless interweaved scenarios. Unless you were on the inside, however, there was only speculation, guesswork, and talk. The only thing that *was* known, concretely, indisputably, was that police had disappeared and a police badge had been found at the site of the *narcofosas*. One rumor had it that the badge had not belonged to one of the disappeared municipal police officers at all but rather that it had fallen off a cop as he was *digging* the graves. No information had been disclosed thus far as to the identity of the person who went with the badge, but one of the contacts within the forensics unit had suggested that the badge was found close to the surface rather than having been buried with the bodies. An alternate theory floating around was that the badge had been slipped in by the federal police to discredit the municipal police, specifically one of three municipal police agents who had been recently arrested and accused of handing people over to the Juárez cartel for execution.

No one really knew where reality lay in Juárez. It clustered around indisputable fragments and artifacts, like a police badge, a weapon, or a cadaver, from which the truth had to be constructed, but those constructions almost always contained as much fiction as they did fact. Life in Juárez was full of such fusions: fact and imagination dovetailed and interpenetrated such that one could not be teased out from the other. Conspiracy theories, big and small, abounded, even among the most sensible people. Every incident carried within itself endless possibilities for speculation and freewheeling conjecture. Hard evidence constantly toyed with perception and understanding. Not uncommonly, for example, when some cartel operation was interdicted (a car stopped on the street, a cocaine lab raided, a cartel safe house uncovered) uniforms belonging to one or another law enforcement agency or the army were found among the drugs, weapons, cell phones, and police scanners. The ready availability of official uniforms (they were easy to purchase, if not steal) often made it difficult to know actors' identities. Criminals wearing law enforcement uniforms of one sort or another routinely abducted people or held up businesses. Then there were the actual abuses committed by the authorities. The circumstance lent itself to confusions and accusations that could never be resolved and that were fodder for endless spin. In Juárez, identities, like motives, were never certain. Over time this circumstance tended to erode people's faith in the manifest. If things were never what they seemed to be, then nothing could be trusted, no matter how obvious.

Conspiracy theories quickly formed themselves in tightly woven clusters that then just as quickly dissipated into nothingness as if never before conceived or uttered. It was said that the governor of Chihuahua, José Reyes Baeza, was owned by the Juárez cartel, for example, and that he was paid two million dollars a year for the Juárez *plaza*. The state prosecutorial people came "bundled" with that, given that they were appointed by the governor and served at his pleasure, although the key people in those slots were being paid for their services separately (these "facts" could be readily found on narco websites, for example). Rumor had it that José Reyes Ferriz was on the outs with the governor, who'd sealed off the mayor's designs on the state governorship (the mayor's job was a historic stepping stone for the politically ambitious). That placed the mayor at odds with the Juárez cartel and was the purported reason behind the mayor's recently announced decision to turn over the municipal police duties, wholesale, to the army. There were rumors that the top tiers of the federal government were in the pay of El Chapo Guzmán, the head of the Sinaloa cartel. According to this line of speculation, the Sinaloa people were losing the fight against the Juárez cartel as they had earlier in Nuevo Laredo against the Gulf cartel. Buying the military, so this reasoning went, allowed Sinaloa to have the military serve as its proxy and wipe out the Juárez cartel, thereby clearing the way for them to take over the *plaza*. This conspiracy theory thus placed the mayor in the hands of the Sinaloa cartel.

It was impossible to know if any of these theories contained substance.

There was no doubt that the cartels had many in their pay, from highly placed officials to cops on the street. That fact permitted the cartels to act with impunity and was reflected in both the police who were caught transporting drugs as well as the narco-messages directed at the police. But who was actually aligned with whom was much more difficult to discern. Everyone could conjure up wild scenarios and far-fetched motives, but really knowing was a near-impossible feat for anyone outside of the cartels. Most people were satisfied with that arrangement, because knowing too much in Juárez was a death sentence. Everyone in this town knew that as an axiom; it was one of those rules one learned early and lived faithfully. But rumor, gossip, and innuendo were another matter altogether.

The entire circumstance produced a pervasive cynicism. Faith in any government action was difficult to find or even justify. No act, no matter how apparently well intentioned or effective, could escape the stain of this cynicism, which had become a national disease. Thus, there was nothing of which one could take hold, no tether to serve as a guide through this social unraveling and confusion. Instead, people all too often turned inward, detaching themselves from the threads that give a neighborhood or city its vitality, its cohesion. The very essence of what makes civil society work was under threat of annihilation because of the evil in the streets and the cynicism that rendered every action suspect before it could hope to have any transformative effect. Most Juarenses had long ago stopped feeling that there was anything reliably good out there other than family and a few friends.

■ ■ ■

The morning of March 15, the ides of March, was crisp and sunny as wave upon wave of Mexican Army units entered Ciudad Juárez. It was an impressive sight: the columns of brand-new olive-green trucks, each numbered in sequence, approaching the city through the main highway to the south. "They're at the Pancho Villa monument," one of Raymundo Ruiz's fellow journalists reported over the Nextel phone. We rushed down the Juárez side streets trying to guess where the Mexican forces would garrison, guided by the incoming communications. There had been no official statement except for a press announcement that the federal forces would be arriving sometime during the day.

Raymundo Ruiz was born in Ciudad Juárez and grew up in one of the hardscrabble neighborhoods now rife with *sicarios* and addicts and, all too often, dead bodies. But his attitude toward it all was strangely accepting, as if it were dictated by fate. "I was a *cholo* as a teenager," he told me, using the Mexican slang for a gangbanger. The implication was that he could just as easily have been one of the victims he photographed as the one taking their images. He'd always been intrigued with photography, even though his family's poverty was so severe that they spent years living in a shack

Swearing-in ceremony for Municipal Police Chief General Julián David Rivera Bretón (left), with Mayor José Reyes Ferriz (center), and Arturo Domínguez, city administrator (right). Photo copyright © Ricardo Ainslie.

made of wood pallets and other found materials. As an adolescent, he'd managed to scrape together enough money to buy a camera and eventually, through a mixture of good fortune and diligence, he became a videographer for birthdays, *quinceañera* parties, and weddings, before becoming a videographer for a news organization. But his true passion was the camera and documenting the tragedy that had befallen his city. His images now graced the pages of the world's leading newspapers and magazines.

Later that day I'd gone to the Police Academy, where José Reyes Ferriz was swearing in the new chief of police. The federal government, and, in particular, the army, had delivered on their promise to help the mayor find a replacement for Roberto Orduña. The new chief of police was another ex-military man who had come out of retirement to take the job. His name was General Julián David Rivera Bretón, and he was a veteran of military campaigns in Chiapas and Sinaloa. The mayor introduced General Rivera Bretón to the press and announced that all policing functions in the city would be taken over by the army and the federal police. The municipal police was officially disbanded. Military officers would now head up the various areas of responsibility, including all six of the city's police sectors.

The mayor underscored the fact that the city government remained in charge of public security, but it was clear that the army was now running the law enforcement show in Ciudad Juárez. A few municipal police officers were permitted to ride with the federal forces, mostly because the latter did not know their way around the city.

These extreme steps were unprecedented in modern Mexico. Some questioned the constitutionality of the government's move, arguing that for all intents and purposes it amounted to the imposition of martial law. With the army convoys replacing police patrols and federal roadblocks all over the city, the only thing missing was a curfew. But the city's residents were tired of living on the edge of anarchy, tired of feeling vulnerable and in constant fear. Most welcomed the drastic measures, hoping the federal intervention would finally restore some semblance of law and order to their city so that they could go about their lives.

José Reyes Ferriz was obviously one of those who welcomed the military presence. The problems within the police had been a constant threat to his administration; they'd absorbed the bulk of his attention, and the bulk of his city's resources. The security situation had already placed an enormous strain on the city's budget, a state of affairs that was about to worsen: the agreement that Reyes Ferriz had signed with the federal government stipulated that the city would underwrite the cost of housing and feeding the troops. This circumstance served to further inflame the tensions between the mayor and the governor, given that, despite repeated requests, more than a year into the violence the governor had yet to divert any state resources to help Juárez manage the crisis.

■ ■ ■

A week after the discovery of the *narcofosas* it was announced that none of the bodies found in the shallow graves at Villa de Alcalá were those of current or former police. The police badge remained a mystery. The one piece of evidence that should have been the easiest to track down (presumably the municipal police kept a registry of its officers and their respective badge numbers) proved to be the most elusive. A silence shrouded it. The official report was as terse as it was uninformative: "Under investigation." Everyone in the city knew what that meant: nothing would ever be known beyond what was already known, which was very little. The frightening discovery would simply go down as yet another horrific crime in an endless sequence of unspeakable events that was the backdrop to the lives of the people of Juárez.

CHAPTER 18

Civics Lessons

A poll published in *El Diario* shortly after the army's arrival that spring of 2009 found that 70 percent of the city was in support of the their presence, despite the accusations of abuse of force and human rights violations over the prior year. Historically, attitudes toward the army had varied in Mexico. In the aftermath of 1968, when the army had participated in the massacre of student demonstrators at Tlaltelolco in Mexico City and, later, in the ensuing anti-guerrilla campaigns of the 1970s, many viewed the Mexican Army as an abusive instrument of the state with no regard for human rights and a long record of committing atrocities against *campesinos* and poor, rural people as well as others who were in opposition to the government. Some of the military's top brass had also been arrested for corruption and working in consort with drug lords. But there was a counter-narrative. Many also viewed the army as the most disciplined and least corrupt of the Mexican institutions, and some of the generals had earned the admiration of the nation for standing up to the cartels and fighting them hard while exposing corrupt police and politicians. Many Juarenses had high hopes that the army might solve the crisis of violence that was eviscerating their city.

Raymundo Ruiz wasn't one of them. He was not sanguine about what the army could achieve or even about its intent. His natural skepticism worked against the view that the army could serve a useful purpose in Juárez. One afternoon after the army had taken over the city's policing functions, Ruiz was stopped because his inspection sticker had expired. There was one municipal police officer in the patrol car (the "guide"), along with three soldiers. The police officer had been sent to deal with Ruiz. "Help me out, brother," the photographer had pleaded with him. "I'm in the middle of my work shift." But the cop wouldn't budge. "I can't," he said, motioning back with his head toward the three soldiers standing grimly next to the patrol car. "These guys won't let me." The officer proceeded to take his pliers and detach Ruiz's rear license plate—a means used to ensure that the transgressor will show up and pay the corresponding fine. "My tour's over at twelve thirty," the policeman said to Ruiz. "You can pick it up then after you've paid the infraction."

If it was intended as a strike for a more responsible civic arrangement (taking your lumps and paying your fine down at the city offices rather than participating in the usual bribes), it had the opposite effect. I broached this idea with Ruiz but he smacked it right down. "No, it's not about a more honest society," he said. "These things are so entrenched that you can't change them by issuing tickets. I can't afford the time to go down there to take care of this; I'll lose half of my day of work because of these idiots."

Later that day we went to the city offices, where Ruiz dutifully paid his ticket. However, when he went to the window to retrieve his license plate, a dismissive clerk claimed it wasn't there. "It's there!" Ruiz fumed, noting that the police officer's tour had been over hours ago. Turning to me and still within earshot of the clerk, Ruiz said, "He just wants a bribe." Eventually, Ruiz's plate was returned, but only after he'd found a district attorney walking down the hall whom he'd known from a couple of stories. The DA had gone straight into the room with the license plates and returned ten minutes later with Ruiz's rear plate. "See? What did I tell you?" Ruiz said. The civics lesson was over.

In Mexico, corruption is a creature of many faces and permutations; it can come into play for a few pesos when stopped by a cop on a city street or for millions of pesos in fancy restaurants and richly decorated boardrooms. It is a civics lesson with which an entire nation is wrestling, and it is a circumstance into which narco-corruption readily enters when the opportunity or need arises. An entire way of life, a deeply ingrained cultural stance, is at work. Changing such realities will be a long, slow process in a country where the flush of narco-dollars works a system and attitudes are so deeply ingrained that they are simply accepted as a normal and ordinary way of life.

■ ■ ■

"We had no choice," Eduardo Medina-Mora would later recollect in reference to the intensification and militarization of the Mexican government's tactics against the drug cartels. Medina-Mora was a veteran of Mexico's campaign against the cartels. During his time as federal attorney general, he'd had to fire his subordinate, the former drug czar Noe Ramírez Mandrujano, who had purportedly accepted $450,000 a month from the Beltrán-Leyva faction of the Sinaloa cartel in exchange for information about police operations. After leaving his post, Medina-Mora was appointed Mexico's ambassador to Great Britain by Felipe Calderón. In 2010, I visited the ambassador's private office in the embassy in London's fashionable West End, which was spacious and decorated with an eclectic eye that included modern sculptures and handsome wood-inlaid antique chests. A large painting of a seascape hung over a couch, and an assortment of large-format books (*Haciendas of Mexico, Beauty and Poetry in Mexican Popular Art,* and *The Soul of Mexico,* this latter book by Carlos Fuentes) lay on a coffee table.

Prior to 2004, the cartels had been a problem and a national presence, but they lacked the firepower and infrastructure to deploy systematically, even though by then they had already made enormous inroads into Mexico's police forces as well as the judiciary. The violence had begun to increase precipitously in 2004, Medina-Mora explained. He was unambiguous in his assessment of one of the root causes for that increase: "That's when the Americans allowed the Assault Weapons Ban to lapse," he said. Almost immediately, the cartels had begun their buildup, buying large quantities of assault weapons, thereby dramatically increasing their firepower. Very soon the cartels all over Mexico were much better armed than municipal and state police forces, which tended to carry 38-caliber pistols and the occasional antiquated rifle. That's when the cartel violence shifted in intensity and reached a new level. "They started becoming a real threat to the sovereignty of the Mexican state," Medina-Mora said, adding, "That's why the president had to move in the way he did."

The ambassador had been reluctant to criticize American domestic policies, but it was evident that he viewed the procurement of assault weapons as a critical problem. "I see no contradiction between some regulation of these weapons and their Second Amendment," he noted, referencing the U.S. Constitution. "They don't even keep a database; there is no record of who is buying these weapons in the United States."[1]

To underscore his point, the ambassador handed me a document labeled "Not for public release: Mexico/UK—SENSITIVE." The document included the following statistic: "About 90% of all the weapons seized in Mexico come from the United States."[2] The document also noted that between December 1, 2006, and July 2010 the Mexican government had seized more than 85,551 weapons. Almost 60 percent of these were high-caliber automatic weapons. Indeed, according to an August 2008 article in the *Los Angeles Times* that cited the U.S. Bureau of Alcohol, Tobacco, Firearms, and Explosives, there are 6,700 licensed gun dealers between Brownsville, Texas, and San Diego, California, all within a short drive of the two thousand–mile U.S.-Mexico border. As violence reached an intense pitch all over Mexico, ready access to automatic weapons was playing a key role. Genaro García Luna described these weapons as the gas that was fueling the engine of violence.

In the midst of the ambassador's description of Juárez's intractability, he was interrupted by a call on his cell phone. I asked if he wished for me to step out, but he indicated that there was no need. Standing up and walking to the bank of windows facing the street that ran along the back of the embassy, he had a brief, amiable conversation before returning to the couch. "That was Carlos Fuentes," the ambassador said, adding, "He spends a great deal of time in London. He loves it here."

Without missing a beat, he picked up where he'd left off. "In Tijuana, which was an enormous problem just two years ago, far greater than Juárez

Mexican Army in Ciudad Juárez. Photo copyright © Ricardo Ainslie.

at the time, we were able to retake the city from the criminal groups by disarticulating the Tijuana police that had been in the cartel's hands. Juárez was different," he said. "The problem with Juárez is the culture of local gangs, the power of gang identities, and their territorial disputes. They also seem to have a penchant for engaging in violence for violence's sake," he concluded.

■ ■ ■

In Juárez, the government's lack of success in quelling the violence was beginning to erode the initial enthusiasm for the federal forces. One afternoon I arrived at a crime scene where several men had been executed near the intersection of two streets in a ramshackle neighborhood. The yellow tape that marked the perimeter fluttered in the wind, and the usual players were presiding over the scene: municipal police "guides," federal police, Mexican Army personnel, and forensics people, who had laid out black-numbered yellow markers next to each shell casing that they'd encountered. From my vantage across the way I could see at least thirty such markers, but there were many more: the execution had taken place inside a small auto repair shop so most of the crime scene was out of view. The yellow markers made their way from the street into the darkened space where I was told three men lay dead.

The yellow crime scene tape ran across the street on all four sides of the intersection, creating an interior space, and most of the officials were standing in groups within that space. Federal police and army soldiers stood guard to keep onlookers at a distance. The entire neighborhood was out: children of every age, teenagers on bicycles, adults—all standing along or near the yellow tape, looking. Some were anxious and grim, others chatted as if at a carnival. The only other people inside the perimeter appeared to be relatives of the victims and a few neighbors whose homes were inside the taped-off area.

"They were good people," one of the neighbors said, standing next to me at the tapeline. "They were mechanics, and for a while now they'd been hitting them up for the *cuota*," she said, referring to the extortion fee cartels and local gangs were charging merchants and shopkeepers. Another neighbor chimed in and explained his understanding of what had taken place. He told me that the man who owned the repair shop also employed his son and his two sons-in-law. The *sicarios* had entered the shop and started shooting. Only the man's son had managed to get away, having jumped the wall at the rear of the building.

The son was pointed out to me. He appeared to be in his midtwenties and was tall and thickly built; he was wearing jeans and a gray sweatshirt that still had what looked like garage grime on it. The survivor was standing inside the sealed-off area where two friends consoled him. The man appeared to be in shock; he was distraught, his face flush with tears.

"They need to take him inside somewhere," one of the neighbors said. "If they see him they'll come back to get him." The group of neighbors standing around me murmured their agreement. Just then, three soldiers walked past the man, and in that moment he lost control of himself and started shouting at the soldiers, insulting them. "You people are worthless," he screamed in a mix of rage and tears. "You claim you are here to protect but you do nothing! You aren't worth shit!" The son lunged toward the three soldiers, who stood their ground facing him, but before he could spring loose his two friends caught hold of him and restrained him. After a moment, the soldiers walked away and the man and his two companions made their way to the man's house, which was on the same block. He was not present when the forensics people loaded up the three cadavers for their trip to the morgue.

The scene was tense and hard to digest. The neighbors and other onlookers seemed to take on an angry mood, especially toward the soldiers and federal police. They'd seen too much of this. Whatever promise they may have felt, whatever hope there may have been when the federal forces first arrived in Ciudad Juárez, that optimism appeared to be dissipating rapidly, replaced by a sea of frustration. It was the first time I saw clearly that the federal forces were losing the battle for hearts and minds in Juárez. The city seemed to be losing faith in the possibility that things would get better. And civics lessons, it occurred to me, were as much about such hope and the belief that good and right would prevail, as they were about anything else that a society might offer.

■ ■ ■

"My aim is to have 3,000 new police elements by December," José Reyes Ferriz told me one afternoon in his office at Juárez's Presidencia Municipal in the summer of 2009, after the arrival of the new wave of federal forces. The paradigm had not changed: the army and federal police were buying him time—they were a stopgap measure, placeholders, until the city of Juárez could create a new, reliable force. "We need the army to help contain crime until the police can be cleaned up and begin working," he added.

With the arrival of the latest contingent of federal forces, March and April had seen a reduction in the number of executions in the city. In January and February executions had been running at about eight or nine per day, but in April and May they dipped to three or four per day. The cartels appeared to be taking a wait-and-see approach to the presence of ten thousand federal forces patrolling the city. But by the end of May the tally of the dead was back up and the problem with the federal strategy remained the same: the army was not trained to do police work, and even as it succeeded in arresting narcos and other criminals, the interface between the army and the civilian judiciary system was so deficient that for a variety of reasons most of the criminals simply walked once they were turned over to civilian authorities. An added complication was that their bread-and-butter tactic was bare-fisted engagements, and these were beginning to create a backlash of protest and accusations of human rights violations.

■ ■ ■

The mayor and the police chief, General Bretón, had set out to reach their goal of almost doubling the size of the police to three thousand. This time, they focused their recruitment efforts in Juárez. In order to induce men and women to sign up, the city launched campaigns that promised recruits higher pay, a $7,500 peso (about $700) bonus, scholarships for their children's schooling, and credits that would help them purchase a house. By September of 2009, they had succeeded in bringing in the 2,250 or so recruits for what they were now officially calling the "New Police." In addition to having passed the Confidence Tests, these recruits had been subjected to rigorous, boot camp–style training similar to what an earlier wave had received at a Mexican Army training camp in nearby Santa Gertrudis, but this time the recruits were trained in Juárez. They also received extensive instruction in the use of automatic weapons. In collaboration with the Universidad Autónoma de Ciudad Juárez, the city also developed a four-month-long law enforcement curriculum that was incorporated into the police academy instruction. Between the weeding out of the questionable officers, the creation of a new training scheme, and the recruitment and training of new officers, the yearlong process had represented a massive undertaking, but the New Police were now ready to be launched.

Mayor José Reyes Ferriz inaugurated the New Police with great fanfare at an event in the auditorium at the Universidad Autónoma de Ciudad Juárez on September 14, 2009. The entire force was mustered, in their new, starched, silver-gray uniforms, specifically designed to be easily distinguishable from the uniforms used by the earlier incarnation of the discredited and infamous Juárez municipal police. At the outset of the ceremony, the new officers stood at attention and saluted sharply. In his introduction, the mayor spoke about Juárez's historic reputation as an industrious and progressive center, a reputation that was recognized worldwide, he said. The mayor acknowledged that over the course of the last decade the city had undergone a steady deterioration, increasingly becoming a place that was at the mercy of criminals. The city's reputation was now on a par with that of some of the most violent places on the globe, the mayor continued. "We had to act," he told the newly minted police officers. There was pride in the mayor's voice as he summarized the accomplishments of the preceding year; it had taken an enormous effort to rebuild the police, a force that had been under the control of the Juárez cartel for at least a decade and that had then been decimated by the Sinaloa cartel's efforts to take it over. In little more than a year, scores of officers had been assassinated, including three of the force's top commanders. Two chiefs had resigned, ultimately eventuating in the army's takeover of policing functions. For these reasons, in addition to a sense accomplishment, that September 14 ceremony brought enormous relief to the mayor, who dared once again to entertain the notion that the city could be saved, that it was on the cusp of a change, a change that would deliver it from the grips of the ungovernability it had endured for so long.

Notes

1. In Texas, New Mexico, and Arizona, there are few restrictions for gun dealers selling assault weapons. As long as a purchaser has a valid driver's license and does not have a criminal record, these dealers can sell an unlimited number of assault weapons without reporting the sales to the government.

2. This figure has been a source of controversy. A sample of the total weapons seized was submitted to U.S. authorities, and 90 percent of these were found to have U.S. origins. On this basis, William Hoover, assistant director for ATF field operations, testified before the House of Representatives on February 7, 2008, that "there is more than enough evidence to indicate that over 90 percent of the firearms that have either been recovered in or interdicted in transport to Mexico originated from various sources within the United States." More recently, in July 2011, an ATF report indicated that authorities in Mexico recovered 29,284 firearms in 2009 and 2010. Of these, 20,504 came from the United States (that is, approximately 70 percent).

CHAPTER 19

The Other War

The Juárez mayor had another war to contend with: politics. The July 2010 elections, only a year away, were beginning to loom large. The city would be voting for a new mayor and the state for a new governor (by law, neither Reyes Ferriz nor Reyes Baeza could be reelected). There was already intense jockeying for these and other positions. Reyes Ferriz's party, the PRI, was divided into two factions. One faction was derisively known as "The Dinosaurs." Composed of remnants of the party that had ruled Mexico with an iron fist for over seventy years, it had a well-earned reputation for corruption and prepotency. The other faction within the party was made up of younger, college-educated, professional people with more of a democratic vision. Reyes Ferriz belonged to the latter faction.

The stakes were high for the coming elections. One of the old guard who was jockeying for the PRI candidacy for governor was Héctor "Teto" Murguía. Murguía was Reyes Ferriz's predecessor in the mayor's job; he had imposed Saulo Reyes on the police department in January of 2007. The man that Murguía wanted in the Juárez mayor's job was named Víctor Valencia. Valencia was Reyes Ferriz's nemesis—a street fighter of a politician with a sketchy background. Reyes Baeza, Murguía, and Valencia formed the old-guard troika, a package deal wrapped in innuendo and rumor. Reyes Ferriz was convinced that this lineup would undermine his efforts to save Juárez from the current crisis; at stake was everything that he had been trying to achieve since becoming mayor of Juárez.

■ ■ ■

By chance, I had encountered Víctor Valencia one day at a standoff between police and residents in an upscale residential subdivision. In Ciudad Juárez the rich and the poor alike braced themselves every time they left their homes, no matter what time of day or night. Living in the most violent city in the Americas (perhaps in the world) was to live in a constant state of fear even for the city's elite, who lived in the Campestre neighborhood. The older part of the Campestre was dotted with opulent mansions arrayed around the exclusive Club Campestre, with its emerald-green, well-manicured golf course and the usual country club amenities. The homes had expansive lawns; expensive, late-model cars and armored SUVs sat parked behind tall walls and elaborate wrought-iron gates. It was the fashion that a good number of these homes had private chapels. In addition to the ever-present bodyguards, elaborate security systems were in evidence.

Not far from the heart of the Campestre was a more recent and comparatively more modest subdivision of the neighborhood. It was still upper middle class, home to assembly plant managers and successful professionals, but clearly a rung below the original Campestre, where the city's mega-wealthy lived. If less luxurious, the homes here were still quite nice, ample with gated entryways and tall walls surrounding interior gardens. The newer neighborhood lacked the panache of the original Campestre; it had a nouveau riche feel rather than the air of established money. A long wall that ran several blocks separated the older Campestre from the new, further reinforcing the sense that the latter was not to be confused with the former. I had come to this upscale part of the city because I'd been told that the residents had taken to putting up impromptu obstructions in the streets in an effort to dissuade *sicarios* and kidnappers from coming through the neighborhood. It struck me as an indication that notwithstanding their bodyguards and armored vehicles, the rich were also affected by the climate of fear that permeated the city. In the older, wealthier Campestre, residents had trucked in enormous boulders to block the streets; in the newer subdivision, residents were using both boulders and sand from the desert to create berms.

In an all-too-premature effort to bring an air of normality back to the streets, the city administration, in conjunction with the federal police, ordered the Department of Public Works to remove the berms and boulders so that traffic could flow freely. Under the watchful eyes of two dozen municipal[1] and federal police officers, who lined the street to protect the city crew, a mustard-yellow Caterpillar backhoe loader was at work scooping up the sand from the berms and dumping it into the bed of a waiting truck. Black diesel smoke gushed from the backhoe's exhaust as its operator maneuvered the heavy scoop, which scraped loudly as it moved across the pavement.

The residents of the newer Campestre were out in the street and they were irate. A tense standoff had developed between them, the city crew, and the police officers. The residents had not been informed that the barriers they'd thrown up over a year ago in a desperate act of self-protection had been slated for removal. It was only the scraping sound of the backhoe and the sight of the dump truck and police that had alerted some to what was taking place, and as word spread in the neighborhood that their defenses were being dismantled, the number of angry onlookers grew. It was noon and some thirty or forty neighbors were out in the street demanding that the work stop, but so far their efforts were to no avail.

The tension was growing with each scoop of sand that was removed and each boulder that was pushed on to the edge of the street. In desperation, one middle-aged man in a brown designer jogging suit jumped in front of the backhoe, daring the driver to run him over. The crowd screamed, imploring the Caterpillar operator to stop, which he did just as the thick steel bucket came within inches of the defiant man's face. The jogger held his ground in this Juárez Tiananmen Square moment as the crowd erupted in applause and cheers and the Caterpillar operator looked on helplessly.

When a federal police officer approached the jogger, the crowd drew close, shouting "Don't touch him! We are all witnesses!" Several made it a point to show that they were filming the incident with their video cameras. The officer calmly explained that the orders were to clear the street, that this was no way to handle security issues, but his appeals drew a chorus of howls and derision. By this juncture, in solidarity with the Tiananmen man, some residents had laid themselves down under the enormous wheels of the backhoe. "Calm down," the officer appealed, but to no avail.

A municipal police officer named Lieutenant Villalobos now stepped forward to try to address the crowd. "I'm in charge, and I will ensure you are safe," he told the men and women who'd left their nearby homes in what was already a sweltering-hot summer day. "That's not true," a woman shouted into the lieutenant's face. "You're a liar," another shouted.

"You tell me the time of danger and I'll have a patrol car assigned to be here," the officer said. "What time?"

A middle-aged woman in a T-shirt and shorts, her hair braided down her back, spoke up: "They kidnapped me at four in the afternoon," she said, her words breaking up with emotion. "They kidnapped my sister at ten o'clock at night, and they shot my father to death at eight in the morning!" She continued, angry and upset. "There is no safe time in this city!" Soon another neighbor replaced this woman, recounting his version of the city's horror. "Please don't use my name," the first woman told me when I spoke to her later. "There could be reprisals."

The police pulled back, regrouping to the side as the stalemate continued. At that moment, a young man who had been standing in the wings stepped forward. He was no older than twenty-five, dressed in a purple striped dress shirt, black pants, and sunglasses. He was modest in stature and soft-spoken as he attempted to address the group, identifying himself as a city engineer here to monitor the job. He was apologetic and understanding of the residents' concerns, but he also underscored that clearing the street was in keeping with a recent directive from the federal police. Such obstructions were not a good security strategy, he maintained. The city engineer was clearly a newbie, not long out of college and still wet behind the ears. He was perspiring in the summer heat and in the face of the responsibility he'd been given to oversee the order to clear the street. He was trying his best, but he was no match for the agitated crowd.

As the engineer was speaking, a man in a navy blue blazer and a pink shirt with no tie briskly entered the fray. He did not bother to identify himself, but the engineer no doubt recognized him as Víctor Valencia, the governor's representative in Ciudad Juárez. I thought that perhaps Valencia lived in the neighborhood. He had a thick moustache and black curly hair that was combed straight back; whatever product he used in his hair made it gleam in the summer sun. The crowd opened a path for Valencia, who in a matter of moments was in the engineer's face, brusque and imperious. Valencia's voice was loud and carried easily through the crowd. His tactic was to jab his finger into the young man's chest while publicly humiliating him. The engineer was clearly out of his depth. "Who called the police?" Valencia demanded to know. He called the engineer a "coward" for "coming in here to beat up on the public." The engineer made one or two efforts to respectfully counter Valencia, invoking the fact that he was just doing his job, but Valencia shouted him down, accusing him of "working for other interests" and alleging that the real reason he was here was that the city was clearing the road so people could cut through the neighborhood to get to the new shopping mall on the other side. He repeatedly called the man a coward and a "collaborator" with the police, who, he said, "have done nothing." The latter drew cheers from the residents, who by now had formed a tight circle around the encounter, savoring every word. People clapped every time Valencia made a point. Valencia appeared to have a need to fan the flames; he was theatrical, playing to the audience.

"There are killings all over this city," Valencia continued, now speaking to the neighbors rather than the engineer, "and look how many police they have with them. We must be very important," he said mockingly. Some people laughed, but Valencia's excesses were beginning to make even those who had at first enthusiastically welcomed him now begin to feel a degree of awkwardness. The tight knot of people that had encircled the exchange began to loosen, and some even began to head home. It had become clear that the city was not going to proceed with the orders to dismantle the barriers on this day, and they'd had enough of the spectacle. Off at the edge of the crowd, I eavesdropped on a conversation between two federal police officers remarking on the scene that had just unfolded. "When are you going to see people of that class behaving that way? That's how out of control this is," one officer said. He was referring to the fact that in Mexico, with its tight class structure, it was unusual to see upper-middle-class people out on the streets screaming and shouting. Then, in reference to Valencia, the same federal officer observed that the situation had turned into political grandstanding. "I heard this guy is going to be put in charge of the CIPOL," said another officer. The CIPOL, the intelligence and investigative agency for the state police, was known to be under the control of the Juárez cartel.

Valencia had succeeded in throwing a wrench in the process. The engineer ordered the city's crew to stop their work and most of the berms and boulders remained in place. As the city vehicles exited down the street, the remaining residents cheered. Having accomplished his goal, Valencia exited the stage as abruptly as he'd arrived.

At the time of the Campestre confrontation, I did not know who Víctor Valencia was, much less of the animosity that existed between him and the mayor of Juárez. But it was impossible to miss the man's arrogance, an attribute that had eventually soured even those who'd initially cheered him that day.

■ ■ ■

Conflict between José Reyes Ferriz and Víctor Valencia dated back to Reyes Ferriz's nine-month tenure as interim mayor in 2001. The day following Reyes Ferriz's interim appointment, Valencia had called ostensibly at the then-governor's behest. "He said, 'The governor wants my *compadre* to be secretary of social development,'" Reyes Ferriz recalled. This was an important post, because it controlled many of the city's purchases. The entire arrangement had the look and feel of an insider deal (the kind of deal that Saulo Reyes would subsequently get in 2005, when he opened the companies through which a third of the city's business flowed). Reyes Ferriz wasn't comfortable with it. "I refused," he told me. "I knew [Valencia] and didn't trust him." The mayor's refusal put him on a collision course with the governor and Valencia's other allies.

Governor Reyes Baeza had installed Víctor Valencia as his personal representative in Juárez in July of 2009. It was a step meant to set the stage for the latter's mayoral candidacy, positioning Valencia for the upcoming 2010 elections. The tensions between Reyes Ferriz and Valencia had simmered for years and the governor knew it. In the prior mayoral election, in 2007, both the governor and Héctor Murguía had picked Valencia to succeed Murguía as the Juárez mayor. At the time, Valencia had begun spreading rumors that José Reyes Ferriz actually lived in El Paso, not Juárez, a fact that, if true, would have disqualified Reyes Ferriz from running for office. Reyes Ferriz did, indeed, own a home in El Paso, but that was not uncommon among the people who occupied Juárez's upper social strata.[2] Paying Texas property taxes made it possible for their children to cross the river every day to attend school on the U.S. side. Having such homes was also a symbol of status within Juárez's upper social circles.

Reyes Ferriz discounts the allegations that he lived in El Paso as outright falsehoods. "We lived our lives in Juárez," he said in reference to himself and his family. But as a precaution, in the six-month run-up to the mayoral elections in 2007, Reyes Ferriz made sure he did not so much as cross the river. "I did not go to El Paso, not even for a single day, during that time because if they had photographed me there they would have used it against me," he told me.

But Valencia's accusations stuck. Reyes Ferriz claims that *El Norte*, which backed Valencia's candidacy, was primarily responsible for endlessly repeating the rumor, which took on the status of fact and was repeated as such in both Mexican newspapers and the international media, in part because it lent itself to the dramatic picture of an embattled mayor whose life was under siege. However, in Juárez, the Valencia-inspired rumor had a different connotation: it implied that the mayor was cowardly, and for some it also bred resentment because it implied that the mayor's privilege gave him the luxury of seeking refuge across the river while the rest of the populace lived trapped in crime-ridden neighborhoods from which there was no escape.

Reyes Ferriz had succeeded in outflanking his adversaries within his party and garnered the nomination for mayor. But the animosities remained. There was no love lost between José Reyes Ferriz and Víctor Valencia.

■ ■ ■

I had read many newspaper accounts over the course of researching Juárez, and during my first interview with José Reyes Ferriz, I, too, remarked that it was my understanding that he was living in El Paso due to concerns for his own and his family's personal safety. The mayor's reaction was immediate: "I must correct you," he responded, politely but firmly. "I do not live in El Paso. My wife and children stay in El Paso because we have been the object of many death threats. But I live in Ciudad Juárez. I live in *this* city, not over there," he said definitively, gesturing toward the north-facing window behind his desk with a view of the Rio Grande and downtown El Paso. I was surprised by the mayor's correction, and not altogether convinced of it given that the contrary view was common currency in the local, national, and international media.

Across the street from my hotel, the Lucerna, was a Sanborns restaurant. One evening not long after that first interview with the mayor, I joined a group of Juárez journalists who were decompressing from a day's work over a few beers. The discussion was lively and far ranging. At one point the conversation drifted to the mayor, with whom the journalists did not seem to be particularly enamored. They were aware of the fact that I'd interviewed him and asked me what he had to say about what was taking place in Juárez. I volunteered at one point that the mayor had told me that he did not live in El Paso, as had been so frequently reported in the media. "He says he lives in Juárez," I told them. The journalists were emphatic: "He lives in El Paso!" they asserted.

The mayor had been so adamant about living in Juárez, however, that I pressed the journalists. "Why don't you investigate it?" I asked. "It would be easy enough to do, you know where he works; you could trail him."

That suggestion drew protests. "We might be killed," one of them volunteered. No one was interested in pursuing the question of the mayor's domicile, even as they strenuously upheld the common view that he lived across the river.

Some months later, on a Saturday afternoon, I was interviewing the mayor again in his offices. He seemed to feel beleaguered. Despite his efforts, he had yet to succeed in dampening the rate of the killings or other crime in Juárez. He knew the city was growing restive about the situation, and he threw in the press's insistence on the notion that he actually lived in El Paso as a reproach against the media. In response, I suggested that perhaps he could show me where he lived in Juárez and, to my surprise, he readily agreed. Within minutes we were headed out of his office.

The convoy exited the Presidencia Municipal and roared down the border thruway until we turned right onto a boulevard off of which were a series of relatively new housing developments. One bore a large stone marker that said Bosques de Aragón; fifty yards past the marker we pulled up to a gated community. The security detail deployed to strategic spots as the gate opened slowly and we passed through. Once inside, we came to a stop in front of what Reyes Ferriz said was his house.

The gated community was nice but not ostentatious; the homes were arrayed around a central, expansive lawn, at one end of which was a well-worn children's playscape. The mayor exited the Suburban and made his way over to greet some neighbors clustered near the playscape, their children entertaining themselves on the swings and slides.

Next we headed inside the house, where the mayor gave me a tour. There was a living room/dining room area partitioned by an iron railing. In the living room were family pictures of his wife and children. The decorations were modest, some appearing to be gifts he had received over the course of his term in office, but there were also paintings and other artwork on the walls. In the kitchen the mayor offered me something to drink. I noticed that the refrigerator held food, the condiments shelf was full, and there was a case of water bottles and a six-pack of Dos Equis beer. On the kitchen counter, next to a toaster, I spotted half-consumed bottles of DayQuil and NyQuil, which suggested that the mayor had been battling a cold. Also on the counter I spotted two letters addressed to him at this address: one from a bank and the other from his telephone service.

The landing at the foot of the stairway took me by surprise. An enormous steel door, like one would find at a bank vault, was used to seal off access to the stairway. It was easily one inch thick. "I close this when I go upstairs for the night," the mayor said, adding that this door and one upstairs had been installed following a rash of death threats against him when he'd fired the police after the Confidence Tests in the fall of 2008.

Upstairs, there were several bedrooms and a workout area. The master bedroom was somewhat in disarray. One of the nightstands had a stack of DVD movies as well as books and what appeared to be an assortment of medications. There was also a handheld electronic device with an LCD screen and numerous security cameras that Reyes Ferriz could control with the device. "I can see what's going on downstairs with this," he explained. To illustrate, he changed stations. The door to the house came into view on the LCD screen, then the living room, then the landing by the stairs. Standing in front of the only bedroom window was a three-quarter-inch steel plate that spanned the length of the window. "When the death threats against me intensified, we installed this in order to prevent a sniper from shooting through the window," he said matter-of-factly. Finally, the mayor showed me his "panic room." It was actually a large master closet with rows of suits, shirts, and trousers, and shoes haphazardly arrayed on the floor. "I've got food and water in here," he told me. "I've also got a weapon in case of an emergency," he said, referring to the AR-15 that he had begun keeping when he'd fortified the house. The panic room had an enormous vault-like steel door, like the one that sealed off the stairway downstairs. The house had the unmistakable feel of a bunker.

José Reyes Ferriz's residence was more like a professional person's bachelor pad than the home of the mayor of an important city. But all indications were that he lived here, at least during the week, visiting his wife and children on weekends, as commitments permitted. It was evident that in the steady chorus of "He lives over there," the mayor felt maligned.

I asked him why he hadn't brought other people here. "In Juárez it's dangerous to talk openly about death threats," he answered. "It is easy for the cartels to take that as an act of defiance, as a challenge to them. That can make them feel that they *have* to take you out. It has not been worthwhile for me to do that. People can think what they want. I know the truth."

Notes

1. A skeleton force of municipal police had been retained.

2. Héctor Murguía owned a home in El Paso as well, but his "residency" was never an issue in his campaign.

CHAPTER 20

Addicts

Juárez was awash in drugs and addicts (150,000 of them by one official count).[1] Drugs were being sold all over the city—on street corners, in parks, in bars, even from street vendors' push carts, which ostensibly sold tamales or steamed sweet potatoes but whose owners made their real profit selling drugs. As a result, drug addiction had metastasized. The explosion of *picaderos* was paralleled, if not exactly matched, by an increase in the number of treatment centers catering to strung-out addicts seeking help; they had sprung up everywhere, most supported by churches and nonprofits, others by government programs.

Casa Aliviane, the Center for Attention to the Health of Addicts, was on Uranio Street in Norponiente, just a short walk south of the Rio Grande and within sight of downtown El Paso. The center was not difficult to find: the entrance to the building, which had once been a private residence, had a distinctive arabesque-shaped narrow doorway, as if one were entering a set from *1001 Arabian Nights*. The exterior was painted bright pink and purple, its barred windows outlined in bold burgundy stripes. A short, red-tiled ledge sheltered the entryway, and above it "Casa Aliviane, A.C." was painted in large red and orange block letters. The center had multiple rooms that served as dormitories, as well as a kitchen and dining room area, an office space, classrooms, and a space that served as a large meeting room. Twenty addicts were living at the center. Some of them had day jobs, returning in the evenings for dinner, prayer, and the group classes and meetings that were part of their recovery program. Others spent the day at Casa Aliviane, performing a variety of jobs that kept the center going.

The staff at Casa Aliviane knew that theirs was dangerous work. The men who walked through their doors were not only strung out, many also had complex ties to Juárez's drug world, which was rife with gang warfare and killings. Not all of the clientele were there in good faith. The staff at the treatment centers often worked in fear that gang members had infiltrated the centers and were living among the addicts who were genuinely trying to work their recovery programs. For example, gang members who were on a rival gang's hit list sometimes sought refuge in the rehabilitation centers, masquerading as addicts seeking treatment, when in fact they were merely trying to hide out until the heat was past. And as often as not, the pushers themselves were addicts. By virtue of their gang affiliation, the pusher-addicts retained their predatory edge within the rehabilitation centers. It gave them power; they represented an ever-present threat of violence. Ordinary addicts feared them. Thus, within the rehabilitation centers there was often a great deal of tension.

The addicts were part of a chain of realities that could be traced back to the cartels and the vicious battles taking place between their proxy gangs for control of the retail drug markets. Each rehab center had its own place within the ecology of the Juárez drug world. Pushers and addicts had alliances or arrangements with specific gangs by virtue of where they lived and the source of their drugs. If you were an addict living in a twenty-block area in Bellavista that was controlled by Los Aztecas, then you purchased your drugs from one of their pushers. You were living out your addiction within a Los Aztecas–controlled universe, but rival gangs (from a few blocks over, or perhaps even from the same neighborhood) were constantly trying to move into this piece of turf to push their own product on the neighborhood's residents. Each of the substantive players in this game pressed people into service. Upcoming wannabes had to prove their mettle by pushing drugs and were sometimes forced to test rivals' terrain. They also shared responsibility for identifying the incursions of rival gangs into their part of the *colonia*. All of this created flux and tension between gangs and within neighborhoods, and addicts were caught in between. It was a combustible mix that was producing many of the Juárez dead.

The fratricidal hatreds between the Juárez street gangs ran so deep that treatment centers could not cater to addicts from rival gangs. In the natural course of things and not by design, there was an informal sorting of the centers. As often as not, specific centers became associated with particular gangs and the addicts that they served.

■ ■ ■

The *sicarios* arrived at Casa Aliviane on the night of September 2, just as the evening prayers had begun. They wore ski masks and brandished assault weapons. There were eight in all, and they broke down the door and moved briskly, in single file, through the narrow arabesque entryway and into the hallway, where they encountered the first residents. They eventually rounded up twenty men, whom they lined up and forced to their knees before shooting. All told, seventeen people were executed that night at Casa Aliviane. Sixteen were found dead in the interior hallway amid pools of blood and another died later that night at a nearby hospital (the remaining three were gravely wounded). One of the treatment center's two pit bulls, ostensibly there to protect the facilities, had also been gunned down. The other dog, later found cowering in the courtyard, was spared for some reason.

The Casa Aliviane killing was the third such attack on a drug treatment center in Juárez in recent months. It was also the biggest massacre on record for a city that had already witnessed more than its share of violence.

■ ■ ■

An operative of the Juárez cartel from the Amado Carrillo Fuentes days during the 1990s[2] told me that at that time the culture within the cartel dictated that few of them used cocaine. People who violated that ethos were demoted and pushed to the margins, and if they persisted and their substance abuse interfered with their duties, they were executed. A decade later that ethos had all but disappeared. In fact, cocaine use had become extensive. In April 2010, state ministerial police intelligence video cameras caught a ninety-minute narco-takeover of Creel, Chihuahua, a small town on the edge of the Copper Canyon. The raid involved a dozen SUVs and a score of *sicarios*. At the beginning of the raid the *sicarios*, assault weapons in tow, are clearly visible coming up to a capo's car—a man subsequently identified as Jesús Ernesto Chávez Castillo, an important Juárez cartel operative—and reaching through the car window into the bag of cocaine in Castillo's hand before heading off to assassinate their targets. (In the course of the massacre fifteen people were killed, and yet, even as a state police agent in the Command and Control Center tracked the commando group's actions, zooming in and out, there was no response by the state police. It clarified what everyone in Chihuahua already knew: the Juárez cartel ran the state ministerial police.)

■ ■ ■

Hernán was one of those who'd begun using the product he ran across the river. He had been a heavy drinker, but he had never been a cocaine user. Now, more and more cartel members were using coke and, as a consequence, some were becoming addicts themselves. Over the last year of Hernán and Elena's relationship, his violence had intensified, very likely as a function of his cocaine abuse. For a long time Hernán denied it, but Elena felt she could always tell when he came home coked up. He was hyper and restless, his eyes constantly darting around. He could not sleep, he was agitated. She worried that he was losing it. He also became hyper-suspicious and increasingly vigilant, but Elena was never clear whether the paranoia was a function of something real or imagined, given that in his line of work there was the ever-present threat of being ripped off; cocaine loads could have "bunk" mixed in among the kilos. You had to worry about getting paid for loads you delivered and you had to worry about paying up the line in a timely fashion. You had to worry about rivals stealing money or product from you, or your people defecting to work for someone else. You had to worry about getting busted every time you or your people crossed the river. And you had to worry about the shifting politics and alliances within the cartel. Misreading any of these variables got people killed, and, with the changing terrain, as the Sinaloa cartel people started making inroads in Juárez, many of Hernán's associates were turning up dead. The cocaine didn't help Hernán manage these complexities, it just helped him forget about them in fits and spurts, even as it compromised his judgment.

Hernán became erratic. On one occasion he wrestled Elena to the floor in the kitchen and put a gun to her head in front of their boy. It was the one thing she would never forgive. She told him to go ahead and kill her. "You'd be doing me a favor," she said. But she also fantasized killing him; she imagined poisoning his food. Things had reached bottom for them.

One incident captured her sense that things were unraveling for Hernán, that he was losing his footing. She had always made a habit of noting the numbers on the police patrol cars that were parked in front of her house. One day Hernán found the list and asked her what it was. She told him. His reaction suggested a problem. There was something in his tone, or in the glint in his eyes, that made her think that some of the patrol cars watching the house were not from his group. She had never liked having the police at her house, and now their presence made her feel anxious.

One morning she received a call from Hernán. He was tense and not himself. He gave her very clear, specific instructions: Take Pedro to your mother's and stay there until you hear from me. Under no circumstances was she to go near the house. There was no mistaking his apprehension and sense of danger. Something big was taking place, although he refused to say anything more about it. Later that afternoon Hernán called again, only to repeat the instructions that she and the children were not to return to the house.

The next call Elena received was from one of Hernán's brothers, telling her he was dead. He had been shot down in the street, ambushed by an unidentified narco-commando group. Killed like a dog, she said.

At Hernán's funeral, Elena discovered that he had at least a dozen children, only four of which were with his wife. She had always assumed that he had other lovers, but discovering that her child was not the only one outside of his marriage surprised her. Elena consoled herself with the fact that she was the only one of his consorts for whom he'd purchased a home, and with the knowledge that he had participated in the boy's baptism. She also consoled herself with the knowledge that she had had Hernán for eight years. "He defied the odds," she told me. "Most of them don't live more than five years." Hernán's execution was either a sad fact or earned justice, depending on how one looked at it.

Whatever purchase such reassurances gave Elena, it was short-lived. She returned to her house two days after Hernán's execution to find it in shambles. It was obvious that the people involved believed that Hernán had hidden either drugs or money at the house. No drawer was left in a dresser or cabinet; no mattress was left unturned. Every piece of furniture had been moved, some of it broken. The closets and drawers had all been emptied onto the floor. In fact, no crevice had escaped the havoc of their thoroughness. Elena inferred from this that Hernán had betrayed someone. She also knew that had she been home she would have been assassinated or lifted and tortured to see if she knew something. That is why Hernán had been so insistent that she and Pedro leave the house. There was something else that Elena noticed: the ever-present police cars were gone. They never returned.

■ ■ ■

In the wake of the Casa Aliviane killings, officials weighed in on what they believed had transpired. Víctor Valencia had only remained as the governor's personal representative in Ciudad Juárez for a short time, given the conflicts between Valencia and Reyes Ferriz. In another effort to further Valencia's political prospects, the governor had appointed Valencia the Chihuahua state secretary for public safety, which meant that he was essentially the head of the state police. In that new capacity, Valencia's response to the killings was to say that drug centers like Casa Aliviane were sometimes fronts for criminal gangs. Patricia González, the state attorney general, noted that such centers "had become hideouts from police or rival gang members." Whether or not there were one or several gang members among the Casa Aliviane dead, there was also every indication that the dead included addicts who had sought to remedy their suffering in one of the city's bona fide treatment programs, a fact that would probably have a chilling effect on other addicts similarly in need of help. A few days after the massacre at Casa Aliviane, mayor Reyes Ferriz announced that the army had arrested three of the people believed responsible for the killings.[3]

Notes

1. A 2008 Consejo Nacional de Adicciones report noted that Juárez had the highest number of addicts of any city in Mexico.

2. This individual requested anonymity for fear of reprisal, even though it had been over a decade since he had been actively involved with the cartel.

3. On March 19, 2011, eighteen months after the massacre, the state prosecutor in Chihuahua released the three men on the grounds that there was insufficient evidence to convict them.

CHAPTER 21

Los NiNi

On a hot June day in 2009 I was at a crime scene in Norponiente. The federal police and the army had secured the area, which was a short block with an elementary school (its fence painted in bright primary colors) along one side, and modest homes along the other. Behind and above those houses were two layers of desert, like shelves, upon which other working class homes sat, constructed of rough, bleached-out cinderblock or red brick. The homes had barred windows and were surrounded by patches of scrubby, dusty vegetation.

It was a grim landscape even without the victim lying face-up on the pavement next to a recent-model, silver-gray Chevrolet sedan that he had been about to board. The driver's door was still wide open. The man, dressed in jeans, white tennis shoes, and a clean white T-shirt, had fallen backward such that his head lay next to the vehicle's rear tire. His legs splayed out in the opposite direction. I was mystified by the whiteness of his T-shirt; there was no trace of blood on it, at least not that I could see from my remove of twenty yards. The man had been shot in the face and, mercifully, someone had covered his head.

One of the federal police officers guarding the scene told me that the victim was twenty years old. The assassin had shot fifteen bullets—at least that was the highest number on the yellow markers that indicated the location of shell casings. Off to the side, standing along a chain-link fence, the victim's mother wailed mournfully. She was flanked by two people who attempted to console her: a teenage boy in a light-blue T-shirt, who rubbed her shoulder as her right hand extended behind her and touched his face appreciatively; and a young woman in a white blouse looking on in silence, whose thick black hair was braided straight down the middle of her back. I surmised that these were her other children.

At one end of the street there was a pickup truck full of brooms that someone had been peddling at the time of the execution and an ice-cream vendor whose cart sat under a large faded umbrella. The entire neighborhood appeared to be standing at the yellow crime scene tape that enclosed the area where the dead man lay. As always, there were children and stray

Juárez execution. Photo copyright © Raymundo Ruiz.

dogs. Some of the people had solemn looks; others were cutting up, having grown bored waiting for something to happen (the forensics people had to finish their work before the body was removed to the morgue). At both ends of the street people chatted intermittently or stared blankly in the direction of the victim. There was nothing to do but wait for the quotidian scene to play out so they could go on pretending their lives were normal.

Around the time of this execution, José Reyes Ferriz pointed out a curious fact: most of the victims being executed all over the city were young. Like the executed man I encountered that day, 60 percent of the dead were under twenty-five years of age. The mayor and the federal authorities attributed that fact to a transformation in the Juárez war. The victims now included more drug retailers and young gangbangers fighting for turf and fewer traditional cartel operatives (men who were executed in more orchestrated ambushes and selective, targeted assassinations). Juárez's massive unemployment, especially among the ranks of young men, had created an explosive mix of youth, drugs, and a sense of hopelessness about the future. Therein lay the core of the problem for Juárez, or at least the part of the problem that didn't have to do with the quantity of drugs Americans were consuming.

■ ■ ■

Boys and Girls First! was one of the programs run by Organización Popular Independiente, a small nonprofit in Altavista, a neighborhood where the dead appeared daily. The program was operated out of a rundown building and it targeted elementary school–aged kids and young adolescents. So did the gang members who ran the *picadero* across the street, one of many that supplied the addicts in the neighborhood. Inside the Organización Popular Independiente, the main room had tables where classes were taught and kids could work on projects after school and on weekends. The walls were mostly bare except for a poster of Christ (Laurencio Barraza, the NGO's director, was a religious man who made the sign of the cross every morning before leaving his home; he knew his work in gang-infested neighborhoods was dangerous). A stack of donated food sat in the corner: fifty-pound sacks of El Globo wheat flower, beans, and rice, along with bags of corn masa for making tortillas, cooking oil, and boxes of "fine" cookies. The administrative offices were in an adjoining room and consisted of a series of workstations with a blackboard and a few old computers.

Barraza's group described itself as an "independent organization for the people." The day I visited, there were but two staff members present and no kids (I was there during school hours). Barraza and I sat at one of the computers reviewing photographs that the kids had taken for a photo contest they'd titled "Change in the Wind." Forty kids from Altavista had participated. They were provided with ten weeks of instruction by a professional photographer covering light, composition, action, and mood, and then sent into their neighborhood to document their worlds with disposable cameras. Once the film was processed, each child had been permitted to submit three images to the contest.

Some of the images were whimsical. A photograph taken in the interior of a public bus was captioned *The People's Limousine*. Another image was of two Mexican soldiers walking through shops that typically catered to Americans, with piñatas and colorful dresses hanging above and an assortment of Mexican curios all around. It was titled *The New Tourists* (a reference to the fact that the tourists from across the river had long since stopped coming). Most of the photographs spoke to the violence that had overtaken the city. One image was of a girl lying on the floor, ketchup on her neck to simulate blood, with a knife beside her. It was titled *Man with a Knife*. An exterior window with bars had a *calavera* (a Day of the Dead sugar skull), a small, brightly painted casket, and chrysanthemums (the ceremonial flower for the Day of the Dead). It was titled *The Face of Juárez*. A picture of two soldiers at nearby Altavista Park, their automatic weapons resting on sandbags, was titled *The Surveillance*. The most moving image was of a young girl standing with arms outstretched, reaching for the sky, a flash of sunlight caught between her fingers. It was titled *Liberty*. The photographer had added the following caption to this image: "I want to be able to go out in peace, I wish the afternoons were like they used to be, when I could go to the park."

The images were hung in various locations throughout the city—at the Camino Real hotel, at the main city library, at the historic Presidencia Municipal—and the media had covered the events. The contest's wining image, *Liberty*, had been exhibited in Mexico City.

Laurencio Barraza was a man with a calling. He was an energetic activist in his late forties, on the corpulent side, with a dark complexion and graying hair made starker by his thick, black-framed glasses. Barraza had been a child advocate most of his life. He and his organization were rabidly independent; he refused support from the usual government sources because, in his view, "there are too many strings attached."

Barraza leaned back in his chair and described the world within which most of his charges lived: the poverty, the abandonment, the absence of schools and social services. He was extremely concerned about the impact of the violence on Juárez's youth. "How can they process all of it?" he asked. "How do the daily images of violence affect their values? . . . You can't imagine how saturated their lives are with fear," Barraza continued. During Holy Week a year earlier rumors that the cartels were going to make the week the bloodiest ever had gone viral on the Internet, and everyone had been afraid to leave their homes.

In the Altavista neighborhood most parents either worked in the assembly plants or in the "informal" economy, which meant vendors in the streets. Barraza summarized the explosion of *picaderos* in the city. He told me that in 1997 there were seven hundred, but by 2005 there were almost 3,200. "It has to have happened with the consent of the authorities," Barraza told me. (As he spoke I was reminded that the estimates I'd been given for the number of *picaderos* varied depending on the source; what didn't change was the universal understanding that drugs had taken over the city, especially its poor and working-class neighborhoods.)

In 2000 there were six hundred elementary schools in Juárez, three hundred middle schools, and ten high schools. Norponiente, where 40 percent of the city lived, had but one public high school. "There's been a systematic policy of exclusion for this population," Barraza argued. "They push them toward the *maquiladoras*, at $70 pesos a day. They leave elementary school when they're twelve or thirteen but by law they're not permitted to work until they are fifteen. What do they do?" The question hung there. "There are few parks, no public institutions that address their needs, no *tools*. What these kids have is what the streets offer them—criminal activity." He was describing what in Mexico had emerged as a new social phenomenon: "Los NiNi,"[1] a term used to describe the growing number of youth who are neither in school nor working. Los NiNi had become synonymous with a lost generation, a generation whose lives were increasingly defined by gang affiliations and existence outside of the conventional social structures.

Barraza stood up and walked over to the blackboard. He sketched out a rough map of the city's neighborhoods. The areas of dense poverty formed an arc, like a sliver of moon, curving from top-left (Norponiente) to a tip at the southeast corner of the city. "What you have in this corridor are the least amount of city resources: single mothers, no childcare centers, no infrastructure, no parks. And you've got a proliferation of gangs throughout this entire area," he said.

The city was caught in a vise grip, he told me. There were seven hundred gangs, according to one study conducted by a local university. "That's why 90 percent of the people are in favor of the military being here," Barraza said, adding that he wasn't particularly taken with them. "They're from the south; they are burning up in this heat yet they don't bathe." But the real critique was what he perceived as inaction: "There haven't been that many skirmishes between the army and the narcos. It's more the narcos killing each other off," he told me, adding that the gangs were extorting everyone: pharmacies, hardware stores, stationary stores. "They're all hit with the 'mochate o te va ir mal' [pay up or it's going to go poorly for you]."

Barraza added that the army had lost its moment of opportunity as far as public opinion was concerned. "The first time the army entered the city en masse there was a sense of hope and possibility, even a sense of respect," Barraza recalled. But those hopes had been dashed with time: "The ever-present road blocks have produced very little other than being a major hassle for us."

■ ■ ■

Growing up, Elena never had the benefit of Boys and Girls First! or any other such program. She was a NiNi who'd been fortunate enough to have the looks to hook up with a narco. But in the aftermath of Hernán's execution, Elena was left alone. For all the conflict between them, her life had revolved around Hernán. Now he was gone. There was both relief and sadness in it. She felt that Hernán's executioners had done her a favor; she felt unburdened even as she felt deeply mournful. Life is always so full of contradiction, she thought. She missed him and she knew Pedro missed him. Her cell phone was all but mute, as his insistent, stalking calls had ceased. The enormity of his emotional baggage was no longer upon her. Hernán, the father of her son, was dead.

But that absence had consequences. He had purchased the house outright, so she owned it free and clear, but suddenly she was broke. He had always been clear with her: "I don't want you to have money because I want the guy who has you after I'm dead to have to work for you like I've worked for you." At the time it seemed like something theoretical, a "what if" scenario. But the "what if" was now a reality. She had no money and an elementary school–aged son. In fact, Pedro was in a private school. For the last eight years Hernán had typically arrived at the house with a wad of cash in his pocket that she tapped to pay the bills, shop for groceries, or go to the mall. That was gone.

"I was alone and had nowhere to turn," Elena told me at one of our meetings. Her family was impoverished; her brothers had their own families to feed, clothe, and otherwise support, and all of them lived hand-to-mouth lives as it was. Elena's first strategy was to sell her things. The house had nice furnishings, artwork, three computers, several televisions, and appliances and knickknacks. Elena organized a series of garage sales and started selling off what she had. A close friend, another narco-widow whose man had also been executed and who was now prostituting herself at an expensive brothel to pay her bills, offered a proposition: "Don't sell your stuff, come work with me. I'll set you up," she told Elena. But Elena couldn't bring herself to do it. "My pride got in the way," she told me. Over the first few months she sold everything she had in the house except for worn-out modular couches, the beds, and one of the televisions. She pulled her son out of private school and put him in the neighborhood public school.

For a year, Elena cobbled together a month-to-month subsistence, borrowing what she could from family members and selling everything she could. In the end she could not stay afloat. A year later, broke and in debt, Elena swallowed her pride, called her narco-widow friend, and asked her what she needed to do. Her friend's response was not heartening: "You should have called me a year ago; you wouldn't have had to sell all your shit." Elena started prostituting herself.

It was not an easy transition. Elena had been fast and loose for years, but always in control. Sex had been her terrain and a source of power. This was different. She was forced to relinquish that sense of agency. She had to make herself desired rather than dictating the terms of engagement. She had to acquiesce to other's desires and play a game she had never wanted or needed to play. The very essence, the thing that made prostitution what it was, ran counter to the way in which Elena had used sex. She felt defeated and depressed.

The man who ran the shop stopped her one night and told her to cut out the moping. "This is just a job," he told her. "What you do here is not your identity, it's just what you do to earn money. When you leave here and go home, leave this behind; separate yourself out from it." It was simple advice, proffered with a mix of sympathy and this-is-the-school-of-hard-knocks straightforwardness. It was advice she tried to take to heart. Somehow it relieved her. She stopped feeling sorry for herself and worked.

The bordello where Elena worked catered to Juárez's professional class:

dentists, veterinarians, accountants, lawyers, and plant managers. She says she made six hundred to seven hundred pesos (roughly fifty to sixty dollars) an hour, although that didn't include the house "cut." Still, it was far more than she could make in a week at any of the local assembly plants. Her only costs were wardrobe—buying the outfits that made her alluring and desirable to the clientele. Between her family and friends she tried to find people to take care of Pedro, but he also spent nights alone sometimes.

After a year of turning tricks Elena talked the owner into letting her be part of the management team. She started recruiting girls for the brothel. "I just returned from a recruitment trip to Parral," she told me once. She had discovered that she had a talent for talking girls into prostitution. She would enter a bar, scan the place, and target girls that she intuited were vulnerable or amenable to her pitch. She offered them base salaries that were far and above what they made in regular jobs, and she brought them to Juárez and trained them. Most had to be taught how to dress for this clientele, how to act, how to make themselves interesting to the men of Juárez's professional class. They were unsophisticated; most had never traveled anywhere beyond Chihuahua. Elena claimed she was straight with them about the job and what it entailed. They came willingly, she said, and she described herself as a kind of sponsor or protector who made sure the owners lived up to their promises. Of course, I had no way of confirming her representations of this world or her role within it.

One evening Elena and I met at a Chinese restaurant for an interview. The place was dimly lit, with ersatz Chinese decorations of gold tassels and gold, red, and black trim. At the buffet line the warmers appeared to have kept the same food hot since the lunch rush. The Chinese are more plentiful in Juárez than many would expect. They'd come in the nineteenth century after the California Gold Rush; some opened opium dens that became the nucleus of the local drug world. Eventually, the other netherworld types like La Nacha, the infamous drug queen who ran La Cima for many years beginning in the 1920s and 1930s, decided to wipe out the Chinese, and they did it in a most brutal way. In the 1930s there was a massacre of Chinese involved in the drug business that has not been forgotten. The descendants of these immigrants went on to do what immigrants do: some became university professors, others doctors, others ranchers, and still others policemen. More than a few opened restaurants like this one, although there were also upscale Chinese restaurants with excellent food.

We sat at a corner table, our backs to the rest of the restaurant in an instinctive attempt at discretion. Elena placed her cell phone on the table, as she had been receiving a steady flow of calls from the girls working or scheduled to work at the brothel that night. The calls covered a range of pressing needs; two of the girls called for a wardrobe consultation ("I think the striped blouse looks good on you!"; "No, that's not sexy enough"). Elena was like a mother hen to them. One of the girls called to ask whether there would be sufficient clients that night to make it worthwhile to show up for work (it was a Tuesday, typically a slow night). Elena responded like a harsh schoolmarm. "You're damn right you have to show up," she told her. "And if you don't show, you know I'll have someone behind you who really wants the work."

She gave the girls no quarter. She told me these conversations were frustrating because she'd made it clear over and over: the schedule is the schedule. You don't always get the prime-time nights; you have to take your turn on the slow nights, just like everyone else, and so on. No matter how many times she reiterated the message, she still got the calls, often just before someone was expected to report for work. She had to threaten them with firing or else she'd have anarchy on her hands, she said. Elena also was convinced that if she took a more lenient, soft approach, if she placated or indulged the girls, they would take advantage of her. Elena's greatest fear was that one of them would "jump" her, as she put it, meaning try to take over her job. Being a manager was far preferable to having to turn tricks.

In the midst of these reflections Elena surprised me with an insight about herself. She'd been describing her knack for recruiting girls, for going into bars and knowing, intuitively, which girls might be amenable to this work and just how to sweet talk them into signing up. "I really learned this from him," she offered at one point, referring to Hernán. It was then that she described Hernán as a narco-pimp because of his skill at seducing and recruiting young women to be his mules. He ran those women like a pimp runs his whores, she observed, aware that this was exactly how she now recruited and ran her girls at the brothel.

Within the chaos, Elena had somehow found the turns her life had taken to be oddly empowering. She dreamed of starting her own brothel. Maybe she'd send Pedro off to the nuns and turn the house into a members-only, exclusive "club." She could pilfer the membership list from her current workplace and bribe the cops from her precinct so that she wouldn't have any problems. She was convinced that the girls would come with her rather than stay with the current brothel owner. "He's got his head up his ass," she said. "And he's always trying to renege on the base pay he promised them." She was brainstorming ideas. For the first time in her life, she told me, she felt she had a skill, she knew she could run a business, manage employees, keep track of money. She was already doing it at the brothel, where as time went on she had less and less respect for the owner and where she increasingly felt that he needed her to run a successful business, given that he relied on her for everything. It gave her a measure of control over him. The only thing that intruded upon and ruptured this feeling of agency was the ever-present anxiety of being "jumped." She feared that if she pushed too hard, one of the other girls would take her place and the owner would drop her.

■ ■ ■

The *cuota* (extortion fee) was said to have begun as a strategy for replacing lost income, given the increased effectiveness of American efforts to seal the border. That effort was making it more difficult to cross product, which, in turn, meant lower profits. Extortion of businesses had become epidemic. That, in turn, had encouraged other gangs and neighborhood punks to emulate the lucrative strategy. It was impossible to know for sure, but it was assumed that the cartels were extorting higher-end businesses and perhaps professional people, while lesser gangs were extorting neighborhood shops, bus drivers, and street vendors.

Elena's shop had cameras through which they could monitor the entrance to the brothel, which had an outer door, then a hallway to the interior, and then a second door that led into the brothel itself. One night a man opened the outer door and walked calmly toward the second door. Elena watched him enter. He looked like one of their typical clients. He was well dressed, in his thirties. "Not bad looking," had been Elena's initial assessment. There was a panic button that Elena could press when something suspicious happened, and she could have some muscle at the desk in a matter of seconds, but this man did not raise her concerns until he was through the second door and walking up to the desk, where Elena sat with another woman. It was his face, which was tight and severe, and especially his eyes, which made her feel instinctively that he was malevolent.

The two women froze. Just as he reached the desk the man's hand went into his coat pocket and he said, "Your time has come." Elena and her companion feared they were going to be executed. Instead he pulled out a slip of paper, which he put on the desk. "Have the owner call this number in the morning," he said, before turning around and exiting the building. The next morning the boss called the number and was told that he was to begin paying a *cuota* of one thousand dollars a week. Someone would be picking up the payments every Monday night. Failure to pay up would lead to dire consequences: the owner or a member of his family might be killed, the establishment might be burned to the ground, or the girls would be murdered one by one. He'd know soon enough which outcome it might be.

Like most of the other businesses in Juárez, the brothel owner started making his weekly *cuota* payments. He assumed it was one of the cartels, but of course they never identified themselves and at the end of the day he had no way of knowing. It was part of the Juárez terror. Even the brothels were being hit up by organized crime. Later, when I ventured the thesis that perhaps the brothel was owned by someone with links to the Juárez cartel,

Elena assured me that if the owner was hooked up with them, he would not be paying the *cuota*.

■ ■ ■

Across town from the Altavista neighborhood where Laurencio Barraza ran the Boys and Girls First! program, Father Mario Manríquez, a forty-one-year-old priest at the Santa Teresa de Jesús church, tended to his sprawling, impoverished parish. The church was in another hardscrabble *colonia* called Oasis Revolución. Father Manríquez was tall and lanky, with jet-black hair that matched his vestments. He was an activist whose ideological views I found to be an odd mix of liberation theology and hardcore, old-school Catholicism. His office at the church was cluttered with religious artifacts—statues of saints, busts of Jesus, rosaries. One of his parishioners had given the priest a globe of the world and it sat on his desk; each of the continents had been cut out, painted by hand, and pasted onto it.

The priest had grown up in Parral, Chihuahua, a small town of less than 100,000 famous for the fact that Pancho Villa was assassinated there. Mario Manríquez was the eleventh of twelve children in a close, religious family of modest means. One of his older brothers was severely impaired, having suffered acute oxygen deprivation at birth. That tragedy was part of the day-to-day culture of the Manríquez family, and Father Manríquez described it as formative for him.

The family moved to Juárez after his father lost his job when Mario was very young. Not long thereafter, when Manríquez was fourteen years old, a gang assaulted his cousin as he was leaving a party with his girlfriend, crushing the boy's skull with stones. Manríquez had grown up with this cousin; they'd attended elementary school together in Parral and were quite close. His murder affected the young Mario profoundly. Four years later, when Mario Manríquez was eighteen, he went to seminary, joining the Order of the Sacred Hearts. Initially he studied philosophy in Mexico City, before going to Mérida and Guadalajara to study theology. At the completion of his seminary studies he returned to Juárez.

Father Manríquez was to be ordained on February 17, 1996. His father was quite ill and he told Mario that he feared he would be unable to make his ordination. Indeed, Mario awoke to the news that his father had died on the morning of the sixteenth. Mario was given his father's Bible on the day of his ordination and discovered that a priest who was very close to the family had written the following inscription: "May God grant you the opportunity to see your son ordained as a priest."

Thirteen years later, as we sat in his parish office at the Santa Teresa de Jesús church, Father Manríquez reflected on what was happening to Juárez. "What we're living is the end of a political, social, and economic epoch," the priest told me. He believed that the violence in Juárez and Mexico was a symptom of an unraveling society. "We've had laws since 1917 [when the Constitution of Mexico was signed, signaling the end of the Mexican Revolution] that were made just to be broken time and again," he averred. For decades the government had distributed resources with an eye toward enriching members of the ruling party and with little regard for the needs of the broader citizenry, he continued. Laws and institutions weren't transparent. "The corruption starts at the top," he said. "When you construct an edifice with so many incoherencies, it's going to collapse." That was his diagnosis for what was taking place not only in Juárez, but also, in myriad forms, throughout the country.

Like Laurencio Barraza at Organización Popular Independiente, Father Manríquez viewed Los NiNi both as the root of the problem and as victims of a dysfunctional society. "We've lived in a crisis for decades now," he continued. He put out some confirmatory evidence: for every ten families, four fall apart within the first five years, and there is no support for the children, he told me. Fathers frequently abandoned families and mothers were forced to work to support their children. "The typical shift at the maquiladora starts at five thirty and ends at three thirty," he noted, "but children enter school at eight o'clock and finish at one in the afternoon. The kids are home alone; there's a high incidence of child abuse in our homes," he said.

Father Manríquez decried the fact that the country's educational level had been on a steady decline for decades. Moral values had all but evaporated, the priest argued, rattling off a litany of evidence: "When you tie into the electric grid to circumvent having to pay for electricity; when you pay transit cops a bribe; when the group that oversees reconciliation and mediation of disputes between workers and companies is bribed by the companies so there is no justice for workers; when you open businesses without licenses or security and safety measures because you bribe officials; when students pay teachers for grades; when judges sell themselves; when the Mexican soccer selection uses false birth certificates for its team who are over-age and they are disqualified by FIFA; when Mexican banks charge some of the highest interest rates in the world; when corruption in the legislature is at a high level; and when you have a company like TelMex, owned by Mexico's richest man, charging some of the highest service fees in the world because of government concessions . . . that's corruption!" the priest exclaimed. "The list is interminable," he concluded after a moment's pause. "Mexico isn't free. It's a slave to corruption," he said. "What we're living in Mexico is the death of a system that was started in 1917."

Manríquez wasn't simply spouting ideology; he was speaking from experience. The Santa Teresa de Jesús church covered the Oasis Revolución neighborhood, a large area of seventy thousand residents in which there were few services and little infrastructure. Forty percent of the streets were unpaved and 70 percent of the area had no drainage. There was no potable drinking water; families had to go to public pipes with buckets for their water, which had to be boiled, although Father Manríquez maintained that despite public information campaigns many families still did not boil their water. "We have lots of intestinal problems for that reason," he said. Forty-five percent of the parents living within the parish had only an elementary-school education and another 30 percent had only a middle-school education. In other words, three-quarters of the adults had not completed high school. "There are no jobs for these people," Father Manríquez noted. "They have no hope." The priest summed up that lack of hope in this way: "There are no artists, mimes, clowns, or musical groups," he said forlornly. "There are no places where people can play sports. It's like the soul of the community is atrophying."

Father Manríquez spent most of his time going house to house trying to visit every family in the parish. "The health needs are enormous," he told me. There was a high incidence of diabetes, for example. "The church decided to enter at the ground floor, to start with families. We're trying to rebuild the social fabric," he said, noting that 40 percent of the population in the parish was under fourteen years of age. "There's a great opportunity here," he observed. The church held soccer camps with five hundred children and put on workshops to combat family violence. Father Manríquez was especially proud of the church's efforts to intervene with adult men through a "masculinity course" for fathers, which attempted to teach men to be more involved with their families and more sensitive to their wives and children.

The priest was not a fan of the maquiladora industry. On the contrary, he blamed it for some of the ills that Juárez was suffering. "They changed the family," he lamented. "They changed the root of everything when they brought women into the workforce. And the children? You changed the model, but you didn't prepare men or women for the new model." The officials who were so eager to institute the maquiladora system failed to factor in the social toll of having women become the breadwinners while men were left unemployed in great numbers. That fact, he theorized, had a lot to do with the explosion in domestic violence: men were simply not prepared for these profound social changes.

One of Father Mario Manríquez best-known programs had been instituted in the spring of 2007; it was called "After Ten Home Is Best." In an effort to decrease gang membership and gang violence in the neighborhood around the parish, he had convinced then-mayor Héctor Murguía and the police chief to decree that children under the age of eighteen would not be permitted to be in the streets after ten p.m. The logic was that children should be home with their families, and that taking them off the streets would reduce their exposure to gang pressure and influence. If a minor was spotted out after ten at night the police were instructed to pick him up. He was not cited or detained; he was simply driven home. For multiple transgressions, parents were required to come to the police station to retrieve their child. The program was launched on May 1, 2007, and that week the streets of Colonia Oasis Revolución were unusually calm. The program was an overnight success and received considerable media coverage. Other neighborhoods in the city were soon requesting that "After Ten Home Is Best" be implemented in their communities as well.

"It all came to a stop on October 10, 2007," Father Manríquez told me, still annoyed. He pulled a scrapbook from a nearby shelf. It contained pictures and newspaper clippings relating to the parish's different community projects. We came to a picture of the priest standing next to José Reyes Ferriz, who at the time was a candidate for mayor. "The mayor signed this pledge," Father Manríquez said, flipping a few more pages until he arrived at a photocopy of the document. The mayoral candidate had apparently committed himself to continuing the "After Ten Home Is Best" program, but had reneged upon assuming office. "He said that it was unconstitutional and he could not continue implementing it," the priest said with frustration.

The mayor was not the only one who did not like the "After Ten Home Is Best" program. Neighborhood gangs took to defacing the church, scrawling all manner of commentary and obscenities on its walls, like, "You fucking dick!" and "Who says '10'?" and "The clock strikes SHIT! Ha! Ha! Ha!" But the program had enjoyed the support of "90 percent" of the community, according to Manríquez, who claimed crime and drug consumption were reduced significantly during the period the program was in force.

By the fall of 2009 Father Manríquez had grown disillusioned with the government's efforts to quell the violence in the city. The cartels and their gangs had grown more bloodthirsty. "We have 2,200 dead so far this year, even with the New Police," he noted. He had mixed feelings about the army. He cited the infamous case of General Gutiérrez Rebollo, who'd headed the Mexican government's National Institute for Combating Drugs (INCD) between 1996 and 1997 until he was discovered to be in the pay of Amado Carrillo Fuentes, the head of the Juárez cartel. But the army also lacked the skills and training to intervene in a situation like the one in Juárez. "Their initiation rites are that they bring you into a room and beat you up," the priest claimed, implying that sensitivities to human rights and due process were not high priorities. They were good at looking for weapons and setting up roadblocks, but the incidence of robbery and extortion was higher than ever. Manríquez was of the opinion that corruption within the army was not wholesale, but that "there are a few cells within the military that are acting outside the law."

What the government was not seeing, the activist priest noted, was that any efforts to engage this problem must be accompanied and supported by social investment that ensures social and economic development. "Without that we have a perversion," he said. There were three fronts to this war, he asserted: the war against the cartels and the gangs; the war against the municipal, state, and federal authorities who for various reasons were not doing what they needed to do; and the war against the poverty that was an incubator for the violence.

■ ■ ■

The crush of poverty was obvious in many of the city's neighborhoods, where a lost generation, Los NiNi, was growing up without direction or hope, caught in a social fragmentation that was devouring them. They comprised the bulk of the killed and they comprised the bulk of the killers, and it was their desperate, convulsive violence that had brought the once-proud and glorious Ciudad Juárez to its knees and perhaps to the verge of extinction. From within these neighborhoods it was increasingly easy to see the obvious: Juárez's problem transcended the issues of crime and law enforcement. It ran much deeper and was more interlaced with the particulars, like the fact that fathers were absent and mothers left home before their children awoke and worked until three thirty or four in the afternoon. Their children came home from school at one p.m., and day after day, week after week, the prevailing reality for the kids was the friendships and alliances formed on the streets, which took on their own meanings, meanings that eclipsed the dreams that mothers and fathers held for their children, dreams that, in any event, families could not support and which thus became hollow, inert, and unreal. Father Manríquez and Laurencio Barraza were men whose calling seemed to be to try to reinvigorate those dreams, to give them plausibility in the eyes of the children and teenagers who were being ground up by a fraying society that seemed to have no place for them.

Mayor José Reyes Ferriz was a man with a different calling, but a calling nonetheless. In the span of two years his life had been thrust into a register that he could have never anticipated or imagined. He was presiding over a city that was unraveling, and he was grasping at everything he could think of to try to alter the course of the nightmare. Increasingly, out of the unrelenting violence, he had begun to understand something that the priest and the city's social activists had known all along, namely that military and police operations alone were never going to save Juárez. Around the time of my first visit to Father Manríquez's parish, the mayor flew to Costa Rica to meet for the first time with representatives from the Inter-American Development Bank in hopes of securing funds to help address the social catastrophe that was Juárez. It was a new approach, and the mayor had begun to believe that it might just offer the missing piece to solve the Juárez conundrum.

Note

1. From "*Ni estudian ni trabajan* (they neither study nor work)."

CHAPTER 22

The Eagle's Hill

Gustavo de la Rosa had become the Chihuahua Human Rights Commission representative for Juárez in April of 2008. He was the perfect man for the job. His credentials as a human rights activist were impeccable, going back decades to his days as a law student in the 1960s. His mercurial personality, though, had gotten in the way of his being named state commissioner for human rights; Governor Reyes Baeza had nixed that possibility, even though de la Rosa had been the odds-on favorite for the job. "He's too controversial," the governor had said. Instead, de la Rosa was given the Juárez post.

Between the time when the 1990s femicides receded from the headlines and the cartel wars began, being the human rights representative in Juárez had meant the occasional complaint for maltreatment at the hands of the municipal police, things of that sort. The arrival of thousands of troops, who were patrolling the city's neighborhoods and engaging in often rough confrontations with anyone they believed to have a suspicious mien, translated into a substantial increase in human rights complaints against the military.

One of these complaints involved the murder of a twenty-one-year-old man named Javier Eduardo Rosales Rosales, who worked as a radiology technician at a hospital called Ángeles, located in a poor neighborhood called Vista Hermosa. On the night of Monday, April 6, 2008, Javier and a friend named Sergio Fernández, also twenty-one, had been drinking beer with a woman they knew. The drinking had gone on all night, and the next morning Javier and Sergio set out for a nearby store to purchase some more beer. They'd made it just a couple of blocks before they were stopped by a military patrol. The army had been focusing a great deal of attention on this neighborhood in recent weeks, and residents described the prior week as one marked by an unusually high military presence. One source told *El Diario* that the soldiers found each of the men to have a small amount of marijuana in his possession, and on that basis took them away.

The two men were purportedly taken to a safe house (though others allege that they were taken to the military garrison), where their clothes were removed save their boxers and they were beaten and tortured. According to *El Diario*, the men were repeatedly asked where drugs were being sold in the neighborhood. Javier was abused most severely, because his captors took his extensive tattoos to mean that he was a member of Los Aztecas.

Thursday morning, after two days in captivity, Javier and Sergio were hooded and taken to the nearby deserted foothills of Cerro del Águila (The Eagle's Hill), on the southwestern side of the city. Javier was severely hurt. In the fog of confusion and disorientation, accounts of what the men were wearing differed. In one, they were naked save their boxers; in the other, they were given clothes that did not belong to them. In any event, once they were out of the vehicles the soldiers reputedly mocked them and pelted them with rocks, telling them to move. Traumatized, Javier and Sergio made their way as best they could, barefoot amid the cactus and rocks, seeking to distance themselves as quickly as they could from the men taunting them. Shortly thereafter, Javier collapsed and Sergio noticed that his eyes had "gone blank" and he'd stopped breathing. He knew Javier was dead. Sergio covered Javier's body with some torn pieces of cardboard he found nearby before continuing.

It took Sergio a long time to pick his way back home, even though the distance was not far. He finally showed up at his mother's house later on that Thursday morning, torn, bloody, and dazed. Despite his state, Sergio managed to give her an account of what had transpired over the previous two days, including Javier's death on Cerro del Águila.

Sergio's mother took him to the hospital. She then called Javier's mother and told her what had transpired. Javier's mother is said to have gone out to the street and stopped a military patrol, seeking their help. A search party of family members and friends was quickly rounded up, and they made their way to the Cerro del Águila, where they spent four fruitless hours in search of Javier's remains.

Thursday evening, Javier's mother came back into the city to file a report with the state and federal authorities. It was an exercise in frustration, the typical buck-passing. At the offices of the state attorney general and again at the federal attorney general's offices, she was told to file a complaint against the military at a separate location across town. The family chose not to do that, fearing retaliation. Later that evening, they returned home; their efforts to muster official help had been futile.

Friday morning a new search party was mounted and again it scoured the foothills of Cerro del Águila looking for Javier. A little after noon, one of Javier's friends shouted out "He's here!" as he stood over the stiff remains of Javier Eduardo Rosales Rosales, still lying beneath the weathered scraps of cardboard that Sergio had put over him. His body showed telltale signs of torture: severe abrasions to his face, body, and feet.

It took the authorities an hour and a half to reach the location; they came en masse, nearly fifty in all. When they arrived, the collection of friends and family greeted them with a chorus of "Assassin soldiers!"

In the aftermath of the discovery of Javier Rosales's remains there was more confusion. "The previous day we had already searched in the area where we found him," Javier's mother told *El Diario*. "He wasn't there the day before." She also noted that Javier was dressed in clothes that did not belong to him, whereas Sergio Fernández had indicated that the soldiers had left them at the location in boxers after pelting them with stones. Javier's mother accused the military of having replaced her son's body there after the previous day's search.

A woman named Raquel García presented herself before the Juárez media to say that the two young men had been drinking at her home Monday evening and Tuesday morning before they were picked up. She accused an officer named "Captain Molina" of leading the unit that had lifted the two men, and she identified their vehicle as unit number 2321370. She went further. "I know them, they're with the Red Berets. I know that because I work with a group of women who 'service' the military and they asked me to send them girls." Raquel García accused the military of threatening her since the events had come to light, saying that they would plant drugs on her, so she'd decided to go public, including disclosing the nature of her work and why she knew the soldiers as well as she did.

After two days of silence, the *secretaría de la defensa nacional* issued a terse press statement:

> In relation to the newspaper article published on the 11th day of April of 2009 in the newspaper *El Diario* of Ciudad Juárez, Chihuahua, and the stories aired on Channel 2 of the local station "Televisa Juárez," regarding the presumed participation of military personnel in the actions that eventuated in the death of the civilian JAVIER EDUARDO ROSALES ROSALES: The command of Operación Conjunto Chihuahua roundly denies that military personnel had any role whatsoever in the said actions, which are turned over to the corresponding authorities for investigation and so that the identity of those responsible for the murder of the young Rosales Rosales man may be clarified.

As soon as Sergio's medical condition stabilized, his family transferred him to a hospital in El Paso (he was an American citizen). Javier Rosales's family was afraid that there would be reprisals against them for speaking out; when asked if they were going to press charges, they said they would not appear at the attorney general's office but that they would present themselves at the office of the Chihuahua Human Rights Commission in Juárez to file a complaint against the military.

This was the dark underbelly of the government's efforts in Juárez. Since March 1, 2009, the date that marked the official outset of Operación Conjunto Chihuahua, 140 complaints had been filed against the military at the Juárez office. This fact placed Gustavo de la Rosa on a collision course with the federal forces.

In mid-April, the Mexican Army issued a statement, ostensibly unrelated but clearly in response to the firestorm over the allegations against them, in which they noted that it was not uncommon to discover military uniforms as well as federal, state, and municipal police uniforms in the narco safe houses that they raided. The implication was that perhaps narcos dressed in army uniforms had lifted Fernández and Rosales, generating unfounded accusations against the military.

In this instance, the explanation was implausible. The military and the other federal forces were sometimes overplaying their hands, entering homes without search warrants and lifting people to garner information, some of whom were tortured and some of whom died in the process. But it was also the case that the cartels and gangs kept stashes of official uniforms that they sometimes donned in an effort to disguise their identities; caches of such uniforms had been reported by the press covering raids on safe houses long before the human rights accusations against the federal forces had begun gaining traction. Regardless, the mounting opinion in Juárez in relation to the Rosales case was that it was, indeed, an example of human rights violations on behalf of the military.

Such abuse was an inevitable outcome of the circumstances. When Calderón initiated the war against the cartels, the military was the only tool in the shed. The federal police were a force of but a few thousand, and local and state police were in the control of the cartels. There were no law enforcement resources to use in the declared war; only Mexico's 240,000 army troops[1] were available for the purpose. In Juárez, the military set up roadblocks and patrolled neighborhoods, but there was a circumstantial quality to their work. If they happened to see someone suspicious as they patrolled, they stopped them. If cartel operatives or gang members stumbled into one of the army roadblocks, they apprehended them. But there was no systematic approach to their engagements with the cartels and their minions, and very little intelligence work. The seizing of Sergio Fernández and Javier Rosales (two males in their early twenties, one of them tattooed up, hanging out in a hardscrabble neighborhood that was full of gang action) fit the profile of how the military worked perfectly. Taking them to a safe house or, as it was alleged, to the military garrison, where they were beaten, may have been a product of the soldiers' conviction that the men were gangbangers doing cartel work. This was the military's "intelligence" work. This was how they extracted information and learned whom to go after next, or where the drug sales were occurring in the neighborhood. Similarly, if a suspect ran into a house, the military pursued him. If they suspected that a cartel operative lived in a given house or that drugs were being sold there, they simply went into the house and turned it inside out. Though Mexican law requires that a search warrant be obtained from a judge or a prosecutor's office for that kind of entry and search, it was rare for the military to resort to such legal niceties. Everything was spur of the moment, driven by circumstances on the ground. Soldiers weren't about to call in for such permissions every time they came across something suspicious. Then there was the problem that they had every reason to believe that the local and state judicial system had been compromised, penetrated by the cartels.

As the human rights complaints against the military accrued, most were about these tactics: that the soldiers were beating people up in the streets, and that the soldiers were entering people's homes without a search warrant and trashing them looking for drugs. And as often as not, such incursions resulted in human rights complaints against the military. The Javier Rosales cases, where the victim was held at some location, tortured, and purpose-fully or inadvertently killed in the process, represented a handful of the hundreds of complaints against the military, but they were so egregious that they became emblematic of the military's transgressions.

■ ■ ■

The first leg of the Mérida Initiative, the United States government's three-year, 1.5 billion dollar financial package proposed by the Bush administra-tion to aid Mexico (primarily) in the war against the drug cartels, was finally coming online after traversing an arduous path through the American con-gress. A complex assortment of groups from a variety of political perspec-tives opposed the aid, but a strong, persistent voice among these was that of human rights activists opposed to funding Mexico's military and law enforcement, given their records of corruption and human rights abuses. Patrick Leahy, the Democratic chair of the Senate's appropriations and foreign operations subcommittee, was one of those who were not convinced that helping underwrite Mexico's antidrug war made sense given Mexico's human rights record. Cases such as Javier Rosales's were prime exhibits in the arguments against such support. Only a handful of the Mexican mili-tary had been prosecuted for these violations, a fact not lost on the anti–Mérida Initiative camp. Senator Leahy used his position to temporarily put the brakes on the release of the Mérida Initiative funds, and opponents launched a full-bore assault on the aid program, including letter-writing campaigns to American officials and reports and presentations by groups such as Amnesty International and Human Rights Watch that assailed the Mexican track record on human rights.

Human rights were shaping up to be a defining issue. The U.S. Con-gress added stipulations to the Mérida Initiative to pressure the Mexican government to do more on this front and to give teeth to accountability efforts. A key issue was the fact that Mexican law did not allow military personnel to be tried in civilian courts and military tribunals were not sympathetic to civilian accusations. In fact, the military judicial system had sent very few soldiers to prison for abuses against civilians.

A lawsuit in which the military had killed a civilian in 2008 at a checkpoint in the municipality of Badiraguato, Sinaloa (the birthplace of El Chapo Guzmán and an area infamous for its poppy fields and narco-culture), argued that military abuses of civilians should be tried in civil rather than military courts. The suit had made it all the way to the Mexican Supreme Court, but on August 11, 2009, the court rejected the case on a technicality. The case had been followed closely by Javier Rosales's mother, given that its outcome would have direct implications for her effort to prosecute the soldiers presumably involved in her son's murder. She told *El Diario* that in her opinion the Supreme Court's decision would simply lead to "cover-ups." "I don't think anything will happen [to resolve the case] because they're just going to protect themselves," she added. She told the paper that she was against the military presence in Ciudad Juárez because the only outcome of Operación Conjunto Chihuahua was the death of innocent people.

The stage was set for a confrontation regarding Mexico's use of the army in the war against the cartels in a scathing seventy-six-page report issued by Human Rights Watch, which detailed seventeen cases from various parts of the country (none, in fact, was from Juárez) involving military abuses against more than seventy victims, including several cases from 2007 and 2008. Human Rights Watch argued that the abuses included killings, torture, rapes, and arbitrary detentions. They further noted that the military investigations into these crimes had not led to a single conviction.

Gustavo de la Rosa was an especially vocal critic of the military's tactics in the city. In mid-September, de la Rosa told the Mexico City newspaper *El Universal* that "the troops are committing excesses in the same way that the Holy Inquisition did during the Colonial Period, extracting confessions from innocent people based on torture."

The human rights activist was becoming a spokesperson of sorts for critics of the military's activities and the government's strategy in Juárez. He accused the army of "disappearing" people and said that there was a rising tide of voices calling for the military to leave Chihuahua because of the army's excesses. De la Rosa went as far as to imply that the military was perhaps in cahoots with the narcos: "I get the impression that they only pretend to be fighting organized crime," he told *El Universal*, "but basically they are in accord, and we're seeing the wholesale failure of president Felipe Calderón's strategy of bringing the army into the streets." It was powerful rhetoric, and it posed a direct challenge to the government's policies.

In contrast, Mayor José Reyes Ferriz championed the military's actions in the city as indispensable, given the circumstances. There was no love lost between de la Rosa and the mayor. They'd known each other for years, taught law together at the Universidad Autónoma de Ciudad Juárez, and been thrown together by developments in the city, but everything about their personal styles and ideological commitments dictated that they be antagonists. The rather disheveled, garrulous de la Rosa, with his unmistakable 1960s look, was the polar opposite of the somewhat reserved Reyes Ferriz, who had the starched, tailored-suit look of a successful businessman. Reyes Ferriz was not naive about what it meant to have the Mexican military patrolling the city. Some human rights violations were a given and not entirely unanticipated; such accusations had followed the military in all of its campaigns, whether against the Zapatistas in Chiapas, marijuana growers in Guerrero, or poppy cultivations in Sinaloa. Having five thousand military-aged men in the city for an extended period of time, away from their families, had even involved frank discussions during planning meetings about an increase in prostitution and other potential problems. For the mayor these were part of a cost-benefit analysis. Realistically, there was no way to have the army in the city without these attendant problems. It was a matter of degree; a matter of what was tolerable in exchange for the presence of a force that could help check the cartel violence.

For this reason, the mayor defended the army in public. "We should make every effort to make Ciudad Juárez a safe city and open our doors so that [the military] can do the necessary searches," he said. He went further, stating that in his view the great majority of Juarenses supported the army's activities, including home searches, because they were hard working, law-abiding citizens who had nothing to hide. "I believe we should not be against the military searching homes," the mayor said in mid-September 2009, amid growing human rights complaints of illegal searches. The army was routinely ignoring constitutional provisions that required a search warrant, and while not in support of such tactics, the mayor seemed to justify them for two reasons. First, the city was in a state of war. There were many months when the deaths in Juárez matched or surpassed those in war-torn cities like Baghdad, in Iraq, for example. The hard reality on the ground, with so many people being executed every day, was akin to a guerrilla campaign, with narco-commandos all over the city bearing assault weapons. In the heat of the moment there often was no time to make a run to the district attorney's office to secure a search warrant. But the second reason was equally to the point. "The military also knew that the people in the DA's office were reporting everything to the cartel," the mayor told me. The army's excesses, which rankled idealists like Gustavo de la Rosa, were rationalized by pragmatists like Reyes Ferriz, although the latter did not condone the fate that had befallen Javier Rosales any more than did Gustavo de la Rosa.

Human rights groups in Mexico and the United States, as well as international groups such as Amnesty International and Human Rights Watch, kept the pressure on the Mexican government to address complaints related to the army's activities. On September 9, Gustavo de la Rosa met with attorneys who were fellow members of the Barra y Colegio de Abogados (an organization akin to a state bar association). He had already established himself as a vocal antagonist of the military, publicly demanding that the army leave the city. At the meeting, de la Rosa roundly criticized the military's actions in Juárez and said that "the army is losing the opportunity to cover itself in glory and if they continue torturing people they are going to have to retreat covered in manure."

De la Rosa's statement was leaked to the press. There was already a great deal of hostility between the human rights activist and General Felipe de Jesús Espitia, the commander of Operación Conjunto Chihuahua. The latter had stated, in relation to complaints against the military, that there were "ties" between the drug traffickers and the human rights commissions. He'd all but accused de la Rosa of being in league with the Juárez cartel. Gustavo de la Rosa told me that General Espitia had become irate upon learning of de la Rosa's "manure" comment at the bar association meeting.

Around this time, de la Rosa had the unnerving encounter at the stoplight in which a man had walked up to his car, made his hand into the shape of a gun, and pretended to shoot him before saying, "You need to tone things down or we're going to kill you." On another occasion, de la Rosa pulled into a gas station. While his car was being gassed up, he went into the restroom. A man entered behind him and said, "You know, I respect you and what you do, but if you don't tone it down you're going to be assassinated." The man's tone was anything but respectful—it, too, was a direct threat.

■ ■ ■

The Valley of Juárez, southeast of the city, was once a rich, vibrant farming area, until American agricultural runoff eventually left so much salt in the Rio Grande that much of the land on the Mexican side became useless for farming. Federal Highway 2 heads out of Juárez through the Valley of Juárez, running roughly parallel to the Rio Grande toward Ojinaga, some 250 miles to the southeast, the famed base of operations for Pablo Acosta, who'd mentored Amado Carrillo Fuentes in the ways of the drug business prior to Acosta's assassination in 1987. A score of little villages and hamlets in the Valley of Juárez along Federal Highway 2 was renowned for its history of smuggling, given that most of the towns were arrayed within easy access of the river and Interstate Highway 10, which follows the river on the Texas side for some seventy miles until it veers northward southeast of Fort Hancock, Texas. For decades, this geographical circumstance had made the Valley of Juárez prime territory for the Juárez cartel, which used it to smuggle drugs across the river with the same regularity that it used Juárez itself. That fact had turned the Valley of Juárez into a killing zone, where entire families were being wiped out. The Sinaloa cartel had issued instructions to move on anyone affiliated with the Juárez cartel in the Valley. According to de la Rosa, the instructions were to exterminate "anyone who'd had an economic tie or a familial tie to the captains of La Línea." Those people had operated freely in the area prior to 2008. In fact, almost all of the families in the Valley had such direct or indirect ties. "They sold them alfalfa, they rented out or sold parcels of land, sold cattle, or worked on their ranches," de la Rosa said.

Gustavo de la Rosa knew the Valley of Juárez well. He lived in the small town of San Agustín, less than thirty kilometers from Juárez. He raised prize-winning goats and enjoyed his country life, which was a welcome change from the dark realities he dealt with on a daily basis in Juárez. De la Rosa described the developments in a letter to the Inter-American Human Rights Commission (IAHRC) as follows: "Beginning on the 15th of August 2009, the climate of violence intensified in the area around my home . . . This is due to the war between the cartels which, in this area, has taken on the character of open warfare and the authorities have abandoned their responsibilities to provide security; there's but a single checkpoint at the entrance to San Agustín." In de la Rosa's small community, people were being killed, their homes were being razed, and there was widespread fear. Around this time, someone came to de la Rosa's home to tell him that he was on a hit list. "People from San Isidro, the next town over [two kilometers away], came to tell me that I was getting too involved with things," he said.

De la Rosa asked the state director of the Chihuahua Human Rights Commission to ensure that he and his family were protected. His boss failed to act. On September 11, de la Rosa asked Víctor Valencia, now the commander of the state police following his disastrous stint as the governor's representative in Ciudad Juárez, to provide protection, but Valencia told him he didn't have the personnel available and, in any event, the Valley of Juárez was under the army's jurisdiction, not his. The state attorney general, Patricia González, said perhaps she could help, but he'd have to file formal requests. In short, de la Rosa, the controversial Juárez human rights representative, was on his own. "We're in a state of war," de la Rosa told the head of the Inter-American Human Rights Commission, "and I have received no institutional backing with respect to my personal security." He requested that the IAHRC intercede on his behalf with the Mexican government in order to "safeguard my life and physical integrity as well as those of my wife, Laura Carrillo Moreno, and son, Alejo de la Rosa Carrillo, given the state of risk in which we find ourselves." The desperation could not have been clearer.

On Tuesday, September 22, de la Rosa decided he'd had enough. He had ready access to El Paso by virtue of a SENTRI permit that allowed him entry into the United States at any time for stays of up to thirty days. (Such permits are standard issue for Mexicans living along the border who have steady jobs and do not appear likely to violate U.S. immigration laws.) Meeting with journalists in El Paso, de la Rosa gave them a summary of the ordeal he'd endured over the recent months, including the incessant death threats. He said he would continue carrying out his responsibilities as the Juárez representative of the state human rights commission, but he would do it via the phone and Internet. He dared not set foot in Juárez for fear he would be killed. De la Rosa was incensed, noting that twenty bodyguards protected Víctor Valencia. "I'm not returning to Juárez until [president] Calderón and [governor] Baeza can guarantee my safety and that of my family," de la Rosa told journalists.

De la Rosa accused the state human rights commissioner, José Luis Armendáriz, of threatening him with administrative action for the declarations he had made at the state bar association meeting, in which he'd openly criticized the military. Armendáriz had also taken de la Rosa off of the open cases pending against the military that he had been working over the prior eighteen months. De la Rosa was, for all intents and purposes, fired, although officially his status was "under review."

Almost immediately, a hue and cry went up in support of the human rights activist. On both sides of the border, human rights organizations and NGOs mobilized campaigns to publicize what was happening to de la Rosa, including letter-writing campaigns addressed to national and international groups. A showdown between de la Rosa and the Chihuahua state officials was inevitable. The state human rights leadership gave de la Rosa until October 7 to resume his responsibilities in Juárez or be fired.

De la Rosa initially blamed the military for the death threats against him, although in subsequent interviews he was more equivocal: "The possible culprits," de la Rosa told *El Diario*, "are two groups: one is, if not the army, then soldiers." The other potential culprit, the human rights activist said, "is a commando of killers, not more than 10," who are operating in the Valley of Juárez. De la Rosa also distanced himself from earlier suggestions that the army was involved with the cartels. "I'm not saying that the army has ties to them or that they are engaged in social cleansing," de la Rosa said. "But, personally I believe that some of them could be part of the bloodiest groups of *sicarios*."

The outpouring of support for Gustavo de la Rosa saved his job. Following a tense meeting in Juárez with municipal, state, and federal representatives, including the army, he was allowed to continue working out of El Paso and Juárez, as dictated by the state of his personal security. Two state ministerial police were assigned to protect him, and a panic button was installed in his Juárez office. The latter de la Rosa found laughable. There was obviously a deep split between de la Rosa and the state human rights commissioner. "He hasn't even bothered to call me," de la Rosa complained. But de la Rosa left the meeting with an agreement signed by the army and the federal government in which they vowed to ensure the security of him and his family. De la Rosa was officially reinstated in his position.

■ ■ ■

Gustavo de la Rosa was described as a "civic treasure" in the border region for his activism and work on behalf of those whose rights were trampled by the authorities. A report titled "Defending Human Rights: Caught between Commitment and Risk," by the Mexico office of the United Nations High Commissioner for Human Rights, described de la Rosa as "an example of the perilous situation faced by human rights activists in this country." The head of the Mexican Academy of Human Rights protested that the government was vilifying the work of human rights defenders. De la Rosa had become a cause célèbre.

The human rights activist had taken to sleeping in El Paso every night. On October 16, 2009, following a meeting in Juárez, he was making his way back across the Santa Fe Bridge into El Paso when a U.S. border official asked him if he feared for his life. De la Rosa answered in the affirmative, thinking he was acknowledging the obvious. But American officials decided to take the human rights activist into custody "for his own protection," taking him to a detention center in El Paso for undocumented immigrants and people seeking asylum. De la Rosa immediately contacted his attorney in El Paso, who within hours had filed a protest with U.S. Homeland Security authorities. The latter claimed that, under U.S. law, foreign nationals who declared that they were in fear for their lives in their country of origin were immediately treated as individuals seeking asylum. The problem was that de la Rosa had been explicit about the fact that he was not seeking asylum; he had merely stated that he felt fear regarding his safety. "He entered the United States legally and he has committed no crimes or violated U.S. law," his attorney, Carlos Spector, said. De la Rosa was in the U.S. legally under his SENTRI permit.

U.S. officials appeared defensive and flatfooted. "If someone arrives at a port of entry and makes it known that they are in fear, they are detained," a U.S. Customs and Border Protection official told El Paso's KFOX news. Gustavo de la Rosa was once again on the front pages, and his supporters launched a furious international campaign to secure his release. Perhaps the declaration that he was temporarily fleeing Juárez because of death threats had placed de la Rosa in uncharted legal territory as far as the American authorities were concerned, given that he had made it clear in repeated press interviews that he was in El Paso out of fear that he would be executed in Juárez. He wasn't a mere tourist, in other words. A more conspiratorial thesis suggested that the U.S. government, in collusion with the Mexican federal authorities, was trying to silence the human rights activist. This theory suggested that given that congressional support of the Mérida Initiative had become entangled in Congress because of the human rights issues, and given that Gustavo de la Rosa had become a voice of protest regarding Mexico's human rights shortcomings, both the U.S. and Mexican governments were finding de la Rosa to be a thorn in their sides. Whatever the reasons or motives, de la Rosa was released from the El Paso detention center after five days and permitted to continue using his SENTRI pass to enter the U.S. at will.

Note

1. Mexico has one of the smallest armed forces per capita in the Western Hemisphere.

CHAPTER 23

Villas de Salvárcar

Villas de Salvárcar, a working-class enclave in southeastern Juárez, is entirely surrounded by assembly plants and only accessible via two streets. The homes were government subsidized and are quite small, resting on narrow plots backing up onto each other. Many have no yards. Though modest, most are clean and well maintained, and some are brightly painted. The subdivision had been built ten years earlier and there were families that had been living there since the beginning. Quite a few had come to Juárez from other towns and cities in Chihuahua, and most of the adults worked in the nearby maquiladora plants.

The evening of January 30, 2010, a Saturday, was cool and crisp and an episodic wind blew up through the desert, raking across the city, gripping it in a deep winter chill. The moon was brilliant and large; the night before it had been full. On Villa del Portal Street people were out, and the atmosphere was festive despite the cold. A kid named Jesús Enríquez was celebrating his eighteenth birthday, and most of the high-school and college-aged kids in the neighborhood were coming to the party. Villas de Salvárcar was close in that way. The people who lived on Villa del Portal Street were especially close; their children had grown up together.

The *colonia* had many vacant houses at the time. Massive unemployment, a product of the American recession and the city's violence, had driven many residents back to where they'd come from prior to migrating to Juárez to work in the maquiladoras. Others had fled across the border to El Paso. One of the vacant houses was in the middle of the 1300 block of Villa del Portal. The family had moved to El Paso, but entrusted the neighbor across the street with the house keys. The neighbor had agreed to let the teenagers hold the birthday party in the empty house, as she'd done numerous times in the past. "We were happy not to have the kids going off into the city at night," one of the parents would later tell me. "With so much violence, we preferred to have them celebrating the birthday here in the neighborhood."

Alonso Encina, a man with a gentle face and sad eyes, was one of the parents happy to have the party in the neighborhood. A wiry man with silver-rimmed glasses, a moustache, and dark, short-cropped hair, Encina spent his adolescence as a gangbanger until he was saved by art. He always had a talent for drawing and sketching, mostly self-taught although over the years he'd taken a few classes and participated in the occasional workshop. He started drawing and painting as an adolescent and found something in it that helped him transcend the circumstances of a poor young man from a small town with a limited education.

At the age of twenty-one, Encina moved to Juárez from Torreón, Coahuila, a city in the neighboring state to the southeast. He came looking for opportunities, but his heart remained in his native Torreón: "It's a beautiful city!" he exclaimed spontaneously at the mention of it. "The people work hard, and it's very forward-thinking." It was obvious that Encina was still nostalgic for his hometown.

Alonso Encina had painted murals all over Juárez. Some were part of collective efforts sponsored by government programs, others simply inspired by the fact that he'd encountered an available wall—his version of the current-day "graff" man. Encina and his wife and kids had lived in a poor *colonia* named Independencia prior to moving to Villas de Salvárcar. He'd painted murals on his own in the old neighborhood and was especially proud of some of them. Showing me a photo album containing his work, he drew my attention to several images where he was posing in front of the murals with his family. One of them had been torn down within days of completion. "The authorities didn't like the content," he told me. It included a Catholic bishop wearing a miter that was decorated with dollar signs and greedy industrialists ravaging the landscape. The style and content reminded me of the work of David Álfaro Siqueiros or Diego Rivera. Encina's other murals had survived longer, but most had been torn down. Others might still exist, he thought, but he was reluctant to take me to see them, saying it was too dangerous because the neighborhood was rife with gangs.

One of the more stunning murals he showed me had been painted on a solitary wall in the old, run-down Independencia neighborhood. The mural was titled in English, *Light and Shadow,* and the center of the piece consisted of three identical images of the face of a young *cholo* gangbanger wearing a red headscarf. One of the images was looking straight at the viewer, and the other two were looking left and right. Above these faces were the two Greek masks of comedy and tragedy, with the smiling mask above the word "Light," and the grimacing mask, with a distinctive tear running down its cheek, above the word "Shadow." Above the masks was an all-knowing eye from which two beams emanated, bathing the "Light" side in a shaft of white light and the "Shadow" side in blood-red. On the "Light" side of the mural, the face oriented to the left was connected to a chain that led to a woman holding a child in her arms and a little boy with angel wings pulling on the chain, attempting to bring the *cholo* dad closer to the family circle.

The face oriented to the right had a chain that was being pulled in the opposite direction by a devilish creature, above whom were tormented, tattooed men imprisoned by dripping needles with the caption (in Spanish) "False Time" ("That's drug time," Encina told me). The upper two-thirds of the mural was supported from below by an enormous eagle, the emblem found on the Mexican flag, except that rather than devouring a snake the eagle was devouring a chain, like the chains that were tearing the young *cholo* apart. The psychological complexity of the mural was gripping; it was apparent that Alonso Encina knew something about the human condition.

In November of 1990, with his wife eight months pregnant, Encina took a maquila job, working at the COCLISA assembly plant, making radiators and condensers for Ford vehicles so as to have insurance to cover the delivery. His art took a back seat to the practical necessities of supporting a family, although he continued doing what he could. The Encina children were born at two-year intervals: Ángel Alonso was born in 1990, followed by José Adrián in 1992, and Oscar Alan in 1994. The boys were close, and by the time the family moved to Villas de Salvárcar they were old enough to be all over the neighborhood. There was never concern or worry about their safety. The neighborhood was the village, and the children were in and out of people's houses or playing in the street every day. Villa del Portal Street was as close to communal life as it gets in Mexico.

Alonso Encina had been successful beyond his dreams as far as his art was concerned. At the age of twenty-two he'd won a statewide contest and his prize was the opportunity to exhibit some of his pieces in Mexico City. He had never been to the Mexican capital before. He visited museums, he saw art, and he met fellow artists. "It was an amazing exchange of ideas," he told me. In 1993, after he'd begun working at the assembly plant, he was selected to be one of the artists representing contemporary Mexican folk art at the Smithsonian museum in Washington, DC. It was exhilarating, and, to his surprise, the maquiladora gave him time off and helped pay his travel expenses.

Alonso Encina took night courses and eventually managed to get himself promoted to the position of coordinator of quality control, which was easier work and better paid. He says that the maquila was supportive of his art and allowed him to sell his pieces to fellow employees at the plant. These were not conceptual pieces in the spirit of his *Light and Shadow* mural. Reflections on the human condition aren't that marketable. These were kitschy little trinkets with sayings like "You and Me" painted over a red heart for Valentines Day. The Virgin of Guadalupe was always a big seller.

By 2009, though, Alonso Encina was unemployed. Years of dedicated service had amounted to nothing when it came to laying off workers under the press of the economic recession that was grinding Juárez down to a nub.

Presently, Encina was eking out a living as best he could selling his trinkets and small paintings on wood or plastic—things he could mass-produce at a workbench in his covered carport. He and his father-in-law, who had a shaved-ice cart, made their way to the nearby high school every day, where they sold his wares and his father-in-law's ices at recess and after school. Occasionally, Alonso made it to fairs and markets in the city to sell his things, but it all added up to a meager income with which to support a family. Adrián, his middle son, was encouraging him to go back to Torreón and find a job so that the family could follow. They were all worn out by the city's violence and eager for a life outside of the inferno, Alonso Encina told me.

■ ■ ■

The Encinas lived right in the middle of the block on Villa del Portal Street, almost directly across from the house where the birthday party was to be held. Alonso Jr. had just turned twenty and was at university, Adrián was seventeen and in high school, and Oscar Alan, fifteen, was in junior high. All of them were dedicated students. Adrián was especially promising. Just a few weeks earlier he'd been named to the prestigious Governor's Excellence List for the second consecutive year, and he had his sights set on studying either engineering or medicine when he got to college. Adrián was well liked among the friends at the party, some of whom attended the CBTIS-128 technical school and played on the school's football team, Los Jaguares, which was part of Juárez's high-school AA League.

That Saturday night, as the kids made their way over to the party (many from the neighborhood, others school chums from other *colonias*), Alonso arranged his art supplies on the workbench and started painting the pieces he'd be peddling that coming week. It was nearing eleven thirty and from the carport he could see the house at 3010 Villa del Portal, where the party was taking place. All three of his sons were there, and the sounds of the party floated across the street as kids came and went. It was cold, but as teenagers are wont to do, most kids were dressed lightly in jeans and hoodies or sweaters. Alonso's wife poked her head out of the front door and said, "It's after eleven, let's get the kids and go to bed."

Just as Alonso was about to walk across the street, he heard the roar of vehicles round the corner to his right, coming hard and fast before stopping directly in front of his house. There were four SUVs and every instinct told Alonso that something nightmarish was about to take place. A wave of fear swept over him as he saw some two dozen *sicarios* pouring out of their vehicles, all armed with assault weapons. While a few remained posted at the SUVs, the rest rushed into the house where some thirty kids were celebrating the birthday. Immediately, the fusillade brought screams and cries from within the small house, where the attendees were trapped, like fish in a bucket. Some neighbors initially thought that the reports were *palomitas* (a popular Mexican firecracker) being set off at the party, but that illusion was momentary, quickly displaced by the awareness that something horrific was taking place.

Alonso Encina heard the shots and the screams and his only thought was that his three sons were in that house. He exited the carport intending to cross the street but was immediately confronted by a *sicario* who put an AK-47 to his head. "This is an *operativo*, steer clear," said a cold, disembodied voice. Just then, a neighbor exited her house and ran across the street. She was gunned down on the spot. Alonso retreated to his carport; he was helpless, there was nothing he could do but look on in a state of shock and terror.

Inside the party house there was pandemonium. The rat-tat-tat of the assault weapons seemed eternal, and it was entwined with cries of desperation that saturated the space and broadcast from it out into the surround. Anguish, fear, and the smell of gunpowder and death infused the scene. In the confusion, some of the kids tried to exit through a back patio and jump over a wall but they were cut down.

Three students fled to a neighboring house, where the woman who lived there closed the door behind them and attempted to lock it. A *sicario* followed them, kicking in the door. In the meantime, the woman awoke her husband, alerting him to the presence of men with guns. He emerged from the bedroom in his boxer shorts to find an agitated *sicario* waving his assault weapon, shouting almost incoherently, "We've been looking for you!" It was senseless; the man worked at a maquiladora. Before he could respond the *sicario* shot him dead and shot the three students, two boys and a girl, huddling behind him.

The *sicarios* appeared to be on a rampage. They were wild and crazed, lost in a frenzy of death. The owners of the next house over ran a little store out of their home from which they sold candies, sodas, and *bolis* (small plastic bags of flavored chipped ice that they sold for $2.50 pesos, less than an American quarter). A couple on a motorcycle had pulled up to purchase sodas just moments before the commando unit arrived. They were shot dead, as was the owner of the makeshift store. The owner's wife was critically wounded.

The agony of the *operativo*, spasmodic and full of the perpetrators' shouts and the victims' terrified screams, ended in a span of fifteen minutes. The *sicarios* then boarded their vehicles and, in an eerily slow procession, drove down Villa del Portal to the corner, where they turned right and made their way out of the Villas de Salvárcar neighborhood. Behind them they left the gruesome carnage of the dead and wounded. As soon as they cleared the block, Alonso ran across the street and into the house. What he found there was ghoulish. The flow of blood was so profuse that it was difficult to hold one's footing on the thick, viscous fluid covering the floor in large pools. A woody, humid odor permeated the house, along with the sharp, acrid smell of gunpowder. Smoke from the extended fusillade hung motionless, suspended in the middle of the room, equidistant from the ceiling and the floor, giving the scene an infernal cast.

"I entered the house shouting for my three sons," Alonso said. There were bodies everywhere. "No! No! No!" he shouted. In the hallway beyond the small living room area he came upon a mound of bodies, clutched together, as if the victims had sought sanctuary within one another. Then he recognized Adrián, lying face down. "I turned him over. His eyes, his lips . . . I knew he was dead," he told me, full of grief. Adrián had been shot in the head at close range.

The forty-five-year-old stepfather of one of the kids who lived directly across the street from the party had exited his house in order to pull his car into his carport just as the *sicarios* arrived. Rosales had run into the party house trying to save the kids. "When I entered the house his body was on top of the group of dead kids," Alonso said. "It was as if he had been trying to protect them all with his body." Although at the onset of the holocaust the *sicarios* had yelled for all of the girls to leave, a seventeen-year-old named Brenda Escamilla had refused, clutching her boyfriend, in all likelihood knowing what lay in store. They'd shot her, too, and she was in the same pile.

All of the people in that mound of bodies appeared to be dead. Throughout the house there were spent shell casings. Alonso wailed. He shouted the names of his two other boys into the moans of the wounded and the screams of the neighbors and parents who were entering the house, crossing the lagoon of blood in search of their children or intent on lending assistance. The dead and wounded were strewn throughout the house. There was blood splattered on every wall and there was fear and nausea, an overwhelming scene that would never be digested or absorbed by those who witnessed it.

Alonso's youngest son, Oscar, emerged from a back room that was off of the hallway into which the bulk of the dead had been herded and shot. He'd taken refuge in a large closet with a sliding door along with two other kids. The closet had been strafed, and others in the room had been wounded, but, miraculously, the three in the closet emerged unscathed. Alonso's eldest son, his namesake, was nowhere to be found. Alonso allowed himself to entertain the idea that perhaps he'd been spared, but the thought was also present that perhaps he'd just missed him among the contorted bodies, some of whose features the bullets had torn beyond recognition. Then again, maybe the *sicarios* had taken him for some reason. In Alonso's desperation his mind was a jumble of thoughts and fears.

Down on the next block, Luz María Dávila heard the noise coming from the party. She would later tell me that she took the reports to be firecrack-ers. In a city where so many people had died, people's natural defenses still kicked in: firecrackers. Please, firecrackers, not bullets, she thought to herself. Luz María stepped out onto the street and immediately knew that something terribly wrong was taking place. The *sicario* convoy had already rounded the corner near her house on its way out of the neighborhood. What Luz María saw as she looked up the street was people running to the house where the party had taken place. The night was full of the shouts and screams of parents and their wounded children. She panicked; both of her sons had attended the party.

As she ran up the street, someone shouted, "Here they come again!" and she and her husband threw themselves under a parked car. Running up the street again after the false call she encountered the dead in front of the little store and the cruel sight of wounded teenagers, wailing in pain. One girl had the front part of her foot shot off and was screaming in agony. Inside the house she found both of her sons. The older son, nineteen-year-old Marcos, was in the tangle of bodies in the hallway. He was dead. A little farther on she found José Luis, her sixteen-year-old. "He was still breathing," she recalled. He was critically wounded, having taken a shot to the head.

By now it was after midnight and despite repeated, frantic phone calls, neither ambulances nor police had responded to the appeals for help. "There were police two minutes away at the Seguro Social [hospital], but no one came," Alonso said. "Not even the Red Cross." Many of the families soon concluded that they would have to ferry the wounded to the hospi-tal themselves, otherwise their children would surely bleed to death. Luz María Dávila and her husband went home for the family car, into which they loaded their wounded son along with two of the other wounded before rushing them to the Seguro Social Hospital, only five hundred yards away.

Alonso tried to help the others out. He heard a neighbor shouting, "Help! Help! He's still alive!" Alonso went to lend assistance, but it was soon evident that the boy was already dead. Alonso's impression was that he'd been dead all along; the shouting had been a parent's desperate wish that his child still had life. Meanwhile, Alonso Jr. was still nowhere to be found.

In the aftermath, it was difficult to piece a coherent narrative together about what had taken place. There were conflicting reports about how many vehicles were in the *sicario* caravan, for example. Alonso remembered hearing the *sicarios* say, when they'd first arrived and erupted into the house, "This isn't them! It's a bunch of kids!" But another voice shouted back from among the SUVs, "Fuck it! We're here!" Once the killing had begun, some of the kids had managed to run out the front door. Seeing how young they were, one of the *sicarios* guarding the vehicles was heard to say, "Let them go!" There was confusion and perplexity. No one could make sense of it. Why had this happened to their children?

By the time the ambulances arrived along with the army and municipal and federal police, it had been forty minutes since the guns had gone silent. The authorities were received by a wave of outrage. The entire neighborhood was aroused, furious and incensed. They shouted obscenities and told them they were worthless. They demanded to know why there had been no ambulances to ferry the wounded to hospitals; why they had let their children bleed to death. They asked how it was possible that a convoy of multiple vehicles full of heavily armed *sicarios* could have made it to Villas de Salvárcar undetected when there were police and army checkpoints on the main boulevards all over the city. They asked every question and they challenged every soldier and policeman, and all the while the collective wailing of bereaved parents and siblings and neighbors formed a mournful backdrop to the angry interrogatories. "We said to them, 'We hope something like this never happens to you, that they never kill one of your children because you have no idea what that's like, the impotence you feel, the pain, the rage that we feel,'" *El Diario* quoted one of the parents saying to the officers who'd arrived to secure the area.

Mayor José Reyes Ferriz was at home when the first calls came in about what was taking place at Villas de Salvárcar. "It was around midnight and there was a great deal of confusion and misinformation," he recalled. He was initially told that it was a *quinceañera* party. Over the course of the early morning hours he received at least a dozen calls from his police chief and other city officials keeping him apprised of the emerging picture of what had taken place. He issued instructions for the hospitals to receive the wounded (the Seguro Social Hospital, for example, was only supposed to treat patients covered under their auspices) and sent the administrator in charge of city purchases and expenditures to authorize coverage of all medical services for the victims. "The city's response was terribly inadequate," Reyes Ferriz later told me. Despite repeated, desperate calls to the city's emergency response number, no help had come during the critical period in the immediate aftermath of the massacre, a time frame that might have made a difference. It was unconscionable. "It is possible that lives could have been saved," Reyes Ferriz said of the failure of the city's emergency response services.

By Sunday morning the gun smoke had been swept away by the winter winds that continued to blow steady and cold, and the harsh odor of gunpowder had all but evaporated. Only the stench of death and blood remained inside the house at 1310 Villa del Portal Street. There was blood on the sidewalk and in the street; by now hundreds of footsteps had tracked the victims' blood everywhere—the desperate coming and going of parents, family, and neighbors as they rushed in and out of the house looking for their loved ones, attempting to render aid. That had been followed by the arrival of local and state police, as well as the federal police and the army, and finally the media, who were allowed into the house to document the grotesque scene. All had tracked the victims' blood through the house and into the street.

A young man named Julián Contreras, who lived two blocks away and knew many of the Villa del Portal families, walked through the neighborhood that Sunday morning and wrote down the things he heard. They were fragmentary, some from neighbors, others from parents, still others from the kids who'd been inside the house at 1310: "They didn't shoot to kill the girls, they shot at their arms and legs. The guys they shot in the head and chest and the bigger guys they shot repeatedly in the head until they were disfigured"; "One hid behind the television"; "We were awakened by the sound of gunfire"; "This was the happiest street in the neighborhood"; "They won't do anything, it's always the same. They'd already killed my nephew and nothing is ever investigated"; "They killed almost all of my friends"; "Did they kill one of yours, too?" Contreras had documented the voices of a traumatized community.

■ ■ ■

A strange, haunting silence fell over Villa del Portal, where a heavy military and law enforcement presence sealed the street. For hours after the massacre there was no official comment about what had taken place; local, state, and federal authorities were mute. Those whose loved ones had been taken to local hospitals and clinics, some fourteen in all, kept a lonely vigil, praying that their children would not succumb to their wounds. On Villa del Portal the municipal and state police, as well as the federal police and the army units sent to secure the area, were accused of being cold and indifferent to the families whose lives had been destroyed by the tragedy, treating them as just so many more victims of the city's violence. The meaning of the massacre had yet to fully take shape, but already it was becoming clear that what had taken place at Villas de Salvárcar rested on a different plane of experience, something so outrageous that it would soon shake the conscience of the entire nation, stirring indignation even in the most hardened of hearts.

When the mayor's team arrived at Villas de Salvárcar and at the hospitals where the wounded had been taken, they reported back to Reyes Ferriz that they'd met the families of the victims and their impression was that most of the dead, if not all, were innocent victims. For this reason, Reyes Ferriz was one of the only public officials who resisted raising the specter that at least some of the kids were gang members. The next day the mayor went to the Emergency Response Center to find out what had gone wrong, and he ran into Patricia González, the state attorney general. The two had an exchange in which González warned the mayor against saying that the victims were good kids because, she said, the state police had proof that they had weapons "and other things" that suggested otherwise.

González called a press conference in Juárez that afternoon. Mayor Reyes

Ferriz and the new head of the state police (notwithstanding the massacre, Victor Valencia had resigned his post that same morning, announcing his candidacy for mayor of Juárez[1]) joined her. The head of the federal police in Juárez was also there, along with the representative of the PGR (the federal attorney general's office), and a representative of the army. The fact that all of the principals with some responsibility for bringing law and order to the city had been mustered was itself telling. González told the press that, at present, the information was that fourteen people had died on Villa del Portal Street; the wounded, she said, were recovering at various hospitals and clinics, all of which were under the protection of federal forces. González assured the media that the culprits would be tracked down, and that they were already pursuing several lines of investigation regarding what had taken place and why, although the only motive that she mentioned was that perhaps one of the murdered adults had been the target of the *sicarios*. When questioned by the press as to how the convoy had made it to and from the scene of the massacre undetected, the commander of federal forces in Juárez grew defensive, arguing that the *sicarios* no doubt had lookouts that were shadowing the federal forces in the area, including identifying the locations of the federal roadblocks.

Mayor Reyes Ferriz announced a million-peso reward for information leading to the arrest of the authors of the massacre at Villas de Salvárcar. He announced that the city's new Crime Stoppers program was taking anonymous tips, and he also said that the city and state governments would cover the funeral costs for the Villas de Salvárcar victims.

The final toll at Villas de Salvárcar would come to fifteen dead (eleven students and four adults), and as many seriously wounded. Ten died that night on Villa del Portal Street, and five others died at the hospital or in transit in the impromptu caravans of vehicles that had ferried the wounded. Luz María Dávila and her husband lost two sons in the massacre, their only children. Alonso Encina was more fortunate. In addition to Oscar, who'd managed to hide in the closet, his oldest son, Alonso Jr., had also survived, having left the party to walk his girlfriend home just moments before the commando unit arrived.

■ ■ ■

In Mexico it is common for families to bring the dead home to mourn them at a wake the night before they are interred. In Villas de Salvárcar, families readied their homes to receive the coffins of their loved ones on Tuesday morning, but it wasn't until early evening that vehicles from several funeral homes arrived bearing the six coffins of the students from that block who had been killed in the massacre. It had been raining all day, the steady drizzle reflecting the mood of the city. In addition to Adrián Encina and Marcos and José Luis Piña Dávila, the other boys were Jesús Armando Segovia,

José Aguilar, and Horacio Alberto Soto. All had grown up together on this modest street and all had been friends.

Not long after the coffins had been set up in the modest living rooms, surrounded by candles, flowers, and framed pictures of the deceased, Governor Reyes Baeza arrived to pay his condolences to the families. The strain between the governor and the mayor was such that by now the governor was not even giving the mayor the customary courtesy of letting him know when he was in the city. The governor arrived in a white armored Suburban, protected by a half-dozen heavily armed bodyguards, who secured each of the victim's homes before the governor entered. He was accompanied by Mara Galindo, in charge of victim's services for the state of Chihuahua, a woman whose reputation had been marred by her mismanagement of her responsibilities during Juárez's infamous femicides in the 1990s.

The governor and his entourage started at the home of Adrián Encina before making their way down the street to the three homes on the same block where family and friends were mourning the other young men. His reception was tepid at best; the families greeted him politely, enduring the intrusion into their bereavement and allowing him to offer his condolences before he moved on, leaving them once again to their sorrow. But in the street there was obvious anger. The collective rage over the massacre had yet to dissipate, and there were many people out, given that all of the homes had visitors. The charged atmosphere was amplified because of the governor's presence and the fact that every time he entered a home, his bodyguards seized control of the entryways and did not allow anyone to enter or leave until the governor exited and made his way to the next house.

The last stop for the governor on Villa del Portal Street was the home of Luz María Dávila, a half-block away. It was still raining; the street and sidewalk were full of puddles. Whether for that reason or for reasons of security, the governor chose to get back into his Suburban and drive rather than walk the thirty or so yards to the Dávila house. The gesture elicited derisive taunts from the people assembled on the street. "Why don't you get your shoes dirty, governor!" some shouted with obvious contempt.

When Reyes Baeza exited his Suburban at the Dávila house he was met with a chorus of similar taunts: "Get out of the car and give us answers, don't be cowards!" and "What we want is justice! You have no shame!" At the entry to the small house there were at least ten placards on poster board expressing outrage and demanding security, answers, and solutions, although by now the rain-smudged ink had rendered some illegible.

Inside, Luz María Dávila and her husband were standing in the living room next to the coffins in which their sons, Marcos and José Luis, lay. The boys' school friends and family surrounded them in the cramped, almost unadorned living room, and for the governor it proved to be another tense

encounter. Luz María openly chastised him for what she termed the authorities' incapacity and disinterest in solving the crime. She threatened that if progress was not made on the case, she would seek the intervention of American law enforcement, as if this were the ultimate embarrassment for the Mexican authorities. "Because of all that is happening here, I no longer have my children. It may be best for me to seek the assistance of the United States to help us because here I see nothing at all," she said. She was tearful, but she was clear and unequivocal. In a country where power at the top is absolute, it takes unimaginable courage for a working-class citizen to speak so unflinchingly to that power. In her suffering and loss, Luz María had found a powerful voice, a voice that would soon touch the soul of a nation. The governor had no choice but to listen quietly as he was dressed down by this bereaved mother, against the backdrop of shouts emanating from the street as neighbors and visitors who'd been barred entry by the governor's bodyguards loudly voiced their indignation and demanded that the state deliver justice. Unlike the ink on the poster boards, their voices were not the least bit dimmed by the rain.

The governor finally exited the Dávila home and boarded his snow-white Suburban, leaving the families to themselves in their living rooms, where votive candles were lit by the score and rosaries chanted throughout the night. The rain continued to fall upon the poor neighborhood of Villas de Salvárcar, as if the gods themselves were acknowledging the sorrow of what had taken place there.

The next day, there were funeral masses at different churches. Most of the families went to the Iglesia Jesucristo, Sol de Justicia, where Juárez's Catholic vicar, René Blanco, gave a mass assisted by fifteen of his fellow priests. The entire city was in mourning. Later, at the CBTIS-128 high school, full honors were given to Juan Carlos Medrano and Rodrigo Cadena, who had been star players on Los Jaguares, the school's American football team. Brenda Escamilla, the seventeen-year-old ecology student who'd refused to leave Rodrigo Cadena's side when the *sicarios* had ordered the women to leave the house, was also honored. All three had come to the party from other parts of the city, and this was to have been their last semester before graduating from high school.

The students' caskets were rolled through the school for the last time. Their teammates, in uniform, formed two lines at the entrance, receiving the victims' friends and family members. The football coach gave a tender soliloquy, after which he announced that the two players' jerseys, numbers 12 and 62, were being retired. The coach gave the corresponding jersey and a football to each of the families, as the parents stared vacantly at the caskets containing their beloved children. There was a minute of applause, as is customary in Mexico, a ritual meant to honor the lives that had been extinguished in the senselessness that had taken place at Villas de Salvárcar; the applause was intense and full of emotion. It was followed by a minute of silence, after which the students and families again broke into *porras* (school cheers).

In the afternoon, a silent funeral cortege, guarded by army and police units, left the rain-drenched city and headed out of town. The long trail of cars moved at a slow, mournful pace, traveling the thirty kilometers along the Pan-American Highway until reaching the San Rafael cemetery. There, eight of the student victims were to be buried alongside one another. A bitter wind blew over the flat, wide-open desert terrain, and, as it had all day, the rain fell in a steady downpour, leaving the assembled mourners drenched and cold. The names of the dead were read, then the classmates of the fallen chanted school cheers, followed by applause and, again, a moment of silence in which the only sound was the cruel, gripping wind sweeping across the cemetery. The gravesites were festooned with white balloons. Jesús Armando Segovia, a fifteen-year-old junior high school student, was the first to be lowered into the ground, followed by the rest. The families had pitched in to hire a *conjunto norteño*, which sang sorrowful songs like "You're Leaving, My Angel" and "Eternal Love." In the end there was nothing left to do but to trudge back through the puddles and thick mud to parked cars for the long ride home and the lonely silence that would forever wrap itself around the mourners' lives as they continued to endure the day-to-day horror that defined life in Juárez.

■ ■ ■

A cloud of bewilderment hung over the city in the ensuing days. Why? Why had these children been massacred? They were good kids: they were in school; they were athletes. And the party across the street had been clean. A few of the kids were from other *colonias*, but most of them (they ranged between fifteen and twenty years of age) were from the neighborhood, if not Villa del Portal Street itself. All around the neighborhood families had waited for their children to walk back home after the party that night. The tragic irony was that many of these parents did not allow their children to go into town to the nightclubs for fear of violence.

Immediately, a variety of hypotheses emerged. One parent told *El Diario* that he thought one of the kids attending the party was a cocaine user, spurring the theory that the *sicarios* had come after *him*. Various witnesses told reporters that on two occasions they had heard one of the *sicarios* say, "We've been looking for you." Another theory was that Brenda Escamilla had witnessed the assassination of four high school students in November and the *sicarios* had tracked her down to prevent her from testifying against them. But these explanations seemed untenable. It was unlikely that one of the cartels would mount a multi-vehicle operation involving two dozen *sicarios* to kill a witness or a supposed drug user. People were executed with much greater efficiency in the streets of Juárez every day. Those kinds of hits hardly required more than one or two *sicarios* to effect.

■ ■ ■

Two days after the Villas de Salvárcar murders, José Dolores Arroyo and Adrián Rodríguez (who went by the nickname "El Rama") were driving down Popocatepetl Street in a grey 2002 Grand Am that had been stolen in El Paso some months prior. It was three o'clock in the afternoon. Rodríguez was the head of one of the Juárez cartel's *sicario* cells, and the two were on the trail of a man named Daniel Elías Vicencio, who was traveling with his girlfriend in a Ford Explorer just ahead of them. Vicencio was a member of a gang affiliated with the Sinaloa cartel, and Rodríguez and Arroyo were about to execute him. Vicencio had been a member of Los Aztecas until his release from the Juárez city prison, at which time he'd jumped ship and joined the Artistas Asesinos, or the Double A's, as they were sometimes called.

Just as the two vehicles reached the intersection of Popocatepetl and Manuel J. Clouthier streets, the Grand Am pulled up alongside the Explorer and Rodríguez began firing his pistol into the Explorer. Fortunately for Vicencio and his girlfriend, the two vehicles encountered a military convoy at almost the same moment. The soldiers attempted to intervene, and a brief but intense firefight broke out lasting several minutes. When Rodríguez tried to flee on foot he was shot in the back, perishing at the scene. Next to Rodríguez's body the soldiers found a Nextel phone, a cell phone, and an FN Five-Seven "cop killer" pistol (so named because its bullets can pierce bulletproof vests). Arroyo was apprehended, along with Vicencio and his girlfriend, both of whom were wounded.

A black Nokia cell phone was also found in the Grand Am, and it turned out that it had belonged to one of the kids who had been shot at Villas de Salvárcar. It was the first break in the case for the Mexican authorities, and it made José Dolores Arroyo the subject of intense "questioning" to ferret out what he knew about the massacre.

It turned out he knew quite a bit. Arroyo soon gave army intelligence and officers of the federal attorney general's office an account of what had transpired on the night of the Villas de Salvárcar murders. It had begun, he said, when José Antonio Acosta Hernández, a former state ministerial police officer who ran the Juárez *plaza* on behalf of the Juárez cartel, had received a phone tip from one of his *chavos* who lived in Villas de Salvárcar alerting him that there was going to be an Artistas Asesinos party on Villa del Portal Street. Because of their alliance with the Sinaloa cartel, the Artistas Asesinos gang was the nemesis of the Juárez cartel and their gang affiliate, Los Aztecas. Los Aztecas and the Artistas Asesinos had now been at war in the streets of Juárez for two full years. El Diego, as Antonio Acosta Hernández was nicknamed (he also went by El 102[2]), put in a call to El 51, the man who coordinated the cartel's *sicario* cells, ordering him to gather a cell to wipe out the "AAs" or the "Double A's" (all nicknames for the Artistas Asesinos) at the party.

El Diego also called José Dolores Arroyo on the night of January 30 and instructed him to go to a shoeshine shop located outside the Plaza Juárez mall to await further instructions. When Arroyo arrived, he found his boss, El Rama, and ten other *sicarios*. They were told that they were going to go "do" some Double A's that were attending a party in Villas de Salvárcar. Arroyo was sent to drive through the neighborhood and "comb" it: do preliminary reconnaissance to verify the party's location and make sure it was taking place. Upon Arroyo's return to the rendezvous location, El Rama called El 51 to bring a second team to bolster the force. According to Arroyo, the convoy that set out for Villas de Salvárcar consisted of two *sicario* cells riding in four vehicles, each with six *sicarios* aboard. Their instructions were to kill everyone at the party. Arroyo claimed that his role within the cell run by El Rama was as a "hawk," or lookout, and that he was posted at the Little Wings restaurant in the nearby Plaza Las Torres, not far from the rendezvous point, to alert the team in the event that army or other law enforcement neared the *operativo*. Following the massacre, the group had dispersed, he said.

According to Arroyo, he'd had no further word until two days later, when El Rama had contacted him on Monday to participate in the execution of Vicencio. Arroyo told the authorities that he received two thousand pesos a week (less than two hundred dollars) for his services within the *sicario* cell. He was also given a cell phone and the stolen 2002 Grand Am he'd been driving prior to the shootout with the soldiers on Popocatepetl Street.

Perhaps the neighborhood gangbanger who was affiliated with El Diego, the one who tipped him off that the Artistas Asesinos were having a party on Villa del Portal, had simply misunderstood. Or perhaps he was angry at not having been invited to the party. We may never know. El Diego's Villas de Salvárcar *chavo* has never been identified.[3] And, given the heat that he created for the Juárez cartel, he may no longer be alive. But what is clear is that the Double A's who gathered at the Villa del Portal party were members of a high school football team, not a Juárez drug gang. They played in the city's AA league. José Dolores Arroyo's stunning revelations appeared to point to a grotesque and tragic misapprehension, one that had left the street at Villas de Salvárcar stained with the blood of the innocent. And left the howls of agony and mourning permanently seared into the memory of a nation.

■ ■ ■

As if to say that the frenzy of violence had momentarily rendered them exhausted and inert, on Wednesday, February 3, there were no executions in Juárez. Spent by their own savagery and the steady, relentless flow of blood with which they'd stained the lives of everyone who lived in that desert city, the demons took a day to catch their breath.

Notes

1. Valencia's resignation in the midst of such a crisis drew national opprobrium, further hobbling his political aspirations.

2. Cartel members and their gang affiliates often used numbers to identify themselves. This made it more difficult for law enforcement to know who they were and thus helped protect their operations in the event of arrests.

3. El Diego, on the other hand, was arrested by the federal police in Chihuahua City on July 29, 2011, along with his bodyguard.

CHAPTER 24

All the President's Men

The evil that had taken place at Villas de Salvárcar shook a city that had grown increasingly numb to the varieties of death and cruelty to which the cartels routinely subjected it. The teenagers had been slaughtered attending a private party in their own neighborhood while their parents waited nearby for their children to return home.

President Felipe Calderón had just left the World Economic Forum in Davos, Switzerland, and arrived in Japan for a state visit when the news broke about the massacre. Ironically, he'd spent the day promoting Mexico's maquiladora industry, trying to sell Japanese manufacturers on the notion that it was cheaper for them to build appliances bound for U.S. markets in a Mexican border city than it was to build them in China and ship them across the Pacific Ocean.

At an impromptu press conference, the Mexican president deplored the murders in Juárez and suggested that "the most probable hypothesis" was that the executions were related to an inter-gang rivalry, adding that some of the victims may have had "links" to the cartels' gangs. Calderón further decried the enduring "grave problem of insecurity" in Juárez, saying that it was a function of the deterioration of institutions and the presence of organized crime, which had expanded "under the protection of many years of impunity and corruption."

At the same press conference, Calderón also announced what he said was a policy change: his administration was poised to launch a new security strategy in Juárez, because the problems the city faced were beyond what police actions alone could address. "It is a complex problem," the president said in relation to the violence. "And it isn't solely a criminal problem, it's a social problem requiring a broader and more integrated strategy. In the next few days my government will provide ample details of that strategy, which I believe must be deployed to support the authorities." The president concluded his remarks by expressing his condolences to the families of the victims and wishing a speedy recovery to those who were still hospitalized, in addition to reiterating the readiness of his government to support state and local authorities in the investigation and clarification of what had taken place at Villas de Salvárcar.

Felipe Calderón was not alone in assuming a possible linkage between the massacre and the cartel gangs. The killing of "civilians" was relatively rare in cartel violence, the majority of which was score-settling between criminal groups. Most innocent victims tended to be people who, say, happened to be at a bar when *sicarios* arrived to take out a target and were killed in the cross fire. A number of innocent people (no one could say with certainty how many) had been executed for not paying the *cuota* when extorted by the gangs. But even the killings at the rehabilitation centers had turned out to be gang-related, though there were plenty of innocents among the victims. And the teenagers who'd been killed at Villas de Salvárcar fit the profile (adolescents and young adults from poor, working-class neighborhoods) of many of the drug war–related executions. At first glance it was easy to assume that at least some of the victims had links to the cartels and their gangs. To assume otherwise was to venture outside of the paradigm that had become all too familiar, almost axiomatic.

Many of the first pronouncements shared the president's initial formulations. For example, the governor, Reyes Baeza, volunteered that "practically" all of the students were clean kids, leaving room for the possibility of gang involvement. The governor also told the press that the lines of investigation were indicating that "the *sicarios* were after specific people" who were at the scene where, unfortunately, "there also were good students and athletes."

But it was Patricia González, the state attorney general, who several days after the massacre offered the most extensive description at the time of what was believed to have taken place at Villas de Salvárcar, and her explanation, too, emphasized inter-gang conflicts. González noted that the authorities had a man in custody (José Dolores Arroyo) who was providing key information. She indicated that "a criminal group" was attempting to penetrate the Villas de Salvárcar neighborhood and that one of the gangs had attacked because it believed that there were members of the Double A's gang in the house where the party was taking place. Those individuals, she went on, were actually next door, and they were executed that night as well, she said. In other words, the state attorney general underscored the notion that the violence was directly linked to the gangs. González noted that often the *sicarios* were drug-addled when they conducted their operations, which might have contributed to the tragic confusion that night, especially if one of the Double A's gang members had sought refuge in the party house, as they believed to be the case. González concluded by noting that the gang problems in the city's *colonias* had increased tremendously due to the dispute between "the organized crime groups." For some reason she was still reluctant to identify either the Sinaloa or the Juárez cartels by name, even though everyone knew that she was referencing them. Nor did she mention Los Aztecas, the gang running the Juárez cartel's retail drug operations, though it was obvious that they had been the gang hunting down the Double A's.

Similarly, the Chihuahua State Ministerial Police told the media that one of their primary lines of investigation was that the massacre was gang-related, given that "on two occasions the killers, in different houses, had said 'We've been looking for you,'" leading them to conclude that two people were the actual targets of the *sicarios* that night. The second line of investigation revolved around the November 2009 execution of four young men (the execution that Brenda Escamilla, one of the Villas de Salvárcar victims, had witnessed), two of whom lived in the Villas de Salvárcar neighborhood. The state police said that they were investigating the relationship between the two neighborhood kids who'd been executed in November and the current victims of the massacre in order to "clarify the activities of all involved."

In the immediate aftermath of the massacre it was easy to impugn, even if obliquely ("*practically* all of them were good kids"), the teenagers who had been at the party. It not only seemed plausible, it was easy, almost reflexive. But all indications were that such inferences were wrong; everything pointed to the idea that in Juárez there were still good, innocent kids, probably more than the steady drone of raw, brutalizing crime stories would permit most to entertain.

While a number of people, including the governor of Chihuahua and the state attorney general, had already floated similar ideas in their public comments, the president's statement seemed to galvanize the families of the victims, who immediately protested the defamation of their children. In a city with some of the highest dropout rates in the country, the Villas de Salvárcar parents reminded anyone who would listen that their children had been in school. Alonso Encina took out the Governor's Excellence List award that his son Adrián had won for two consecutive years, and the coach of Los Jaguares praised the players who'd been assassinated as spirited and disciplined athletes. Luz María Dávila talked about the fact that her eldest son, Marcos, was enrolled at the university while also working at the maquiladora where she and her husband were employed. They wanted the world to know that theirs were good, hardworking kids, not a bunch of neighborhood *cholos* bent on intimidating others when not otherwise occupied committing crime.

José Reyes Ferriz attempted to defend or at least justify Calderón's remarks. He noted that the president had only suggested that the possible links between a cartel gang or gangs and the massacred adolescents was "a line of investigation." The mayor added that one of the victim's cell phones had contained an image of himself with an assault weapon, ammunition, and chargers. "Of the fifteen victims it's possible that one of them had ties [to a narco-gang]," the mayor said, noting that such a finding would not negate the fact that "the rest of the people attending the party were good, innocent kids." It was evident that the mayor was working hard to defuse the criticism of the president. "The world is aware of the fact that in Juárez there were powerful gangs like Los Aztecas, Los Mexicles, and Los Artistas Asesinos that are at war with one another," Reyes Ferriz continued. This was the reality to which the president was referring, the mayor said.

■ ■ ■

The fact that their nation's president had implied that their children had links to the drug cartels filled the Villas de Salvárcar families with rage. That indignation quickly spread beyond the boundary of the little working-class neighborhood surrounded by maquiladoras and into the city. Soon that same indignation was reverberating loudly throughout the country. In addition to being a deeply tragic incident, the execution of so many innocent became a collective metaphor for a national experience. It was emblematic of the many good, hardworking citizens whose lives were being eviscerated by the ongoing violence, and it highlighted the inability of the government to protect its citizens, who felt vulnerable and exposed, whether they lived in poor *colonias* like Villas de Salvárcar, in middle-class enclaves, or in upscale neighborhoods like Campestre. Many Mexicans felt that there was nowhere to hide and nowhere to turn; such was the brutal reality of life in significant parts of modern Mexico. The massacre on Villa del Portal Street captured that reality all too thoroughly and it struck a nerve. People had had enough.

The massacre became an instant symbol for all that had gone awry in Mexico's drug war. A pent-up cry of fury and rage erupted all over the nation. It was called the drop that brought on the flood, the tipping point. Everywhere, the rage was deep, the frustration profound, and the helplessness pervasive. The deployment of the federal police and the Mexican Army over the course of the last two years had proven useless in containing or inhibiting the violence of the cartels and their gangs. Nothing seemed to turn the tide against the horror that had become daily fare all over Mexico, even in the many communities where violence was not elevated. The steady, unrelenting coverage documenting the violence, often accented by acts of unspeakable cruelty, was pouring into the living rooms of homes all over the country, and there was an inevitable feeling of gloom and futility in the face of it that drained the spirit.

For these reasons, the president's gaffe mobilized an avalanche of criticism, and almost immediately that criticism went beyond the specific tragedy of Villas de Salvárcar. Critics roundly challenged Calderón's vision in the war against the cartels. By the time of the massacre, nearly thirty thousand Mexicans had died in cartel-related violence since Calderón had taken office. While Calderón's strategy had succeeded in disrupting the cartels' ability to operate, it had also left corpses all over the county. Many executions were taking place in the streets and often in broad daylight—in shopping malls and grocery stores, in front of schools, at movie theaters. In other words, all too often the violence was knitted into the day-to-day lives of ordinary citizens. Drug war or no, the most important metric for the Mexican nation was the security of their families, and by this measure the government's policies had fallen far short of their mark.

All over the country, the president was taken to task in the aftermath of Villas de Salvárcar. Joaquín López Dóriga, a respected and well-known television news anchor, labeled the war the president's "failed diagnosis." "They took a gamble and we're the ones who lost," he editorialized, referring to the federal government's strategy in Juárez. In particular, the anchorman derided the president's decision to make Juárez "the benchmark" for the fight against organized crime. Of the resources mobilized by the Mexican government, almost a quarter of the total troops and federal police had been deployed to Juárez, yet the violence continued unabated. There was little to show for the massive effort, he said. Calderón had failed to grasp the depth and dimensions of the problem, López Dóriga argued. Similarly, the influential Mexico City newspaper *El Universal* said that the Villas de Salvárcar massacre made clear that Calderón's war was "an utter failure." The criticism of President Calderón and his strategy against the cartels was as severe as it was widespread. Some were calling Calderón's move against the cartels Mexico's Vietnam, alluding to the quagmire that cost tens of thousands of American lives and depleted the national treasury, but ended in failure and inconclusiveness.

A group of civic and business leaders took it upon themselves to travel to Mexico City to bring attention to the reality that Juárez's citizens were living. They hosted a press conference at the tony Hotel Nikko in Polanco, where María Soledad Maynez, the president of the Juárez Maquiladora Association, demanded that the president address the crisis in Juárez. "With respect to repairing the social fabric, it's going to take us a generation because we've got approximately ten thousand children who've been either victims or victimizers; we have more than ten thousand children who have been abandoned or orphaned because of the number of deaths," she said. The president of the board of directors of the Central de Abastos, the city-run wholesale food market, charged that "the [local, state, and federal] governments have not lived up to their obligations." Eduardo Güereque, the Citizens Watch representative in Juárez, told the national and international press that sixty thousand families had abandoned the city because of the violence. He also chastised the president, saying he'd only been in Juárez on two occasions since becoming the nation's chief executive, and that during those visits he'd only met with the city's business leaders for a total of ninety minutes. The group called for President Calderón to come to Juárez immediately to address the crisis in person.

The pervasive violence conjured images of a lawless wasteland and invoked the one notion that the Mexican government found most irksome: the idea that Mexico, or portions of it, was, in essence, a failed state. Juárez's *El Diario* editorialized: "[The violence] is the reason for the debate over 'failed state' in the pages of the nation's newspapers and on the internet," it read, citing the absence of safety as the most telling evidence of such state failure. "If we don't have a failed state, then show us; guarantee what Mexicans minimally need: our lives," *El Diario* said.

Even members of Calderón's own party had grown restive. Given the extent to which local, state, and federal governments were overwhelmed by the violence, the state president of the PAN, Cruz Pérez Cuéllar, declared that Chihuahua was a "failed state" and appealed for foreign intervention because of the inability of Operación Conjunto Chihuahua and its most recent iteration, Operación Coordinada Chihuahua, to quell the violence. A coalition of civic, business, and academic groups also called for the United Nations to intervene in Juárez. Such calls, in a country long known for having a strong nationalist tradition, reflected the measure of desperation that many felt. "Juárez is a city without life," Cuéllar said. "People live in terror." He called for the "blue helmets," as United Nations forces were referred to in Mexico, to be brought in to establish peace.

The political opposition parties attempted to shift the terms of the debate, arguing that it was the federal government, rather than the cartels, that was the source of the violence. Federal deputies of the PRI demanded that the president remove federal forces from Juárez given the "obvious failures" of his strategy. The left accused the president of fomenting the violence rather than fighting it. Víctor Quintana, a federal deputy from Juárez for the PRD, called for the withdrawal of all federal forces from the state of Chihuahua.

While the president was the focal point of much of the national criticism, he was not the only target. *El Financiero* of Mexico City singled out the governor of Chihuahua for special criticism, describing him as "a man without shame" for allowing Juárez to unravel as it had and accusing him of doing virtually nothing to help the city in the face of its profound crisis. The article cited the fact that ten thousand businesses had closed in a city where nearly 30 percent of the nation's executions had taken place, provoking the exodus of tens of thousands of persons. "He's blamed the federal government," the article said. "But he's done nothing to plug the dike to slow the growth of the gangs associated with the cartels." Reyes Baeza was accused of standing by blithely as the most important city in his state became the most beleaguered city in the nation.

Local and national media took everyone responsible for the safety of the nation's citizens to task, and in some quarters there were calls for President Calderón to resign, along with Governor Reyes Baeza and Mayor Reyes Ferriz. The dimensions of the anger within Juárez were reflected in cold numbers in a survey conducted by *El Diario*: 80 percent of the people sur-veyed were unhappy about the president's remarks and 90 percent blamed all three levels of government (municipal, state, and federal) for the crisis of insecurity. An overwhelming number, almost 85 percent, stated that the violence had had a significant impact on their lives. The findings spoke to the depth of despair that had come to pervade a once-proud city known for its grit.

■ ■ ■

One of those calling for the president to resign was Julián Contreras, the resident of Villas de Salvárcar who'd captured the spontaneous, traumatized comments in the neighborhood following the massacre. Contreras wrote a letter to the editor of *El Norte* several days after the massacre in which he introduced himself as living two blocks from the site where "a death squad" had massacred "almost twenty adolescents." (The death toll from the massacre had come to fifteen, five of whom were adults.) In addition to Calderón, Contreras also demanded the resignations of Governor Reyes Baeza and of Mayor Reyes Ferriz. "As long as these fascists continue being in charge of the government [perpetuating] the lie of its 'war against the narco-traffickers,' the lives of all Juarenses will continue to be in danger," he said. "It's not the *narco-empresarios* or the corrupt politicians who die, the only ones who die here are the poor," Contreras wrote. The next day, in Juárez's *El Mexicano*, Contreras was even more pointed in his accusa-tions. Describing himself as the Juárez representative of a group calling itself the National Front Against Repression (or, by its Spanish acronym, FNCR), Contreras placed responsibility for the massacre not on the cartels and their narco-gangs but rather on what he described as a "paramilitary commando." "The massacres in Ciudad Juárez are actions undertaken by death squads that are operating in the city," Contreras alleged. Contreras said that the death squads were related to Calderón's militarization of the country and that their aim was to intimidate the population and restrict people's rights; he likened the work of the death squads to what had taken place in places like El Salvador, Nicaragua, and Guatemala. He singled out the Zetas as an example. Rather than portraying them as renegade defec-tors from the military who'd been recruited to work as the armed wing of the Gulf cartel (the conventional understanding of the group's origins), he claimed that the Zetas were actually a group still operating within the mili-tary, working simultaneously within and outside of it in collusion with local and federal police. Contreras argued that the death squads in Juárez were operating under the protection of the military.

A coalition of leftist trade union groups, human rights groups, and intel-lectuals, the FNCR had been active during the Mexican government's Dirty War against leftist guerrillas in the 1970s but had dissolved after a decade of

activism until October 2007, when the war against the cartels and the violence breaking out around the country had bred new life into the group. It
now claimed a membership of over one hundred organizations. The FNCR
accused the government of fascism and was especially critical of the military, accusing it of widespread human rights abuses, including torture and
disappearances. The group mocked Calderón's assertion that the cartels and
their violence and corruption were a "cancer" plaguing the nation, arguing
instead that Mexico's problem was that under Calderón's rule the country
was drifting toward a militarized fascism; indeed, they argued that the
country was facing a "new phase of the Dirty War." In this analysis, the violence was not cartel-driven at all; rather, it was an instrument of the government, a device to intimidate and control the population. Along similar lines,
a sister group calling itself the Juárez Citizen's Assembly, which Contreras
also represented, argued that what Juárez was living had nothing to do with
a fight between drug cartels or rival drug gangs. Juárez was living "state ter-
rorism," and the federal government was covering up paramilitary groups
and sending death squads to the border city.

The far-left seemed unable to engage the violence outside of the rubrics
that were left over from the 1960s and 1970s. There was no place within
those frameworks for understanding a relatively new, third force, one that
was neither the government nor a guerrilla/worker resistance movement
but rather a force fueled by the requirements of narco-capitalism, which,
even if driven by similar commercial instincts, was nonetheless an altogether different creature. Narco-capitalism was not run by the traditional
Mexican elites (despite its influence and control over individuals both
within and outside of local, state, and federal government). If in the 1980s
the cartels had had to answer to state and federal law enforcement, there had
now been an inversion of the power structure: today the cartels called the
shots in many of the areas they controlled. But there was a populist patina
to the narco-world given the humble origins of all of the important cartel
players and given the emergence of a narco-culture that romanticized their
exploits and celebrated them in the ever-present *narcocorridos* and *telenove-
las*. That populism shifted the terrain for a political left long accustomed to
an adversary defined as the nation's elites and long accustomed to viewing
itself as a movement that defended the downtrodden. The cartel leadership
and its cadres were mostly uneducated individuals from poor communities.
And the cartels and their gangs were terrorizing poor communities through
their violence and extortions. This was an awkward fact for the left when
it came to framing adversaries. NAFTA and globalization were easy to fold
into the traditional analysis given obvious facts, such as poor wages and an
absence of even basic services in countless neglected communities. But the
war against the cartels was not a new edition of Mexico's infamous Dirty

War, notwithstanding the abuses of the military and other law enforcement agencies. It was a monster the likes of which Mexico had never known.

■ ■ ■

The pressure on Felipe Calderón was enormous given the national reaction following the tragedy at Villas de Salvárcar. There was a clamor for a change, for a pause that might usher in fresh deliberation. The circumstance demanded something beyond apologies delivered from Mexico City, no matter how sincere and heartfelt. The national debate was pushing the administration, forcing federal officials to break with their habits of mind. Even the PAN's state leader, Cruz Pérez Cuéllar, called in an open letter to the president for Calderón to concede that his policies had failed in Juárez. Reeling off statistics on the number of dead, he advised that the president come to Juárez "in humility." If he did so, Cuéllar assured, the president could count on the support of the good people of the city.

Immediately upon his return from Japan and at every subsequent opportunity, Felipe Calderón began signaling a change in course in relation to his government's Juárez strategy. From the state of Aguascalientes, where he was inaugurating a new technical institute, he announced that his government would take the necessary steps to restore peace and tranquility to the city. He again expressed his deep condolences to the families whose children had been massacred and underscored as often as he could that it had become clear that they were good, decent kids. Calderón expressed his "solidarity" with the parents, siblings, and family members of the fallen. This tragedy, he said, had "not only wounded and hurt the nation, it had also aroused its indignation." Calderón indicated that an announcement was imminent regarding "a new strategy" for Juárez that would involve its citizens. "We are all required to renew our commitment to Juárez," the president declared. The new strategy would encompass new educational opportunities and areas such as employment, recreation, and community life, as well as prevention and treatment of addictions. In other words, it promised to be a broad, sweeping proposal.

The notion of a new strategy did little to change the tenor of what was taking place on the ground in Juárez and the rest of the nation. Historically, successive Mexican governments had often presented grand schemes that amounted to very little. In Chihuahua, the initial federal government intervention had been called Operación Conjunto Chihuahua. It had then been given a new name, Operación Coordinada Chihuahua, but for Juarenses living the day to day, the distinction meant nothing at all. So the promise of a new strategy to rescue Juárez, although it was given extensive coverage in local and national media, was received without credulity, much less enthusiasm.

Given the national clamor, President Felipe Calderón and his security cabinet, meeting at Los Pinos (the Mexican White House), soon came to the conclusion that nothing short of a full-on response could contain or absorb the powerful emotions that had been unleashed by the slaughter of the innocent in Juárez. The president's office announced that Calderón would be visiting Juárez on Thursday, February 11, 2010. The communiqué said that the president was undertaking the trip in order to personally address the concerns of the citizenry and to present a new strategy for taking back the city. The secretary of the interior, Fernando Gómez Mont, would lead an advance team that would lay the groundwork for the president's visit to the most violent and aggrieved city in all of Mexico.

■ ■ ■

"I waited until several days after the funerals before visiting the Villas de Salvárcar families," Mayor Reyes Ferriz told me. The visit was private, in a house across the street from the scene of the shootings. "I expected a great deal of anger against the government," he said, "but the overwhelming tone was more one of resignation and loss." The families had just buried their children days before, and the gravity of it still hung in the air. "There was lots of pain," the mayor continued. He recalled two primary complaints. The first was about the delay in the response by the Red Cross and the police. The second was against the president for his remarks in Japan. One of the things that the mayor remembered from that difficult encounter was a mother of a young girl. She had stood at the back of the living room, which was cramped and full of people. In her hands was a framed photograph of her daughter in a *quinceañera* dress. The woman never spoke, but her silent, mournful presence stayed with the mayor.

■ ■ ■

The secretary of the interior arrived in Juárez on Monday, February 8, three days before the president was due to arrive. The mayor had recommended to the president's liaison that Gómez Mont meet with the Villas de Salvárcar families and had provided a brief on his own meeting with the families a few days earlier, conveying that the tone had been somber and the complaints appropriate given what the families had just endured. "They [the advance team] were cautious about not creating problems for the government," the mayor observed. This was especially crucial in light of the governor's recent reception on Villa del Portal Street. Governor Reyes Baeza and Mayor Reyes Ferriz met Gómez Mont at the airport, where the officials conferred and agreed that together they would visit the families of the victims at Villas de Salvárcar. It appeared that the secretary of the interior hoped to defuse the families' anger following the debacle of the president's comments in Japan. They left the airport and their entourage headed directly for the beleaguered *colonia* where, days after the funerals, the entire neighborhood continued to mourn.

The three men met with the families privately at one of the Villa del Portal homes, across the street from the scene of the massacre. In addition to Luz María Dávila and Alonso Encina, the families of the other adolescents who'd been killed that night were represented. Gómez Mont told them that the president had sent him in order to express his deep sorrow for their loss and to give them his personal condolences. During the two-hour meeting the families pleaded for security. They told Gómez Mont that they feared for their lives. Gómez Mont did what he could to reassure them that they would be protected. He promised that representatives of the federal government would continue discussions with them and that their needs would be addressed. The families would get help, he said. The families had prepared a list of actions, including demands that the authorities allow "foreign law enforcement" to investigate the case; that federal, state, and local police as well as the military stop wearing ski masks to cover their faces when on duty; and that they stop pointing weapons at civilians during their *operativos*. Gómez Mont did not respond to those specific petitions.

Luz María Dávila had already shown that she was not one to buckle in the face of the powerful. She took advantage of the meeting with two of the most powerful men in the state of Chihuahua and the president's personal emissary, dressing down the secretary of the interior just as she had the governor days earlier. She told Gómez Mont that there was no trust, even though he'd promised a full and vigorous investigation.

Following the two-hour meeting, Luz María told *El Diario* that she remained angry; she felt there were no solutions to what was taking place in Juárez. She also struck out at the minister and at the president: "[Gómez Mont] said that when the president made his declarations he had erroneous information and that now he knows that it wasn't so, but I do not accept that as an apology." Her sons were good boys, she said, and she demanded that the president publicly retract the comments he'd made at the press conference in Japan. She also pressed for justice: "Mr. President, until the culprits are apprehended I hold you responsible for the murder of these children!"

The secretary of the interior left the gathering in a five-vehicle convoy and headed for what would be a marathon ten-hour meeting with representatives from a variety of groups, including business leaders, human rights activists, and civic organizations. At a subsequent press conference with the governor and the mayor, Gómez Mont sought to sketch out the outlines of the president's new strategy, a strategy, he said, that would rest on support from four pillars: the federal, state, and municipal governments, as well as civil society. The one thing he specified about the president's forthcoming visit was that the president would meet with the families of the victims of the Villas de Salvárcar massacre, whose tragedy, the secretary of the interior insisted, had "moved the president deeply." "The president knows that the dead were innocent victims and they were part of a youth that is involved in sports and their studies, that they represented the way out of the violence in Juárez, and any hypothesis regarding a confrontation between rival gangs has been discarded," Gómez Mont affirmed. It was clearly a continuation of the full-court effort to defuse the public relations gaffe that had brought strenuous criticism against the president both locally and nationally.

The press conference was testy for another reason; the significant tensions between the governor and the federal government were evident. Earlier, the governor had publicly chastised the president for not coming to Juárez sooner. With national elections just five months off, he now said that it was "imperative" that whatever help Juárez was to receive not become part of the forthcoming electoral contest—in other words, that the money from the federal government not be used to further the PAN's political leverage in the city.

Following that meeting, in separate remarks to the press, Governor Reyes Baeza called the federal government to task for "creating victims." This amounted to a public rebuke of President Calderón and the federal government's policies in the war against the cartels. Reyes Baeza said that the dead were not victims of a natural disaster but "of the war [against the cartels] which the president convened two years ago." Referring to Calderón's statements in Aguascalientes and elsewhere since his return from Japan, in which he had expressed condolences and solidarity with the victims and their families, the governor scoffed at "expressions of solidarity" as insufficient. What people needed, he said, was "deeds." Nowhere in the coverage of the governor's remarks was there mention of the fact that over the course of those two years the governor had himself sent virtually no support to Juárez. There had been no additional funding from state coffers to help defer the spiraling security costs (in fact, those expenditures had been reduced), and neither had the governor enhanced the presence of the state ministerial police in the city despite the rampant violence that had enveloped it and despite the mayor's repeated requests for assistance. In his own way, the governor was using the Villas de Salvárcar tragedy to political ends.

Beyond the governor's cynical comments, the massacre became fodder for political positioning both locally and nationally (municipal, state, and federal elections were slated for July 4, 2010). Víctor Quintana, the federal deputy representing Juárez from the PRD, the party that Calderón had defeated by the slimmest of margins in the 2006 presidential election, coined the phrase "youth-icides," playing off of the so-called femicides, as the killings of young maquiladora women in the late 1990s had been termed. He noted that 80 percent of the Juárez deaths since the start of the drug war were young people, and 30 percent were under nineteen years of age. "We're living a youth-icide," Quintana told Mexico City's *Proceso* magazine.

"The youth of Juárez and the nation, whether execution victims or executioners, are victims. And Gómez Mont and Calderón are trying to blame them and make them delinquents." He pointed out that Chihuahua had the highest incidence of youth between the ages of twelve and eighteen who were neither in school nor working (the infamous NiNis). The state had the highest incidence of middle-school and high-school dropouts. It was three times harder for youth between fifteen and twenty-four to find jobs, he argued, and the youth of Chihuahua, and, especially, of Juárez, faced limited alternatives other than forced migration, joining a gang, participating in drug trafficking, or suicide. "All of them," Quintana insisted, "the executioners and the executed alike, are victims."

Similarly, David Penchyna, a PRI congressional deputy, declared that Calderón's security policy and his so-called war against the drug cartels were merely a ruse to "legitimize" a presidency "that was not legitimately won at the ballot box." "Don't be confused, comrades," the legislator said, "*this* is Mexico's cancer" (thus mocking Calderón's oft-invoked metaphor that the drug cartels were a cancer upon the nation). It was as if the cartels, their gangs, and the orgy of violence to which they had subjected the country were a figment of the administration's imagination, invented merely to justify themselves.

Javier Corral Jurado, a federal senator from Juárez affiliated with the president's party, the PAN, in turn blasted Penchyna and the PRI. "That's how the PRI reduces the problem of insecurity," he said. He noted that the PRI held practically every political position of consequence in the state of Chihuahua, yet 31 percent of the victims who had already died in the violence across the nation had been killed in the state (Juárez alone accounted for almost a quarter of the national drug war fatalities). He further noted that the state had a 50 percent higher rate of marijuana use than the national average, and twice the number of people consuming cocaine (4.8 percent in Chihuahua as opposed to 2.4 percent nationally). "Those are hard numbers," the senator noted. "And yet in Chihuahua judicial investigation is almost non-existent, hundreds of dossiers lay unattended."

From the floor of the Mexican Congress, Javier Corral also implied that Governor Reyes Baeza had ties to the narco-traffickers, suggesting that therein lay the reason for his "negligence" in fighting the cartels and, specifically, the unbounded violence that had overtaken Juárez. He accused Reyes Baeza of accommodating the narco-traffickers, arguing that the governor had blocked attempts to clean up the state police apparatus that was known to have close ties to organized crime. "The government of Reyes Baeza is a spectator before the dispute between the narco capos," he said, implying that the inaction was due to the governor being compromised.

The PRD party's state secretary, Hortensia Aragón, declared that Chihuahua was presently "ungovernable" because of the federal forces and announced that the party would propose legislation to force the departure of federal forces from the state. She argued that fifty crimes were committed every day in Chihuahua, a fact that "required" the withdrawal of federal forces. Aragón's pronouncements lacked coherence. As an antidote to the lawlessness, the PRD proposed that neighborhood groups patrol their own streets. It was, at best, a naive strategy, one that ignored the raw brutality of the cartels and their well-armed gangs and the extent to which they were already terrorizing communities. If the government forces had been ineffective, the viable alternative was hardly to create a vacuum that would give the cartels unfettered control of the city and its neighborhoods. The Villas de Salvárcar families, for example, were clamoring for more protection, not less.

In the days after the announcement that the president would soon be arriving in Juárez, the head of the PRD in Chihuahua, Víctor Quintana, accused him of delaying so long that the situation in the city had become "rancid" and "putrid." "He had to wait until we had more than four thousand executions in the state before coming to Chihuahua," Quintana said. Quintana reiterated his call for the removal of all federal forces not only from the city's streets but also from the entire state. Quintana warned that whatever the president imagined his reception would be, the people of Chihuahua would demand an accounting of his actions, of his presidency. "He's not coming as 'The Savior'! The times do not call for the appearance of a 'Messiah!'" Quintana pronounced. But, in truth, the embattled Juárez needed nothing short of that.

■ ■ ■

As the president's team prepared for his visit to Juárez, they appeared to send mixed messages regarding what the city's citizens might expect. For example, they sought to minimize expectations, initially saying that only the president and the secretary of the interior would be coming and implying that the visit would be brief. Most took this to mean a cameo appearance by the president, something akin to what he'd done on two prior occasions when he'd come into Juárez, given a brief talk to business groups, shaken hands, and dispensed a few *abrazos* before departing for another destination. At the same time, at several press conferences, the president and Gómez Mont indicated that the new program would touch all spheres of the city's life, including education, the economy, unemployment, and public spaces—signaling, in other words, an ambitious plan. The latter suggested the possibility of a significant infusion of federal funds.

The governor of Chihuahua apparently felt he was being cut out of the deal. The day that Los Pinos announced the president's trip to Juárez, the governor contacted the state media to convey his displeasure. As the media carried stories about the president's arrival, headlines all over the state simultaneously described the governor as "mad" and "excluded" and "thundering" in his anger. "By excluding local authorities, the president's new plan has started on the left foot," the governor protested. Journalists described the governor as "visibly upset" at having been excluded from the planning for the new strategy. "I wasn't invited," he complained to the media. He went further: "This plan is not going to work without the participation of the state government." However, according to José Reyes Ferriz, each of Gómez Mont's visits, as well as the subsequent president's visits, were preceded by numerous meetings with the president's advance team that included the mayor of Juárez and the governor of Chihuahua. The mayor dismissed the governor's statements as misrepresentations. In fact, he described an atmosphere of contentiousness: "They argued about everything, down to the forks and silverware!" the mayor recalled. "It was all conflict with the state government." The mayor attributed this to Reyes Baeza's electoral worries.

The governor's protestations continued for days. Three days after the announcement of the president's visit, the governor complained that "I still have not received a call [from the president]." The governor thrashed the president and his team. "I don't know how they intend to create new strategies," he said, "when all they do is that some come, others leave, and they just have meetings at Los Pinos, but the governor has not been called to participate." He told the media that, with respect to law enforcement, he had made "unprecedented" efforts, "perhaps even beyond what was constitutionally permissible" (by allowing state police to investigate crimes that fell under the federal purview). His government had invested fiscally to professionalize and clean up the police, the governor maintained. The governor also argued that whatever resources the federal government was sending should be spread across the state and not be limited to the border.

But the fact was that the governor had done relatively little to support the city of Juárez. And even though he declared that it was "strange" that he had not been included, the most likely explanation was that there was significant mistrust of the governor, who had long been hounded by allegations of alignment with the Juárez cartel. The governor accused the federal government of playing election tactics, implying that they were throwing federal funds around in Juárez in order to buy the 2010 election that was just months away. No doubt somewhere political calculations formed part of the Los Pinos thinking; it was only natural. But, unlike the governor, Mayor José Reyes Ferriz, who was also a member of the PRI, appeared to be fully in the loop with the federal people. And in terms of election positioning, it was of far greater utility to the PAN, the president's party, to be able to show a measure of progress and success in Juárez than to have a successful election in Chihuahua per se. The entire nation was looking over Calderón's shoulder, demanding results. From that perspective, perhaps it was more useful to the president's opponents that his policies fail.

■ ■ ■

The Juárez visit by the secretary of the interior had not gone far in calming either the nerves or the rage in the city. A little more than a week after the massacre, the day after Gómez Mont had visited Juárez, Governor Reyes Baeza and Mayor Reyes Ferriz attended a prearranged convocation at the gymnasium at the CBTIS-128, where students from Juárez's four technical schools had come together for a series of crime prevention presentations focusing on avoiding gangs and criminal organizations and preventing drug addictions. The mayor and the governor faced a near-riot at the school. There was a chorus of loud boos when they entered the auditorium and again when they were introduced. The students shouted demands and called for action; they wanted the political leadership to take action not only to solve this case but also to bring peace and security to their communities. Ten students were evicted from the event as they shouted, "We demand justice!" There was pandemonium. Eventually, the students settled. "The students of Ciudad Juárez are not delinquents," Reyes Ferriz assured them in his comments. "They are good people, they are kids who study, they are kids who are going to work for their city and they are the ones who will move Ciudad Juárez forward." For the mayor and governor it was a harrowing experience. The students' wrath was undiluted, pure, and it reflected the sentiments of the entire city.

■ ■ ■

The massacre at Villas de Salvárcar had become a focal point of discussion throughout Mexico. Every newspaper, from the most important and widely read papers in Mexico City to small newspapers in provincial towns, carried the story and reflected on its meaning. Every television newscast in the country had broadcast the gory images from the house on Villa del Portal, and now television stations and radio programs were mustering their best and most respected pundits to analyze what had taken place. Villas de Salvárcar broke down the national denial that previously had accommodated the horror and found ways of avoiding it; it became the stark fact that forced the nation to engage with the brutal realities it was living.

There was an air of gravity as the president of Mexico prepared to board Avión Presidente Juárez, the Mexican version of Air Force One, bound for the northern border city that shared its name, the city on which he'd bet the success or failure of his presidency. The president, as well as the members of his security cabinet and his broader team, knew full well that the stakes for this visit were high and that Juárez remained restive and angry in the aftermath of unspeakable tragedy.

CHAPTER 25

The Visit

President Felipe Calderón was about to enter a maelstrom. Throughout Juárez, people prepared responses to the visitor from Los Pinos. At the high schools, students were going to mount protests against the violence. At Juárez's universities, where nine faculty members and thirty-one students had been assassinated over the previous two years, students would protest for the victims of the violence. At Catholic churches, congregations would gather to pray rosaries for the Juárez dead. Civic groups were planning marches at the international bridges and at the "Mega Flag," a city landmark in the heart of Chamizal Park. The president would be greeted by citywide expressions of protest and discontent.

José Reyes Ferriz told the press that the president would announce a plan that had been in the works for months, in collaboration with the Inter-American Development Bank. He called it the "Juárez Intervention Plan." He said the municipal government had been working on it since April of 2009, and that it had been in negotiations with both the state and the federal governments. Carlos Chavira, the head of the influential business group Coparmex Juárez, announced that the city's business leaders would tell the president that he had six months to show results, otherwise many of them planned to leave the city. Many already had.

The presidency announced that there would be one public event, at Juárez's Cibeles Convention Center, during which the president would meet with representatives of various sectors of the city. For the first time, the president's team referred to the new program that was to be unveiled as "Todos Somos Juárez: Reconstruyamos la Ciudad" (We Are All Juárez: Let Us Rebuild the City). Although it wasn't announced formally, word was leaked that the president also planned to meet with the families that had lost their children at Villas de Salvárcar.

The president's advance men arrived at the Juárez airport at the crack of dawn on Thursday, February 11, 2010, and by early morning there were five military helicopters hovering above the Cibeles Convention Center and the army and federal police had set up new checkpoints all around the city. The immediate vicinity around Cibeles was the object of especially intense security measures. The spokesperson for Operación Coordinada Chihua-hua, Enrique Torres, said that approximately seven thousand army troops and three thousand federal police had been deployed to ensure security during the president's visit.

In a surprise announcement, the president's office said that not only would the president be arriving with his secretary of the interior, Gómez Mont, as had previously been anticipated, but he was also bringing much of his cabinet to Ciudad Juárez. In addition to Gómez Mont, the entourage was to include Secretary of Public Education Alonso Lujambio; Secretary of Social Development Heriberto Félix Guerra; Secretary of Health José Ángel Córdova; Secretary of the Economy Gerardo Ruiz Mateos; Secretary of Agriculture Abelardo Escobar Prieto; and Secretary of Public Security Genaro García Luna. It was a formidable gesture, intended to signal that the president was committed to putting the full resources of the federal government behind changing the realities on the ground in Juárez.

The funding that the federal government would be bringing to bear for the Todos Somos Juárez program was put at 3.3 billion pesos (approximately 260 million dollars).[1] No Mexican government in the country's history had ever invested anything close to that kind of money in a response to a local crisis, with the exception of mobilizations in response to massive natural disasters.

The monies that the federal government was putting into play activated considerable maneuvering by everyone from the state legislature to citizens groups. The governor again insisted that the funds be spread out across the state, which would give him leverage in terms of political favors and influ-ence. The PRD insisted that the monies be overseen and managed only by citizen committees. Still others called for an integrated approach that would combine public and private sectors. With the exception of the governor, most recognized that Juárez was of necessity the focal point for the expen-ditures; it was the site of the tragedy, ground zero of the narco-war, and the prime location of the social and economic catastrophe.[2] Saving Juárez would require that kind of a focused endeavor. Anything less, such as spreading the money across Mexico's largest state, would erase the possibility of a mean-ingful impact.

José Reyes Ferriz told the press that the federal government was condi-tioning the funds on the consensus and agreement of Juárez's civil society. By now it was obvious that although the mayor and the governor were both members of the PRI, they differed markedly in their views. Reyes Ferriz applauded and even championed the federal move, seeing it as a decisive step forward. The mayor said his only concern was that the funds not go "to erecting empty buildings," rather that they be funneled toward projects that society itself requested, adopted, and of which it took ownership, as well as projects that could continue to develop and unfold rather than being one-time wonders.

In a bizarre move, the governor declared that he was temporarily moving the state government to Juárez in order "to support the people of Juárez." The day before President Calderón's arrival, the governor ensconced himself in the Camino Real (the same hotel, not coincidentally, where the federal people would be staying) along with most of the directors of the state's agencies. The governor also met with the city council and the mayor forthwith, promising programs to upgrade the city's image. (The governor had acted precipitously. The state legislature had yet to approve the quixotic move, which would have cost the state millions of dollars, and, in fact, it never did.)

The governor seemed to have reluctantly conceded that utilizing the funds elsewhere in the state was ill-advised or, at any rate, was not going to happen, although he continued to insist that federal funds should flow through the state coffers, meaning the governor would have greater control over them, given that all of the agency heads were his appointees. Curiously, just the day before, the Chihuahua state legislature, over which the governor exerted considerable influence (the PRI was the majority party), had refused to approve an initiative for Juárez that would have funneled extra state resources in the areas of health, education, work, social development, family development, and security. The state government continued to do virtually nothing to help address the crisis in Juárez, leaving Reyes Ferriz frustrated by the governor's posturing and intransigence. Later, the mayor would tell me, "He did everything in his power to block Calderón."

Contrary to the governor's proposals, Reyes Ferriz announced that the government funds would be managed through federal agencies and programs, not those of the state. "We're very excited about President Calderón's visit," he said. "We await his proposals for Ciudad Juárez." Echoing what federal officials had been saying, the mayor emphasized that the specific ways in which the federal funds were to be used would depend on the local consensus in Juárez.

■ ■ ■

Calderón's visit was not only a change in policy, it was a gamble driven forward by desperation. The toll of the dead, not only in Juárez but nationwide, was increasingly weighing on the country. His poll numbers had sunk. Once heralded in many quarters for his courage in taking on the cartels, his policies' lack of success when it came to day-to-day crime and the seemingly inexorable wave of executions was increasingly impossible to ignore. Calderón was faced with a must-do situation in Juárez.

The new strategy represented a radical departure from the actions that the federal government had been undertaking since December of 2006, at the start of Calderón's presidency. That earlier strategy had netted many cartel capos, who were subjected to the classical Mexican perp walk, paraded in front of the media, with the emblems of the Mexican Army or federal police behind them, surrounded by heavily armed officers whose faces were typically covered by ski masks. Many of those capos had been prominent targets. There were also countless images in the national media of drug seizures by the ton, including dramatic footage of discovered tunnels connecting both sides of the U.S.-Mexico border and narco-barges and narco-submarines that had been seized off Mexico's Pacific Coast, their hulls bursting with Colombian "merchandise." Tons of cocaine, tons of marijuana, and tons of methamphetamine, as well as other pharmaceutical drugs, had been seized. But on the ground, in terms of the violence, nothing changed; it only got worse. This was the paradox that Calderón faced: the government's successes did nothing to ease the burden of violence that Mexicans were living daily.

But contrary to the idea that the Calderón government was throwing together a desperate plan at the eleventh hour, the intervention Calderón was bringing to Juárez had been a year in the making. It was modeled closely after the Colombian experience in Medellín, a city that had been similarly ravaged by cartel members and the FARC guerrillas. Calderón had visited Colombia in 2009, and he'd seen firsthand the efforts to rebuild some of Medellín's roughest neighborhoods. A few months later, Mayor Reyes Ferriz and the governor had also visited Colombia. The Inter-American Development Bank had underwritten significant parts of the Medellín effort, and Reyes Ferriz had had numerous meetings with them addressing the Juárez situation. In fact, the Inter-American Development Bank had arranged the mayor's appointments in Medellín to ensure that he visited the most instructive sites.

At Los Pinos, a team had been working on a Colombian-style plan, adapting it to the Juárez situation. This plan had been scheduled for implementation in Juárez in April of 2010. The massacre at Villas de Salvárcar and the national outrage it stirred quickened the pace of the planned intervention. In fact, even before Calderón's return to Mexico City from Japan, he'd instructed that the plan be readied for immediate implementation.

The team developing the specific nuts and bolts of the new program, under the name "Juárez Intervention Plan," started working around the clock. The president said he expected to see a proposal and a working document within days. Every federal agency that would have a hand in the intervention had a representative on the team, people with the power to make decisions. In the final days before the president's departure for Juárez the team worked nonstop in a conference room at Los Pinos. A premium was placed on efficiency. Calderón's style is to micromanage, and some of the participants later told me, "He's a real detail person." Not completing the proposal in time for the Juárez trip was not an option.

On the eve of the president's visit, six people were executed in Juárez. The next day the local newspapers greeted the president with headlines like "Juárez needs profound solutions, Mr. President" and "A devastated city receives the president." And, perhaps the most hopeful, "Calderón to the rescue."

■ ■ ■

It had been decided that the president would meet with the families whose children had been murdered at Villas de Salvárcar. The massacre had become such a rallying point for the nation that a visit to Juárez that did not include direct engagement with the aggrieved families was not only unimaginable on human terms, but on political terms as well. The particulars of the president's meeting with the families were kept secret. The meeting was not listed on the published presidential agenda and the press was not informed. The families had been told a few days earlier, during their meeting with Secretary of the Interior Gómez Mont, that such a meeting was likely, but no details had been given and no firm commitment made. Nonetheless, the families' expectations were heightened the morning of the presidential arrival, when scores of army and federal police units arrived to secure the neighborhood.

The general assumption was that if the president were going to meet with the families, he would come to Villa del Portal Street. As had been the case with the governor's ill-fated visit a few days prior, the neighborhood was already plastered with placards and graffiti protesting the violence, demanding justice and an end to corruption, and protesting the president's visit. Residents for blocks around were milling about, anticipating that the president might arrive at any moment as the possibility of Calderón's presence spread by word of mouth.

No doubt partly influenced by the screaming, taunting mob the governor had encountered on Villa del Portal Street, the president's advance team decided to find an alternate location to meet with the bereaved families. Calderón's people clearly hoped for a more controlled environment, where scores of angry residents would not be descending upon the presidential entourage in front of the national media.

The advance team decided on a place called Casa Amiga Crisis Center, a mustard-yellow building with red trim located just five minutes from the site of the massacre. The center had a reputation for providing exceptional service to the community. It was a nonprofit for women, founded by Esther Chávez Cano, a legendary and much-beloved Juárez social activist (she had received Mexico's National Human Rights Prize in 2008). Although she died on Christmas Day in 2009, a little more than a month prior to the Villas de Salvárcar massacre, Casa Amiga was part of her legacy in the beleaguered border city. Two psychologists, two social workers, and two prevention specialists staffed the center, which offered a variety of programs, including child abuse prevention, art therapy for children, and support programs for women who worked in the city's maquiladoras. There were also educational programs and workshops aimed at preventing domestic and sexual violence.

Mid-morning, the presidential team sent word to the Villas de Salvár-car families confirming the president's visit and informing them that a van would be coming to retrieve them (the location of the meeting remained a secret). All but three of the families whose children had been killed boarded the van for Casa Amiga. Luz María Dávila, the mother who'd lost her only two children, was one of those who refused to meet with the president. "He can come here if he wants to talk to me," she told reporters.

The families arrived at Casa Amiga in advance of the president, who came moments later, accompanied by the governor, the mayor, and a couple of cabinet members, including Abelardo Escobar, Calderón's secretary of agriculture, who was a Juárez native. A surprise was the presence of the president's wife, Margarita Zavala; none of the previsit lists of the officials arriving from Mexico City had included her name and her participation had been a closely guarded secret. Aside from the group accompanying the president, the Los Jaguares coach was the only non–family member at the meeting, which took place in a small auditorium whose walls were decorated, ironically enough, with various posters relating to the prevention of violence, especially domestic violence and violence against women. There were four rows of folding chairs, ten or so seats per row, and the president and the others sat in a line in front of them, also in folding chairs. It was a solemn and oddly intimate encounter, with no microphones and no speeches and no tables separating the presidential party from the families. Once again the president attempted to convey his sorrow for their loss and make amends for the remarks made in Japan that had insulted them.

Initially, the tenor of the meeting was one in which the families expressed their feelings and presented their grievances to the president. They rebuked him for his characterization of their children and for the failure of the city to respond in a timely manner to the crisis. Margarita Zavala took feverish notes, documenting the complaints and what needed to be done. Gradually, though, the meeting became more personal. The parents began to talk about their children's lives, about who they were, about their friends. The meeting lasted nearly two hours, during which the president, his wife, and the aggrieved families talked, as the other officials mostly looked on in respectful silence. "The president expressed his condolences to each of us," one of the parents later told me, saying he now felt satisfied that the president and the nation knew that his children were good kids who'd been victims of an evil act. Calderón promised that they would be taken care of, that the children of the adults who'd died and the siblings of the adolescents who'd been killed would all receive college scholarships, along with other support, including psychological services. But the president also told them that he knew that no government intervention could restore their children or undo the profound loss they had suffered.

At the end of the gathering, as people began to filter out of the room and the president stood surrounded by some of the family members, a woman approached him carrying a framed photograph of her daughter. It was Brenda Escamilla's mother, the same woman whose silent presence had so struck the mayor when he'd gone to give his condolences to the Villas de Salvárcar families a few days after the funerals. Standing in front of President Calderón, Brenda Escamilla's mother raised the framed photograph so that the president could see it clearly. "This is my daughter," she said, "and you implied that she was a gang member." Silence fell across the room. "Look at her! Do you think she looks like a gang member? She was sweet, she was a good student!" Clearly touched, the president again offered his condolences. "For me, that was the hardest, the most moving moment," the mayor would later recall.

Notes

1. The amount equaled the annual Juárez municipal budget.
2. Thirty-nine percent of the Chihuahua population lived in Juárez. The city was a vital economic center, generating 50 percent of the state's economy and 10 percent of the national economy.

CHAPTER 26

Cibeles

At the conclusion of President Calderón's meeting with the Villas de Salvárcar families, the official party left for what was scheduled to be a gathering at the Cibeles Convention Center of some three hundred citizens representing the city's business, religious, academic, and civic organizations. At the Cibeles, demonstrators were out in force to protest the president's visit. The protesters were an eclectic group that included students from the high schools and universities as well as members of various political factions, including the National Front Against Repression (FNCR).

Inside the Cibeles things were no less contentious. The mayor was the first to extend an official welcome to the president and his cabinet. When in his welcoming remarks José Reyes Ferriz summarized what the municipal government had attempted to do to contain the violence, there were boos among the attendees and someone shouted out "Liar!" The tone in the hall was raucous, verging on pandemonium.

Luz María Dávila's sister, Patricia, had called to invite her to come to the Cibeles meeting. Patricia was politically active and she was going with some friends who were human rights activists. When it came time for the president to speak, the five women stood up at their seats and turned their backs to him in protest. No doubt it was unnerving, but Calderón proceeded with his prepared remarks. He told the audience that he had met with most of the Villas de Salvárcar families and reiterated his apologies "for the pain his words might have caused." As the president spoke, several members of the Estado Mayor (the Mexican counterpart to the Secret Service) approached Luz María Dávila, urging her to sit down, but the aggrieved mother refused. The women did not sit down until the president concluded his remarks.

The event was like a town hall meeting, with various individuals taking to the microphones to air their concerns and grievances. Luz María Dávila made a number of attempts to enter an open area directly in front of where the presidential party was seated, but each time she had been intercepted by the Estado Mayor agents. However, she found her opportunity while the governor was speaking. The latter's remarks had reached a crescendo when he declared that everything that took place in the state of Chihuahua was ultimately his responsibility. That statement elicited applause, although the tone was ironic, as if to say, "It's about time you accepted responsibility for what's been taking place." That was the moment, with the Estado Mayor people perhaps distracted by the applause or losing focus after an hour and a half, that Luz María Dávila chose to make her move, slipping by the security and coming to a stop directly in front of the president and his wife, Margarita Zavala.

Belatedly, one of the Estado Mayor men rushed to intercept her, but just as they reached Luz María, the president motioned him to stand clear, before gesturing to her with open palms that she was welcome to speak. "Excuse me, Mr. President," she said—she was clearly anxious and disarmingly sincere. She rocked back and forth on the balls of her feet and gestured, her hands making broad arcs in the air, as she continued, "I can't say you are welcome, because in my opinion you are not welcome; no one is," she said before a spellbound and church-silent crowd.

"It's been more than two years that murders are being committed here, yes? And no one has done anything. I want justice not only for my two sons, but also for the rest of the youth. Mr. President, you say the same thing. Just like Ferriz on down have all said the same thing. Baeza—the same. But nothing happens, it just gets worse. That's the truth," she said, her voice repeatedly breaking.

"My boys are dead. They were not gang members. It cannot be, Mr. President. They were students. If someone were to kill a son of yours you would look under every stone for the assassin. But I don't have resources. My boys have been laid to rest . . . I want justice. Put yourself in my place, what I'm feeling at this moment," she said plaintively.

The president sat in front of her, hands clasped together, nodding. "Don't just say 'yes,'" Luz María excoriated him, "do something to make Juárez what it once was, not the bloody place it is now!" The crowd erupted, clapping their assent, as Luz María, full of grief and anger but now seemingly out of words, turned and walked to a couple of empty chairs at the end of the first line of seats and sat down, face in her hands, obviously distraught. A gaggle of reporters and well-wishers immediately surrounded her, some hugging her, others pressing their microphones and cameras toward her.

Margarita Zavala rose from the proscenium and walked toward Dávila. Momentarily, she seemed hesitant, unsure if approaching the grieving mother would only incite her further, but in the end she pressed through the crowd and wrapped her arms around Dávila, quietly speaking words of support and understanding in an attempt to console her. "I'm fine," Luz María said to Mexico's First Lady. "I'm calm. I expressed to the president what I was feeling."

The sense of incipient disorder that had governed the entire affair finally broke down altogether. All decorum in the auditorium vanished. It was not restored again until Luz María Dávila, still tearful, made her exit from the auditorium amid the crowd's emotional applause.

"At some point I just said to myself, 'Why am I here if I'm not going to say something,'" Luz María told me when I interviewed her in her home a short time after the Cibeles event. In that moment, she'd almost felt possessed, she said: "I didn't plan what I was going to say. I'm not a public person by nature." On the contrary, she said, she was a hardworking woman whose focus centered on her family and her children. "I hardly even hung out with the women in the *colonia*," she told me. The afternoon of the Cibeles meeting, her family had just completed the last day of the Novena prayers for the two boys. The gesture had been spontaneous, she recalled, but once on her feet she could not stop herself, something had taken hold of her. She was a disconsolate mother. Overwhelmed with grief and loss, she had seized the moment to demand justice for her two sons.

■ ■ ■

During the governor's remarks at the Cibeles meeting, just prior to the Luz María Dávila incident, an agitated PRD state delegate had stood up and declared that the federal forces were mauling the students protesting out in the street. The president had dispatched Gómez Mont to see what was happening. Exiting the Cibeles, the secretary of the interior, escorted by a single Estado Mayor agent—in flagrant violation of the security protocols governing the protection of cabinet members—walked to the crowd of students and FNCR sympathizers. "I'm here to dialogue with you," he told them amid shouts of "Assassin!" and "We demand justice!" Gómez Mont faced off with the demonstrators, attempting to stand his ground: "I don't have blood on my hands," he said. The two men had inadvertently waded deep into the sea of angry protesters; a circle closed in around the secretary and his increasingly anxious guard. As the Estado Mayor agent called for additional support via the microphone on his lapel, one of the protesters lunged at Gómez Mont from behind and hit him bare-fisted on the head. "So that's your idea of dialogue!?!" the secretary barked as the guard attempted to pull him from the crowd and back within the safety of the Cibeles security perimeter. The foray was as harrowing as it was ill-conceived, but the secretary and his guard succeeded in extricating themselves from the situation. As for the confrontation between demonstrators and the federal police that had prompted the secretary's intervention, there had been clashes, and some of the protesters had been bloodied. A score were arrested, most for laying down on the street in acts of civil disobedience in an effort to stop the movement of vehicles on the streets around the Cibeles.

Back inside the Cibeles, the president proceeded to detail his Todos Somos Juárez program. The federal government was prepared to invest approximately 260 million dollars into six areas that the president had out-lined: security, health, education, economy, employment, and social devel-opment. The plan included building new schools in marginalized areas as well as paving streets, building childcare centers, programs for the unem-ployed, and prevention and treatment programs for addicts, among other projects. The president's program was as ambitious as it was unprecedented in Mexico; it represented an enormous commitment of resources and per-sonnel. Calderón vowed that the funds would be allocated in full consulta-tion with Juárez's civil society. He also promised to return to Juárez the following week, accompanied by his full cabinet. "We will stay the course until our work is done and Juárez is restored," he promised.

Depleted and exhausted, the president and his wife, along with the bulk of his cabinet, boarded their respective official airplanes at Juárez's Abraham González International Airport and headed back to Mexico City. The senti-ment must have been grim; the challenge before them was daunting. Prior to the visit, Fernando Gómez Mont may have been the only one among them to truly grasp the depth of anger and frustration that had taken possession of the city, given that he'd met with the parents of the victims and listened to the desperate complaints and entreaties of the city's residents during his marathon ten-hour meeting a few days earlier. But it would have been dif-ficult to fully convey that experience to the president and the cabinet; they were operating in what for them was terra incognita. They were accustomed to highly orchestrated, orderly events where the respect for the presidency helped contain the more raw expressions of anger or opposition. But what they had experienced over the course of this day in Ciudad Juárez was something beyond containment. This city had endured too much for too long. Normal conventions no longer held.

■ ■ ■

The week between the president's Cibeles meeting and his return to Juárez was frenetic. In Juárez, local working groups were formed under the rubric of the president's six areas: security, health, education, economy, employ-ment, and social development. Within these were smaller working groups, such as human rights, pubic spaces, the judiciary, and small business owners, among others. These groups met feverishly, with the aim of developing pro-posals for specific communities or sectors of the city. It was a Herculean task and it was carried out under the press of the president's timeline, which called for the proposals to be presented to him at the forthcoming meeting.

The federal cabinet members returned to Juárez two days before the president. They convened their working groups at various hotels through-out the city. The atmosphere was intense, the efforts of the local participants earnest. Each of the working groups was meeting with the respective cabinet member under whose auspices that group's activities were to be moved forward. For example, the secretary of health met with the Juárez working groups composed of physicians, psychologists, nurses, addictions specialists, and NGOs providing services, as well as academics whose research was relevant to health concerns. The meetings were substantive. Each was presided over by the cabinet member in question as well as a phalanx of aides, who did everything from distributing pads and pens to passing microphones around to documenting the proceedings and the topics and recommendations that they generated. The goal for each working group was to develop a set of up to ten specific recommendations or actionable items to be presented to the president at a plenary session two days hence.

I managed to gain entry into the working group focusing on the problems of small- and medium-sized businesses, over which the secretary of the economy, Gerardo Ruiz Mateos, presided. It was a window into the challenges faced by ordinary men and women who owned modest businesses such as restaurants, used car dealerships, appliance stores, and the like. Other than the violence, the most salient concern was that extortions were widespread throughout the city. Virtually every kind of business, large or small, was being victimized by gangs that were extorting them, some of them associated with the big cartel gangs, others not. "Our back is against the wall," one business owner said. "We can pay our taxes or we can pay the *cuota* or we can pay our employees' salaries, but we can't pay all three. We desperately need protection from the pervasive extortions," he said. The head of the Small Business Association chimed in, saying that twenty thousand of their members had received extortion demands. "Even the smallest businesses are having to pay five hundred to one thousand pesos a week in order to keep their doors open," he said. The association received twelve to fifteen calls a day from members whose businesses had been held up by delinquents. The climate of insecurity and the inability to contain crime was hurting every business in the city.

It was evident that the economic cost of the U.S. recession, in combination with the city's violence, was devastating the city. Juárez was the second-most-important maquiladora city in the country, and the maquiladora industry represented 50 percent of the city's economy, but the maquilas were experiencing massive closures because of the American recession. The president of the Hotel Association cited occupancy rates that were at an all-time low. "People have stopped coming to Juárez because of the insecurity," he pointed out. "Our society [in Juárez] is on the verge of collapse," another man said, referring to the massive unemployment and businesses closures. "We've lost eighty thousand jobs in the last two years," he said. The businessmen and businesswomen decried the government's regulations that had made it cheaper for them to purchase goods across the border in El Paso than in Juárez. "We're spending 450 million pesos [a little less than 45 million dollars] a year in El Paso that we could be spending here in Juárez," he said. Given Mexico's massive natural gas reserves, there was outrage at the fact that natural gas cost more in Juárez than it did in El Paso. The reason: a monopoly on natural gas in northern Mexico held by a prominent Juárez family. The head of the Used Car Dealers Association, comparing car imports from the United States for 2008 and 2009, noted that 2009 figures had dropped 80 percent.

But in addition to venting complaints and anxieties, the business owners also put forth specific proposals. One of the most persistent was that Juárez and the border be declared a free trade zone; the argument was that this would allow them to be more competitive with American companies. Among the other proposals was a six-month moratorium on federal taxes. The Hotel Association had numerous proposals for beefing up tourism, including developing the nearby Salamayuca Dunes for ecotourism and designating Juárez one of Mexico's "cultural treasures." The group also proposed that instead of having government conferences in the nation's beach resorts, the government could schedule major conferences in Juárez. They called for a major PR campaign in Mexico, the United States, and Europe to restart the Juárez tourism industry.

However, in all of the forums that I attended, the clamor returned to the same fundamental reality: an awareness that the city's massive crisis was not only the product of a lack of security but also of pervasive social problems whose origins went back decades. Approximately 25 percent of the population was between the ages of eighteen and twenty-two and, not coincidentally, the modal age of the *sicarios* was between seventeen and twenty-four. On the whole, the Juárez youth had no education, no jobs, and no prospects for the future. Given that stark reality, for the NiNis the temptation of two hundred dollars a week, with the bonus of a car and cell phone, was compelling indeed.

I attended several other forums and most had the same format, although the content varied as a function of the sector of the city that each was addressing. The surprise was the forum on the judiciary, at which several of the state supreme court justices were present. The judges defended the work of the Chihuahua judiciary. They seemed apathetic to the fact that the conviction rates were minimal in relation to the tens of thousands of arrests over the course of the last two years. They rationalized the fact that judges had set free some of the most notorious criminals on the basis of "human error." In a state where the problems with the judicial system were obvious and almost universally recognized, the judges' attitudes were entrenched and arrogant.

■ ■ ■

The launch of the Todos Somos Juárez intervention was set to culminate on February 17, when all of the working groups, toiling away feverishly, would present their proposals to the president and his cabinet at a plenary session.

On the day of the meeting, there was a glaring absence from the list of groups scheduled to present: the human rights working group was nowhere to be found on the agenda. According Gustavo de la Rosa, the original members of the working group had included several NGOs working on human rights issues, including Centro de Derechos Humanos Paso del Norte, Red de Mujeres, and Centro de Información y Solidaridad Obrera. Laura Carrera, of the National Commission for the Eradication of Violence against Women, within the Ministry of the Interior, had chaired the group. According to de la Rosa, the group had planned to present twenty cases of human rights abuses committed by the military. "It was shut down by someone in the president's office," de la Rosa said. The day before the presentations the human rights group was deleted from the list. "It was short-sighted, an error on their parts that they couldn't recognize the importance of including them," de la Rosa complained. He argued that the federal government found the human rights issue inconvenient, an "obstacle to their operations."[1]

Security was high that day at the Camino Real Hotel when Felipe Calderón arrived to preside over the forum. Each working group was to present proposals for how federal funds might be spent in Juárez. As had been the case during the president's prior visit, several groups announced that they would mobilize large anti-Calderón protests.

I made my way to the Camino Real, arriving early because it had been predicted that the protests would make it difficult to reach the hotel. The national and international press convened in a parking lot next to the hotel, where they were being accredited for entry into the assembly. The atmosphere was testy. The large group was funneled into a narrow passageway where the first of three security checkpoints lay. We were packed in like fans trying to make their way into a sporting event due to start at any moment. In addition to the many army and federal police, there were also many Estado Mayor agents, all wearing suits and walking around officiously with communications plugs in their ears. In the distance, and at every intersection around the hotel, were teams of federal police dressed in ninja-type uniforms, including black ski masks and kneepads. The riot police were expecting the protesters to converge on the hotel at any moment, and they anticipated that the protests would be violent. Raymundo Ruiz's newspaper had assigned him to cover the protests, so he was out there somewhere beyond the thick cordon of black-uniformed federal police agents. We text-messaged one another periodically to stay in touch.

Inside the enormous auditorium, each of the committees gathered to present its proposals to the president, a process that took over two hours. There were two unanticipated highlights. One came close to the end, when the head of the culture group rose from the sea of attendees and looked

Felipe Calderón at the Camino Real Hotel, February 2010. Photo copyright © Ricardo Ainslie.

straight at the president. He stood erect and spoke with a clear, if impassioned, voice. "Mr. President," he said, "the city is to the point of paralysis due to fear. Artists are more than about theater; they are about a vision, about a capacity to see. I can tell you that the criminals are not going to stop killing because we build swimming pools. The *sicarios* will not stop killing. An exceptional situation requires exceptional actions, Mr. President. I was anticipating proposals that would help us attack this problem because Juárez is something magical and it deserves to be saved. The different workshop groups have met and presented you with their proposals and ideas. In order to change what is taking place we must reconstruct the social fabric. But we're being pusillanimous, not brave. If we're going to believe, to have faith, well, believing is the most serious game in this city. Many of us are so afraid of the killers that we are finding it easier to react against the military rather than against the assassins, it's safer that way."

There were no points, lists of proposals, or "actionable steps" in the culture representative's words, only the truth of the extent to which fear was warping perception, shifting orders of importance. He articulated the fury that lives in the absence of faith, when citizens cease to believe in the greater social project of the city, of the nation. Most of all he spoke to the profound human toll such an absence creates. True to his calling, the artist had broken with the forms and conventions of the plenary session to give expression to what was most important about their having convened. His presentation was dramatic; the president and everyone else in the auditorium were spellbound.

Finally there was the student. A young man named Guillermo Asiaín stood and asked for the president's indulgence, given that he was not on the program. Indeed, he said, that was a problem with the arrangement: while different working groups had presented their ideas on how to save the youth of Juárez, he pointed out that nowhere were the youth of Juárez represented in the working groups. Those assembled in the hall grew silent. "You need to recognize the youth of this city, and the programs aimed at intervening with the youth should have input from us," the young man said. There was a powerful response in the hall to Asiaín's comments. He received a thunderous ovation that was as spontaneous as his remarks had been.

At the end, the president himself addressed the assembly, assuring those present that he had listened closely and that his team would get to work on the proposals immediately. "I believe in Juárez and in the nation," Calderón said. "And I believe that Mexicans will find a solution to the myriad problems that our country is facing at the moment." Calderón emphasized that Ciudad Juárez occupied a special place in his deliberations about the crisis. He set a one hundred–day target for the implementation of the proposals. The three-month timeline seemed unrealistically ambitious given that most government projects involved more than three months of permits and paperwork before breaking ground. The president was promising bullet-train speed on all fronts. Whether Calderón could deliver on these promises, or whether the country was any closer to solving the conundrum of the national violence, remained to be seen.

■ ■ ■

The president's people structured a team that would coordinate and monitor the implementation of the federal government's intervention. Antonio Vivanco, one of the president's closest aides, led the team, and its members included a representative from each of the federal agencies that had been involved in Todos Somos Juárez. Beginning the next week, the twenty people on that team boarded the six a.m. Aeromexico flight every Monday out of Mexico City bound for Juárez, where they stayed all week until returning Thursday evening. "We had people who were in a position to make commitments on behalf of their respective agencies," Adriana Obregón would later tell me. Obregón was one of the key players at Presidencia for the Todos Somos Juárez project, and she had been on those weekly flights.

The team stayed at the Camino Real Hotel, and there was a standing Monday morning meeting at ten o'clock that they called the "weigh-in." "How's it going?" "Why is the school not getting finished?" "What are the obstacles?" I was told by one of the participants that the ethos of the team was "can do" and "must do." If someone on the team from one of the federal agencies wasn't up to the task, that person was replaced. "Send me someone who can push," was the guiding qualification. Vivanco, who cut a tall, imposing figure, chaired the process with a firm hand. The aim was to complete the adopted proposals by the president's one hundred–day target, which meant an enormous undertaking and considerable pressure. The effort to translate the Colombian experience in Medellín into something that would work in Juárez represented a vast expenditure of personnel and resources.

It was a complex challenge; the cities were different, the cultures were different. And yet, conceptually and strategically, public recognition that the solution to the violence in Juárez lay not only in quasi-military police actions but also in social programs addressing the realities in the long-neglected *colonias* that hung around the city's neck like a dead weight represented a vital step forward. For too long the city had deferred a reckoning with those realities, so long, in fact, that parts of the city were near the point of no return.

In all there were 160 formal commitments that became the focus of the one hundred–day target. The federal government created a website for Todos Somos Juárez where the status of each of the commitments could be tracked. Mexico had never seen such a massive mobilization of government resources, a mobilization so closely tethered to the perspectives and demands of the local working groups who knew their city's needs. As one editorial put it: "Todos Somos Juárez is something that we cannot allow to dissipate, it's an exercise in democracy."

For once, the federal government had come to Juárez, breaking with the historical modus operandi in which NGOs and local and state agencies were forced to travel to Mexico City to gain audiences with government officials. For a city long-accustomed to indifference from Mexico City, the intervention represented a profound change. However, the payoff of the enormous undertaking would take a long time to assess. It was unlikely that the violence would drop immediately. A long-term rather than short-term vision had been put into play. It was an indispensable shift in strategy: in order to turn the city of Juárez around, the long-frayed social fabric had to be repaired. Such repair was the cornerstone to the future of a great city. Indeed, to the future of the country.

Note

1. Two months later, in a compromise, Gustavo de la Rosa was named to head an office that would receive complaints of human rights abuses in the city and oversee human rights issues in relation to police operations.

CHAPTER 27

No Accidents

In an article that appeared in the *Washington Post* on February 24, 2010, just a week after president Felipe Calderón's second visit to Juárez in the aftermath of the Villas de Salvárcar killings, William Booth reported that for the first time American intelligence agents would be embedding with Mexican law enforcement in an effort to help pursue drug cartel leaders and their hit men operating in Ciudad Juárez. The agents, the article continued, would be operating out of a Mexican command center, where they would share drug intelligence gathered from informants and intercepted communications.

Just a month earlier I had visited the Intelligence Center, which was on the second floor of the Emergency Response Center (known as the CERI), when José Reyes Ferriz had invited me along to attend a security meeting. The building is a solid, squat structure made of native stone with a sky-blue glass façade. Heavily armed soldiers and federal police guarded the entrance. The bottom floor of the CERI is a large space enclosed by thick glass walls, where army and federal police monitored information coming in on the city's anonymous tip line and from emergency calls. Each workstation had three computer monitors, where pairs of agents were supposed to work the calls, identify their locations, and track the location of nearby law enforcement patrol units (this was the system that had presumably failed to respond to the calls coming from Villa del Portal Street).

The security meeting was held on the second floor, in a large operations room at the front of which was a long oval table covered by a forest-green tablecloth; a bottle of water had been placed in front of each seat. The mayor chaired the meeting, sitting at the head of the table. Seated to his right was the city district attorney; to her right was her immediate predecessor, an army colonel who was transitioning out. A federal police inspector who had been overseeing the placement of three hundred security cameras throughout the city sat at the other end of the table, across from the mayor. Next to him was José Luis Lara, an engineer who was in from Mexico City as the chief consultant on the security camera project. To his right was Gerardo Ortiz Arellano, the head of the municipal prison.[1] Finally, there was Julián

David Rivera Bretón, the former army general who was now heading up the Juárez municipal police following Roberto Orduña's resignation almost a year earlier.

Each of the principals had brought their personal aides to the meeting, who, standing, were arrayed around the table, periodically responding to various requests from their respective bosses. The federal police appeared to be hosting the meeting—their uniformed staff attended to the needs of the participants, offering them coffee and sodas or opening up the bottled waters and pouring them into glasses. The discussion around the table that day centered on how to track convicts once they were released from the municipal prison. The mayor asked if prison personnel were routinely obtaining addresses and if someone was checking in on the ex-cons after their releases. Ortiz Arellano, the director of the prison, noted that social workers were already doing that, but the mayor was insistent that the procedures in place were not adequate—as often as not former prisoners disappeared from the addresses they'd given upon release. The mayor later summarized his frustration, noting that the municipal police arrested approximately three thousand people a year. "The majority," he told me, "are let out within a day or two." Of those three thousand, only 150 or so were ever actually sentenced. "Your chance of getting off for anything from murder to car theft to rape to assault in Juárez is 95 percent" the mayor told me. "Those odds look good to most criminals."

The mayor and the others reviewed the newly implemented Crime Stoppers program. A complication was that it only took calls related to local crime, that is, crime that was under the auspices of municipal police. The federal police were triaging calls to the corresponding authority depending on whether they fell under the federal, state, or municipal purview, but there was considerable confusion in the public's mind about what law enforcement entity was responsible for what kind of crime.

At the conclusion of this meeting, the federal police inspector approached the mayor and asked if he cared to see the progress they had made with the security camera program. The cameras had gone up all over the city and were being used to monitor criminal activity from this site as well as from the federal police command center in Mexico City. The inspector led the way to a workstation, where two federal police officers sat in front of a large computer screen. "We're going to show you an execution that we caught on the cameras last week," one of the officers said as he began rolling video. On one corner of the footage was the date and time code, which whirred as a function of the speed with which the officer ran the footage. The first image was of a city street with a fair amount of traffic at an intersection with a traffic light. The main boulevard was two lanes running in either direction while the other street, perpendicular to it, had a single lane in each direction. As the agent fast-forwarded the video, cars zipped across the screen and beyond in the blink of an eye. "Watch this maroon SUV," the officer said. "It's the car carrying the hit team." The car in question drove up to the stoplight and then made a U-turn, going off-camera. "They're scouting the hit," the agent narrated. "This car," he said, pointing the cursor at a white Mercury, "is also involved. And so is this one," he said, drawing our attention to a pickup truck. Over the course of several minutes, those three vehicles made a series of passes through the target area.

It was evident that the video had been closely studied. "These hits all have the same basic profile," the agent said. The vehicles involved in the execution had first moved through the busy intersection prior to the hit. To the untrained eye, they were easily lost in the ordinary flow of traffic. The officer explained that the team actually carrying out the hit typically traveled aboard one or two vehicles. There were also several scout cars, as well as a car that would block others from pursuing the hit team once it completed its work. "Finally, there's always a car that remains behind to ensure that the targets are all dead before it leaves the crime scene," he added. Each of these players had been identified. The time code at the top of the screen made it clear that the video spanned a little more than ten minutes.

For the execution, the federal police officer rolled the tape in real time. The maroon SUV came into view from the opposite direction it had taken during the first two passes. The lookout cars were positioned on both sides of the street. The escort car then made its way through the intersection. At that point, the maroon SUV pulled up and the *sicarios* could be seen jumping from the vehicle, weapons in hand. A group of six men ran off camera, where they took down their target before scampering back into the SUV, almost leaving one of them behind. The maroon SUV then headed down the cross street to the right, where two getaway cars had already been positioned. The so-called "verification" car was also in position just past the intersection. Just then, the pickup truck that we had seen make several practice runs through the intersection rounded the corner and blocked the street down which the *sicarios* had just made their getaway. To my surprise, at that moment two municipal police cars arrived at the scene of the execution. Rather than giving chase, they jumped out of their patrol cars and ran to the victim. The pickup truck continued to block the getaway route and the police paid it no mind. I found it hard not to draw the inference that the police were either afraid of a confrontation or were in collusion with the *sicarios*. The final image was of the white Mercury, the verification vehicle. Once the blocking vehicle left the crime scene following the getaway path, the verification vehicle proceeded slowly down the street, eerily merging into the afternoon traffic as if nothing had happened. The federal police officer froze the frame at that point, with the Mercury at the top of the screen.

Those of us standing around the workstation fell silent. Even in this city of so many executions, so many deaths, it was rare to actually see one live. Typically, one saw photographs or video taken in the aftermath, or one managed to arrive soon after, but it was unusual to see images of an execution as it was taking place. But the silence also pressed an obvious question. Why had the municipal police done nothing? It seemed to me that perhaps the federal police officers had left the white Mercury floating at the top of the screen as if posing a question.

The mayor broke the silence. "Who is the victim?" he asked. He was told the victim's name, but there was no information as to why this man had been executed. The mayor asked if the vehicles' license plates could be brought into focus. He was told they were working on that. What was perfectly evident, however, was the sophistication and planning that had gone into pulling off this execution. The operation had involved six different vehicles; the federal police agent estimated that the entire team consisted of fifteen to eighteen men. They had carried out a precise, highly choreographed hit wherein every actor knew his exact role. They had rehearsed the hit in every detail, making practice runs before executing their target. Each person had done his job to perfection; the execution was carried out flawlessly.

The Mexican federal agent swiveled in his chair, turning from his computer screen to look at the mayor. "Here's another hit by the same team," he said. We were now looking at a Soriana shopping center. According to the date on the video, this hit had taken place several days later. The maroon SUV, the white Mercury, and the pickup from the prior execution were again playing key roles. The other vehicles were different. This time, two men in a beige pickup truck were sandwiched in between two *sicario* cars at the exit to the shopping center. A hit-team van then closed off the adjacent lane, sealing the unsuspecting vehicle off from any possibility of egress. As before, the *sicario* team's vehicles had made several dry runs through the target area some fifteen minutes prior to the execution. The white Mercury, parked across the street, was again the verification car. Another vehicle pulled up alongside the target, and the smoke from the blazing gun barrels firing at the occupants in the beige pickup truck was plainly evident on-screen. When the shooting stopped, the targeted vehicle coasted out into the boulevard on its own accord, as if piloted by an invisible ghost. The pickup continued rolling slowly through four lanes of traffic until it hit a curb across the street. One of the *sicario* cars had pulled into the intersection, blocking traffic as the other vehicles slipped off down the street and disappeared from view. As before, once they'd verified that the two men in the pickup truck showed no signs of life, the white Mercury exited from the scene, merging into traffic as horrified drivers attempted to maneuver around the bullet-ridden beige pickup, aware, now, that within it lay one or more additions to Juárez's tally of the dead.

■ ■ ■

The CERI, where I saw this footage, was the location of the Intelligence Center to which the February 24 *Washington Post* article had referred, indicating that American FBI, DEA, and possibly other law enforcement agencies would be working in collaboration with Mexican law enforcement, especially the federal police and Mexican Army intelligence personnel. Historically, U.S. law enforcement had kept its Mexican counterparts at arm's length. The legacy of corruption and cartel infiltration into Mexican operations at all levels was too widespread and too well known to allow for meaningful collaboration. Information leaked by corrupt authorities readily endangered the lives of informants and agents in the field. Memories of Enrique "Kiki" Camarena, the DEA agent who was kidnapped in 1985 and tortured extensively prior to dying at the hands of a drug cartel in Guadalajara, formed the backdrop to those fears. U.S. authorities knew that the old federal judicial police had had a hand in the agent's assassination and had played a role in the Mexican government's efforts to cover it up and block a meaningful investigation.

Mexican law enforcement, in turn, had similarly kept the Americans at a distance, if for different reasons. In the past, working too closely with the Americans might have translated into pressure to launch operations that were "inconvenient." While there had long been a DEA and FBI presence in Mexico, along with other American intelligence services, relationships with Mexican officials were typically tense for a variety of reasons, including legitimate Mexican apprehensions about American operations in their territory for reasons of national sovereignty, a long-standing factor in U.S.-Mexican relations. Thus the notion of close collaboration between American and Mexican intelligence agents was jarring and novel to most who came across the *Washington Post* article. The article also reported that recently, U.S. agencies had grown more comfortable with the prospect of such collaboration, having developed a new respect for Mexican law enforcement, at least at the federal level. American agents would now be working closely with Mexican federal police who were recent graduates of DEA and FBI training programs.

A DEA spokesman in El Paso confirmed the *Washington Post* report to *El Diario* the following day, stating that "closed door meetings" had been taking place between American and Mexican federal agencies, not further identified. However, the story appeared to have taken both American and Mexican governments by surprise: the respective ambassadors claimed they knew nothing about the reported development.

It is likely that the national criticism of Felipe Calderón's strategy in the war against the cartels had also made such collaboration more tenable. Calderón was already more inclined to work with the United States than his predecessors. In just the first three years of his administration his government had extradited far more cartel operatives to the United States than any prior Mexican president.[2] Leading up to and especially in the aftermath of the Villas de Salvárcar massacre, the Calderón government had been feeling considerable political pressure over its policies: there was a chorus of people, even within Calderón's own party, who increasingly viewed the federal government's efforts as teetering on failure. In Juárez, two years of federal intervention had produced no change in the violence. On the contrary, there were more and more dead, and people felt less and less safe. Mexico had taken down many big-name cartel capos, but there was otherwise little to show for the government's efforts in terms of a reduction in violence (or, apparently, in the availability of cocaine and other drugs in the United States). Such a circumstance lent itself to permitting greater collaboration between Mexican federal law enforcement and American law enforcement.

■ ■ ■

Saturdays at the Barquito de Papel (Little Paper Boat) were always busy. The two-story, lemon-yellow venue decorated with brightly colored children's blocks on Insurgentes Avenue catered to families with young children, and it was a favorite for birthday parties and special events among Juárez's middle class. On Saturday, March 13, one of the Mexican employees at the U.S. Consulate in Ciudad Juárez was hosting a birthday party for her child at Barquito de Papel, and most of the attendees were fellow consular couples with preschoolers. It was around two in the afternoon, and after the children had had time to romp around on the various playscapes and the usual round of balloons, presents, and cake, the party was breaking up.

Two couples left the Barquito de Papel at the same time. Jorge Salcido and his wife, Hilda, had come in separate cars. Jorge loaded up the Salcidos' three children (two, four, and seven years of age) into the family's white 2009 Honda Pilot and headed out of the establishment's parking lot with Hilda following in her car. Jorge Salcido was thirty-seven years of age and worked as a production manager at a Dallas-based Ciudad Juárez assembly plant called Affiliated Computer Services, Inc. Hilda worked at the consulate. Just moments after the two cars began heading east on Insurgentes Avenue, a wide street with two lanes in each direction, a commando group in a Ford Explorer pulled up to Jorge Salcido's car as he idled at a stoplight and began firing at him, killing him instantly. Hilda jumped out of her car and ran up on the *sicarios*, screaming at them to stop, that her children were in the car, but they paid her no mind. They finished their job and then coolly boarded their vehicle and left. Hilda was fortunate not to have been killed. She was also fortunate that her children were not killed, although two of them, the four-year-old and the seven-year-old, were wounded (one having been grazed by a bullet and the other cut by shards of flying glass from the car's shattered windows).

Lesley Enríquez and her husband, Arthur Redelfs, left the party at the same time as the Salcidos. They'd just strapped their seven-month-old daughter into the back seat of their white Toyota RAV4 before pulling out into the flow of traffic on Insurgentes Avenue. Lesley Enríquez was three months pregnant. She and her husband lived in El Paso, although Lesley commuted into Juárez every day to her job at the U.S. Consulate. They initially headed west on Insurgentes, driving in the opposite direction the Salcidos had been traveling, before jagging north toward Chamizal Park and Malecón Avenue (which runs east-west next to the Rio Grande) on their way toward the international bridge. They were unaware of the fact that all the while they were being followed by a black Suburban.

Just as the couple reached the back side of city hall, less than a hundred feet from the turnoff to the Santa Fe International Bridge, the assassins aboard the Suburban came up on them and raked their vehicle with AK-47 and 9mm fire. With Redelfs dead or mortally wounded, the car veered across the lanes into oncoming traffic, striking two more vehicles before coming to rest almost directly beneath the windows of Mayor Reyes Ferriz's office. Above the crime scene, the Santa Fe International Bridge made its ascent over the Rio Grande before sliding back down into El Paso on the other side. It being Saturday afternoon, typically a heavy day for foot traffic as Juarenses crossed over to shop, a line of pedestrians filled the entire span of the bridge; many of them witnessed the cold-blooded assassination from that vantage. It was 2:40 p.m.; the interval between the two executions had only been ten minutes.

The municipal police, their redoubt only a hundred yards away— testimony to the indifference of the cartel operatives to local law enforcement—quickly arrived at the scene on Malecón Avenue. Both of the adults in the vehicle were clearly dead, Lesley from a shot to the head, Arthur from multiple wounds. But the police could hear the weak cries and whimpers of the little girl still strapped into her car seat behind her parents. They assumed she was wounded and worked feverishly to pry the car's door open, a task made difficult because it had been crushed by the impact with the other vehicles, but it turned out that she was only frightened by the violence and the bloody sight of her bullet-riddled, lifeless parents in the front seat.

There had been some forty documented murders of Americans over the course of the drug war, but none of them had been employees of the U.S. government, with the exception of a U.S. Army soldier murdered in a Juárez bar a year earlier when *sicarios* had killed several people at the establishment.

Scattered across Mexico over the course of three and a half years, those murders had hardly raised a stir, but the targeted assassination of three individuals with ties to the U.S. Consulate in Juárez was another matter.

The executions sent shock waves through both the Mexican and the U.S. governments. In a public statement, President Barack Obama expressed his outrage and sadness, and other American officials vowed to "break the power" of the Mexican drug cartels. But the stronger gesture came from the U.S. State Department. The day following the consulate executions, on March 14, 2010, they released the following statement: "The Department of State has issued this Travel Warning to inform U.S. citizens traveling to and living in Mexico of concerns about the security situation in Mexico, and that it has authorized the departure of the dependents of U.S. government personnel from U.S. consulates in the Northern Mexican border cities of Tijuana, Nogales, Ciudad Juárez, Nuevo Laredo, Monterrey and Matamoros . . ." Further on, the State Department Travel Warning also noted that "recent violent attacks have prompted the U.S. Embassy to urge U.S. citizens to delay unnecessary travel to parts of Durango, Coahuila and Chihuahua states." The U.S. embassy in Mexico City instructed its employees to postpone all travel to the troubled states. In short, the U.S. government was resorting to extreme measures to protect its personnel, the kind of measures it typically employs in war zones like Iraq, Libya, or Pakistan.

Even as the U.S. government updated its travel warnings, both the U.S. and the Mexican governments simultaneously sought to lower the incident's public profile. The U.S. government issued a statement asserting that its directive authorizing the departure of dependents of employees at the six consulates and temporarily postponing all travel to the three states had already been "in the pipeline" prior to the three executions in Juárez.

U.S. officials were also quick to point out that neither Lesley Enríquez nor Hilda Salcido had been involved in "sensitive" operations within the U.S. Consulate in Ciudad Juárez that would have made them cartel targets, underscoring the fact that neither worked in drug- or intelligence-related areas. Lesley Enríquez's job (she had dual citizenship, Mexican and Canadian) was in the American Citizen Services section and involved assisting U.S. citizens needing travel-related documents such as passports and consular reports of births abroad, in addition to occasionally helping American citizens get the remains of loved ones who happened to have died in Mexico back to the United States. Hilda Salcido, also a Mexican citizen, had been employed by the consulate for thirteen years and worked in the Consular Services section, which meant she had some exposure to Mexican citizens seeking visas to travel to the United States. Four days after the murders, the FBI in El Paso issued a statement indicating that "at this point we have no reason to believe any of the three victims were targeted because they were U.S. citizens or because of their jobs, but the investigation is continuing."

In a flurry of hypotheses and freewheeling flights of fancy, each of the victims (or their spouses) was woven into one scenario or another in an attempt to make sense of the executions. One of the primary strategies for defusing the crisis was to suggest that perhaps the *sicarios* had made a mistake. Under this theory, the target had been Jorge Salcido, whose status as a non–U.S. citizen who was also not a U.S. government employee conveniently distanced the killings from anything related to the consulate. The U.S. consul, Raymond McGrath, told *El Diario* that "from the first hours on Saturday, after the attacks, the available information has been that the attack against Lesley Enríquez and Arthur Redelfs was a mistake. . . . As for Mr. Salcido, we don't know yet." Many in the media pounced on that explanation and gave it play. CNN, for example, headlined a story that noted that the authorities had "not ruled out a case of mistaken identity."

Within this narrative, Lesley Enríquez and Arthur Redelfs had been killed because they, like Salcido, had also been traveling in a white SUV, a fact that purportedly had confused the *sicarios*, leading them to wipe out both vehicles rather than running the risk that their prey might elude them. It was also reported that Salcido had been the object of extortion threats, requiring him to change his home, work, and cell phone numbers. One of the Mexican newspapers reported that "it has been said" that Jorge Salcido might have been a former municipal police officer or state ministerial police officer, implying that perhaps he had links to the cartels. But Narco News, a popular website for people following Mexico's narco-war, cited anonymous law enforcement sources suggesting that Lesley Enríquez had perhaps been the main target. On at least two occasions, according to those sources, an individual "in consulate-related settings" had tried to pressure Enríquez into "doing something with a document" without the proper paperwork. Reflecting on the universe of theories, Narco News speculated that Salcido might have been the individual pressing Enríquez.

One of the more persistent theories initially making the rounds centered on Arthur Redelfs, who was a detention officer with the El Paso Sheriff's Office. His job was to ferry prisoners from their holding cells to their courtroom appearances when they had hearings. That meant that Redelfs routinely handcuffed prisoners, which may have meant tense exchanges with prisoners. The idea that Redelfs had been the target as revenge for some unknown conflict with prisoners was seemingly buttressed by the Mexican Army's arrest of a man named Ricardo Valles, purportedly a member of El Paso's Barrio Azteca gang, considered a "sibling" of Juárez's much-feared Los Aztecas. Valles claimed to have received orders from within El Paso's county prison, a Barrio Azteca stronghold, instructing him to kill Arthur Redelfs. He claimed that he then followed Redelfs to the party at Barquito de Papel. The killing of Jorge Salcido had been a mistake, Valles maintained, due to the fact that he was in a white SUV similar to the one that Redelfs was driving. The motive, Valles asserted, was that Redelfs had threatened and mistreated Barrio Azteca prisoners. Redelfs's coworkers in the Sheriff's Office scoffed at that idea, noting that he was too smart to have tangled with Barrio Azteca gang members, and Redelfs's family described him as mild-mannered and friendly, a man whose personal qualities made him anything but prone to hostile interactions.

Finally, one of the more bizarre theories was that perhaps the killings had been a consequence of a directive issued by the consulate the day prior to the murders forbidding consular employees from entering a nearby bar called El Reco. The bar was presumably a narco hangout, but the idea that the bar owner, even if he was affiliated with a cartel, would carry out such an execution out of revenge seemed far-fetched, even though McGrath acknowledged it as merely "a hypothesis" that was "floating around."

It all added up to a tangle of contradictory and irreconcilable theories and speculations, most of which were, on their faces, implausible or simply too far-fetched. The concreteness of the government's theory (emphasizing that since neither of the consulate employees had been working in an area related to security or drug investigations, it was unlikely that they would be cartel targets) ignored everything known about the cartels and how they operate. It pretended that narco-logic was linear, as if it were beyond the cartels to select targets because of their symbolic value or because of the message that they might be intending to send. In fact, both governments knew that the cartels were masters of this kind of communication; there were countless examples of it. But the one theory that neither government put forth, the one theory that the media did not pick up, was the most obvious one: that one of the cartels was sending a message to American authorities that it viewed the high-profile involvement of American FBI and DEA agents in Juárez as an escalation. One of the cartels was answering that escalation with an escalation of its own. The message to the U.S. government was that there were plenty of "soft," vulnerable targets for the cartels to strike (in fact, the U.S. Consulate in Juárez is one of the largest in the world), and they could do so with ease if they so chose.

Supporting this thesis was the fact that the *Washington Post* story was covered extensively in the Juárez and El Paso media for several days. Even though there had been collaboration between American and Mexican federal agents for some time, the public announcement, whether or not it actually signaled a change or escalation, altered the perceived dynamics of the war in Juárez. And the cartels were not easily intimidated; they were brazen and bold and any student of their tactics knew that striking at the underbelly of American interests in Mexico was not beyond them if they deemed it necessary or useful (in March of 2011, cartel operatives killed ICE Special Agent Jaime Zapata in San Luis Potosí, even though the agent had clearly identified himself to the *sicarios*).

The video of the executions I saw during my visit to the CERI left me with an appreciation for the sophistication involved in cartel hits. In fact, when I described the videotape to a former American intelligence official, he said that it was evidence that the *sicarios* had undergone extensive training and were highly disciplined. *Sicarios* did not commit impulsive mistakes. They also knew the difference between a Toyota RAV4 and a Honda Pilot (even if both were white). They knew the difference between a Texas license plate and a Chihuahua license plate. These *sicarios* were professionals, not a ragtag group pumped up on cocaine and armed with AK-47s. There were plenty of the latter among the cartels' hit squads, gangbanger types who were enforcing neighborhood retail drug markets and carrying out petty vendettas against rival groups, but assignments to take down important, high-level targets in coordinated hits were given to seasoned professionals. Those people knew what they were doing.

At this point, in early 2010, Ciudad Juárez was still averaging more than seven or eight executions per day. In 2009 alone, 2,607 people had been killed in the streets of Juárez with hardly a blip on the American government's radar. Now, the execution of three people with links to the consulate sent the U.S. government into a state of heightened alert. For once, the United States seemed to be waking up to the problems that all of Mexico was facing, not only Juárez. "For the Mexican [federal] government, the massacre at Villas de Salvárcar was the turning point, the moment when they finally saw the full dimension of what was taking place here," José Reyes Ferriz later told me. "For the Americans, it was the assassinations of those three people related to the consulate. That was a watershed moment for them."

■ ■ ■

Mexican president Felipe Calderón must have felt thoroughly thwarted once again by the events in Juárez. He was scheduled to arrive in the city on Monday, March 16, to follow up the Todos Somos Juárez efforts, which had now been underway for a month. Calderón had expended great effort to make Todos Somos Juárez a success. The consulate executions of necessity changed the president's agenda. Rather than coming to Juárez to assess the progress of his government's most important initiative, Calderón was arriving amid another political furor; he was stepping into an international crisis that had already elicited comments from President Barack Obama and Secretary of State Hillary Clinton. When Calderón stepped off of the presidential plane, the focus was not on the Mexican federal government's efforts to rebuild the city and reignite its hope; instead, the focus was on the consulate executions and what they portended for the future, not only for Juárez but also for Mexico and U.S.-Mexico relations. Indeed, this may have been an additional motive behind the execution of the three individuals associated with the consulate.

The timing of the U.S. State Department's updated Mexico Travel Warning and war-zone directives regarding consular dependents in six border cities coincided with Calderón's arrival in Juárez. That reality no doubt propelled the Mexican president into an atypically aggressive stance toward the United States. When asked for his reaction, Calderón said pointedly and forcefully that "this is a binational problem and therefore the fight against drug trafficking is a responsibility of both governments."

However, there were other considerations also weighing heavily on the president's mind. With local, regional, and national elections just three months off, the timing of the consulate murders could not have been worse for a president whose poll numbers continued to drop and whose party, therefore, was at risk for losing substantial influence. Calderón himself was not up for reelection. By law, Mexican presidents serve a single six-year term, and the next presidential contest would not be until July 2012. But the stakes in the coming elections were high. In addition to federal congressional seats, mayorships and governorships were up for grabs all over the country, and a weakened president spelled problems for the president's party, the PAN. That, in turn, potentially spelled problems for the United States, who had found in Felipe Calderón a unique and strong ally.

Notes

1. Ortiz Arellano had been appointed by Mayor Reyes Ferriz in October 2009 to run the municipal prison. He was subsequently removed from that post in May 2010. In November 2010, he and his twenty-eight-year-old son were executed in Juárez.

2. Vicente Fox, Calderón's predecessor, had opened the doors to extradition of Mexican citizens to the United States. Under Calderón, extraditions of narco-traffickers had more than doubled.

CHAPTER 28

The Federal Police

In every interview I conducted with Mexican federal officials they were consistent about one fact: from the beginning of Felipe Calderón's administration, the strategy had been to deploy the Mexican Army as a stopgap measure until the federal and local police forces were strong enough to continue the war against the drug cartels. On April 8, 2010, five thousand additional federal police arrived in Juárez to relieve the army of its law enforcement duties. The army would continue patrolling the countryside around the city, as well as the highways, the Juárez airport, and the international bridges, but they would no longer conduct policing activities in Juárez. Since February 2008, when Patricio Patiño had promised José Reyes Ferriz two hundred reinforcements, the federal police had gradually increased its presence in the city to about 2,500. But it was the army that had taken over the city's policing duties when the municipal police was disbanded in March of 2009, and until April 2010 the army had been the most important player in the city's security operations, even as the federal police had gradually increased their profile.

The Juárez municipal police remained, at best, sputtering and inefficient, if not under the same level of cartel influence as in the past; their operations became, in effect, supervised by the federal police as of April 8, 2010. Gustavo de la Rosa, for one, welcomed the change. The army had generated some 1,500 human rights complaints before de la Rosa's Human Rights Commission, far more than the federal police, although those against the federal police were in some ways more severe. There were complaints against the army that included torture and murder, but the preponderance was for abuse of power, forced entry, those sorts of things. Though significantly fewer in number, the complaints against the federal police included extortion and kidnapping. For de la Rosa, a major advantage of having the federal police patrolling the streets was that civilian courts handled the human rights complaints against them, whereas closed military courts handled complaints against the army. This meant that it was more difficult to cover up complaints against the federal police.

The federal police expanded Juárez's historic six zones or precincts to

Federal police arrive in Juárez in force, April 2010. Photo copyright © Raymundo Ruiz.

nine sectors, permitting a more even deployment of resources across the city. They also broke the city down further into a grid consisting of 156 quadrants, with twenty-four-hour response teams, and they assumed control of the city's Emergency Response Center, upgrading the equipment with computerized work stations that helped them identify the GPS-equipped units that were nearest the locations where incidents were taking place. Finally, the federal police built a new command center. The question that remained was whether the investment of forces and upgraded technology would have an impact on what was taking place in the streets.

■ ■ ■

Genaro García Luna had been in Mexican law enforcement for twenty-two years, and for almost half of that time he had been heading efforts to clean up the nation's notoriously corrupt police forces by professionalizing them, raising salaries, and increasing training. During Calderón's tenure, the federal police had gone from roughly 6,500 officers (it had been called the Federal Preventive Police at the time) to its present 35,000 officers. Eight thousand of the agents had university degrees, and the level of training, including coursework with American and European law enforcement services, was unprecedented. The force could not be said to be beyond reproach—numerous officers had been caught participating in organized crime activities, including collaboration with the cartels—but it was far and above better and cleaner than any police force Mexico had ever seen.

Along the way, García Luna had incurred many enemies and found himself at the center of allegations that he was in the pay of El Chapo Guzmán, who, it was alleged, was using the federal police to support the Sinaloa cartel's activities. *Proceso,* a left-of-center magazine with a penchant for publishing grisly, full-color images of the narco horrors, once ran a story claiming that in October 2008 El Chapo had intercepted García Luna's security convoy on a lonely road near Cuernavaca, Morelos. The story claimed that El Chapo's men had disarmed and blindfolded García Luna's twenty-seven bodyguards before escorting him to a four-hour meeting with the Sinaloa cartel's top capo, after which El Chapo purportedly told Mexico's top law enforcement officer, sternly and within earshot of his bodyguards, "This is your first and last warning so that you understand that we can get to you if you don't live up to the agreements."

The account was improbable. García Luna travels with a minimum of ten highly armed men in vehicles with armor that can withstand a bomb blast; it is unlikely that they would have simply pulled over and allowed El Chapo's men to disarm them. Also, people like El Chapo Guzmán worked by way of intermediaries; they didn't suddenly show up in the middle of the night at roadblocks, as the story depicted. The purported source was an unnamed, disgruntled García Luna bodyguard who'd supposedly come forth because he felt "humiliated" at having to surrender his weapon to one of El Chapo's *sicarios*. The story had the ring of fantasy, but it was reported as fact in *Proceso*, without so much as a caveat that it could not be independently verified.

But the allegations were persistent and part of a larger thesis that argued that the federal forces in Juárez, both the army and the federal police, were acting as proxies for the Sinaloa cartel, in an attempt to wrest the *plaza* from the hands of the Juárez cartel. The fact that arrests and seizures appeared to be lopsided, with the Juárez cartel taking a disproportionate percentage of the hits, lent further credence to this allegation.[1] However, it was also true that Juárez was the home base of the Juárez cartel, whereas El Chapo's cartel was based in the state of Sinaloa and its presence in Juárez consisted of what might be termed an expeditionary force. In addition, on a national scale, the federal government had taken down many significant Sinaloa cartel capos and captured a great deal of their weapons and product, including tons of cocaine. The numbers simply did not support the allegations. According to official federal police documents, between December of 2006 (the start of the drug war) and November 2010, 1,919 cartel members had been arrested nationally. Of these, 365 belonged to the Sinaloa cartel and 178 to the Juárez cartel. The Gulf cartel had sustained the greatest number of arrests, at 703, with La Familia running second, with 570.

In a country where for decades the daily bread had been a social order governed by corruption, where almost every citizen had suffered the demands and indignities of predatory officials, from street corner cops to petty bureaucrats, and where citizens had seen the people at the top, including presidents and their cabinet ministers, enriched by insider deals and theft of the national patrimony, it was nearly impossible to view an official like García Luna as not made of the same cloth. The rumors of his narco-alliance with El Chapo were easy enough to believe and, in fact, impossible to discard outright, because the counterexamples were almost nonexistent. And, in any event, Mexico is a country that thrives on such rumors, where the disease of cynicism has sunk deep into the country's innermost tissues. When a magazine like *Proceso* ran front-cover headlines like "García Luna's Farce," well, what else was one to believe? In Mexico, it was difficult to develop a conviction that any politician and, certainly, anyone associated with law enforcement, was clean and had the best interest of the country foremost in his or her heart.

In addition to the fact that many Sinaloa cartel people had been taken down, my hesitation in accepting the otherwise widely accepted premise that federal forces were in the pocket of the Sinaloa cartel stemmed from personal observation: in the two years I'd been traveling to Juárez I had, on numerous occasions, spent time with some of the federal police. Having grown up in Mexico, I had the same instinctive mistrust of police that most Mexicans do. However, in Juárez, whenever possible, I approached federal police at crime scenes and tried to engage them in conversation. I typically found them polite but reserved, especially when they saw that I had a camera and a notebook. At one point, attending an all-day dog-and-pony show (which had not been particularly impressive or revelatory to me), I had found the commander in charge of the day, a man named José Galdino Menera Molina, a veteran, congenial enough. A couple of days before the official tour, twelve federal police officers (eleven men and one woman) had been found brutally tortured and murdered in Michoacán, their bodies dumped on a desolate road. A significant part of the Juárez federal police contingent was being redeployed to Michoacán, where, in ten separate attacks, members of the La Familia cartel had also ambushed patrols and shot up hotels where federal agents were bivouacked. I spent a couple of hours on the tarmac talking to the officers waiting to board the airplanes that would ferry them to Michoacán. They did not impress me as thugs; most were young men who planned careers in law enforcement and believed in what they were doing. They were outraged at what had happened to their comrades and aware that they were heading straight into harm's way. No doubt there were thieves, extortionists, and brutal men among them, but most were simply law enforcement officers doing their jobs.

One officer who I encountered at a narco-lab, where the federal police had found twenty kilos of cocaine, had initially been standoffish and even brusque, but over the course of the four hours that I was there (a rumor had circulated that they were going to permit a tour of the lab once they had secured its contents), he eventually warmed up. He was a young man, only on the force for two years. "The girls here won't even look at us," he lamented. "They all want narco-boyfriends, not men like us who are trying to do something for our country." It was a moment of candor from a man far away from home on what was an increasingly thankless mission.

I also spent time on three different occasions with a federal police intelligence inspector (the man who'd hosted the meeting at the Intelligence Center where I'd seen the videotaped executions). He was a career officer who was disenchanted with the force and nearing retirement. He'd taken me under his wing, twice inviting me to lunch with him and his troops at one of the hotels temporarily housing deployed federal police (the hotel obviously catered to by-the-hour clientele when there wasn't a narco-war going on in town). I'd seen the respect with which his people treated him, and he them. He'd talked candidly about his views regarding the expensive security cameras that had gone up all over the city. ("They're useless," he said. "They haven't helped us solve a single crime.") He'd given me books about Juárez and shown me books he was reading, one about unorthodox European approaches to rehabilitating prisoners and the concept of prisons without walls, and one about the history of drug use that argued that every civilization had used drugs and that they should be legalized. "That would put an end to most of this insanity," he'd said. The man was humble, and of humble origins; he was one of the older generation, the generation that had not gone to college, although his children were now at university.

I was aware of the fact that there were allegations that some of the federal police were extorting individuals and shopkeepers, competing with the local gangs for the *cuota*. Indeed, subsequently, in August of 2010, a group of 250 federal police officers mutinied in Juárez, accusing their commander, Salomón Alarcón Olvera, and his lieutenants of planting drugs and guns on people in order to extort them, while pressing the officers of their unit, the Third Group, to participate in their activities under penalty of losing their jobs. Those who did not comply were accused of crimes and arrested. In fact, the mutiny had been sparked by the arrest of an officer named Víctor Manuel Desid, who, his fellow officers maintained, had had drugs planted on him for not going along with Commander Alarcón Olvera's schemes. The mutineers had called the Juárez media after Desid's arrest, and when they arrived, the officers kicked in the door to the commander's quarters, where they found drugs and confiscated weapons that the officers said the commander and his people planted on innocent victims.

Alarcón Olvera and three of his lieutenants were immediately relieved of their duties.[2] Later that same month, Facundo Rosas, the director of the federal police and Genaro García Luna's right-hand man, announced that 3,200 officers had been relieved of their duties in recent months in a house-cleaning effort that had been underway since May of 2010. That represented nearly 10 percent of the federal police force. Of these, 465 had been charged with breaking the law, while another 1,020 faced disciplinary actions after failing portions of the Confidence Test.

I asked José Reyes Ferriz about his views regarding the federal police. "Some of them came to Juárez to do their jobs," he told me. "Others saw it as a 'business opportunity.'" He was well aware that there were federal police who were of the Alarcón Olvera mold, corrupt and, through that corruption, contributing to the losing battle for hearts and minds in Juárez. But in his view these were the exception. He said the federal police rotated through the city for three-month stints, after which the units were sent elsewhere, precisely in an effort to make it more difficult for them to be corrupted or engage in criminal activity. He also said that there had been several occasions on which he had asked Facundo Rosas to remove a unit because of allegations against it, and that Rosas had obliged every time he'd made such a request.

The mayor liked Genaro García Luna; he described him as strong, a man on a mission to leave his mark on Mexican law enforcement. "That's been his goal for years, everything he's trained for, aimed for, pushed for," Reyes Ferriz said. He also described him as a man with a strong need for control, which had led to skirmishes within Calderón's security cabinet, skirmishes that García Luna invariably won.

The fact that the federal police were taking over in Juárez was an example of that influence. Reyes Ferriz recalled arriving at the military garrison for a security meeting in January of 2010. "It was the top dogs," he said, given that the meeting included Guillermo Valdés, the head of the CISEN; Jorge Tello Peón, Calderón's national security advisor; Facundo Rosas, the director of the federal police; General Felipe de Jesús Espitia, commander of the 5th Military Zone; Governor Reyes Baeza; and the state prosecutor, Patricia González, among others. The surprise, however, was the presence of the U.S. ambassador to Mexico, Carlos Pascual, as well as representatives from the DEA and the FBI.[3] It was the mayor's impression that the Americans were pushing for the federal police to take over the Juárez operations, which is what was announced at the meeting. The shift was news to the army, which apparently did not take it well. General Espitia was furious, according to the mayor. "I thought it was a mistake," Reyes Ferriz said. "The army was becoming more and more effective." Reyes Ferriz suspected that the shift had not been implemented until April precisely because of the tensions it had created with the army. "WikiLeaks later confirmed it," the mayor added. "The U.S. was backing the federal police over the army."[4] Reyes Ferriz's point was that Genaro García Luna had won; "He clearly had the ear of the president," he observed.

When I asked the mayor his opinion regarding the allegations that García Luna was in league with El Chapo Guzmán and the Sinaloa cartel, he remarked that his gut instincts were that it was not so, with the caveat that in Mexico anything was possible. As for corruption within the federal police, his response was, "Look, there's corruption everywhere. That's just a fact." Mexico was engaged in a slow process of trying to change the mindset that fostered and lived within the culture of corruption, he noted. Sometimes it was also difficult to know with certainty what constituted corruption. He mentioned the famous security cameras that had been installed in Juárez. In his view, the price paid per camera had been excessive. Was that an artifact of corruption? "It's impossible to know," he said. The same was true for the upgrade of the municipal police's communications equipment from analog to digital. The police had Motorola equipment, which could have been upgraded by buying inserts and new keyboards—everything else required to go digital, including the towers, was already in place. Reyes Ferriz said that the federal police had insisted instead on French equipment that was more expensive. Perhaps there had been an insider deal there, or technological issues that justified the decision; there was no way of knowing, the mayor said. Was García Luna aware of this? Was it underlings? Were there other pressures to go that route? "Who knows," Reyes Ferriz said. "In Mexico it's still impossible to make deals without some of that. It's just inherent in the system. It's the way it all works," he concluded. But Reyes Ferriz distinguished this kind of business culture or this kind of corruption, if indeed it played a role, from being owned by one or another of the cartels. Reyes Ferriz told me that he trusted García Luna. Though he described him as ambitious, in his view those ambitions were in line with the good of the country and the effort to change the world of Mexican law enforcement from top to bottom. "I think he's a good policeman, a policeman with a vision," he concluded.

■ ■ ■

It took me a year and a half to secure an interview with Genaro García Luna. We met at the SSP (Secretariat for Public Security, SSP by its Spanish initials) headquarters—a recently refurbished and smartly designed compound in Mexico City that had once housed the Secretariat for Social Development. The SSP consisted of three administrative areas: the federal police, the federal prison system, and a unit responsible for providing security to federal buildings and administrative units such as the Mexican executive, legislative, and judicial branches. García Luna was one of the most influential players in Calderón's security cabinet; his ideas had held sway from the beginning of the administration and he'd survived a great deal of criticism as it became clear that the war against the drug cartels was not reducing the violence across the nation.

His office was an ample corner space with commanding views of the compound's well-maintained lawns, which were dotted with tall trees and crisscrossed by crisp paths. The walls in the office had a blond, beechwood veneer and the overall design of the room was quite modern, with clean lines throughout. His desk was large and orderly, with the telltale red phones via which he could reach the president at a moment's notice. I sat at a conference table, accompanied by his director of communications, Lizeth Parra, and her assistant.

García Luna strode into the room after I was seated. A man of medium stature with a sturdy frame, he sported a burr haircut and wore a navy blue suit, white shirt, and a fashionable electric-green tie. He was amiable and straightforward, talking at a quick pace with a modest speech impediment that the Mexican media has widely caricatured. In the interview, García Luna described his law enforcement philosophy, as well as his analysis as to why the situation in Juárez had proven to be so intractable. He talked law enforcement theory—the relationship between law and order and the state, civil society, and democracy, for example. He also described the evolution of the drug cartels in Mexico, referencing how the closing of the Caribbean by U.S. law enforcement had transformed Mexico into the primary funnel for Colombian cocaine headed to U.S. markets.

García Luna was especially animated when talking about the central role the federal police were playing in the war against the cartels country-wide, as it increasingly took the place of the army, and his plans to export the model of the federal police to state and municipal police forces. "It's obvious that you can't have a democracy if you don't have functioning police forces," he said, noting that the process of transforming the culture of the police and, especially, the public's perceptions of the police, was proving slow and difficult.

As for Juárez, García Luna spoke about how the enormous migration to the city of people seeking jobs at the maquiladoras in the 1980s had transformed the city. "You had countless families where the fathers were away working in the United States and the mothers were working in the maquiladoras," he noted, invoking Los NiNi without calling them such. He described Juárez as a city with the economy of a small country but one lacking in infrastructure, where streets had no lights, communities had no schools. He also described how the logistics of moving merchandise across the border (whether legal or not) were part of the city's identity, which is what had made it so indispensable to the cartels. Finally, he talked about the fact that the cartels had killed twenty-three federal police officers in the nine months preceding the interview, in what he described as a clear change in cartel tactics.

The head of the Secretariat for Public Security was very enthusiastic about the still-new Plataforma México, a national law enforcement database for tracking criminals with their police records, fingerprints, and other information; data about municipal, state, and federal police officers was also kept on Plataforma México, as were Interpol alerts and other information such as car registrations and license plates.

As the interview wound down, I told García Luna I had one last question. We both knew, I said, that there were allegations accusing him of links to the Sinaloa cartel. What did he have to say in relation to those? There was a pause and I braced myself for an angry response. Instead, he was surprisingly non-defensive. "Look," he said. "That goes with this territory. It is impossible to be in this position and not have these kinds of accusations. And it is all but impossible to defend yourself against them," he said. He cited the fact that his people had arrested many of El Chapo's men, including top capos, and he rattled off the quantity of drugs seized from the Sinaloa cartel. "I arrested El Chapo's brother," García Luna added.[5]

After a moment he continued, telling me that recently *Reforma*, the respected and politically moderate Mexico City newspaper, had printed an allegation that he lived in a two-million-dollar house (clearly beyond what was commensurate with his salary). The article further implied that there was no bill of sale for his prior home (suggesting, in other words, that the funds for the new house must have come from elsewhere) and that another home he owned in Juitepec, Morelos, was worth in excess of a million dollars. García Luna cited this to illustrate that he had been the object of "systematic calumny and defamation" because of his position, in addition to sustaining death threats against him and his family. "Any journalist could have tracked down the facts by searching public documents," he told me. García Luna had written a rebuttal to the allegations, noting his annual salary over the prior three years (for the most recent, 2009, his salary had been the equivalent of $327,000 U.S. dollars), as well as bonuses and a severance package from the PGR over the same interval. I was subsequently shown purchase documents, and a copy of his mortgage on his home. The purchase price for the home, including renovations, came to $808,000 (less than half the value alleged in the *Reforma* piece). A portion of that had been paid for by the sale of his prior home, which he'd sold for a modest profit (there was a copy of the bill of sale documenting the transaction). An outstanding mortgage covered the difference. *Reforma* had subsequently published García Luna's response to the piece. I later found several references in other media accounts to the original allegations that García Luna lived in a two-million-dollar home, with no reference to his rebuttal and without supporting documentation.

As with everything in Mexico, it was impossible to know with certainty what was factual and true beyond doubt. Not being an accountant, not having been privy to the transactions, and having no way of evaluating the validity of documents I'd been shown, I had no way of certifying what I was told by García Luna and his people. What was undeniable, however, was that Mexico's war against the cartels turned as much on what people believed to be true as it did on what was actually taking place. Another way of framing the problem, however, was just as true: if people had been living relatively free of fear in their communities, rumors such as those that impugned Genaro García Luna would have found much less traction.

Notes

1. In Juárez, federal authorities had arrested 262 people affiliated with the Juárez cartel and only sixty affiliated with the Sinaloa cartel.

2. Alarcón and the three lieutenants were subsequently charged and sent to federal prison.

3. This meeting took place a month prior to the February 24 *Washington Post* story disclosing just this kind of collaboration.

4. WikiLeaks suggested that part of the U.S. government's rationale was that the federal police were better positioned to interface with Mexico's judicial institutions and thus were the logical ones to be in the forefront of the cartel war—which, in any event, had been the strategy from the beginning.

5. Arturo Guzmán Loera, whose nickname was "The Chicken," had been arrested in 2001. During the seven years that El Chapo was in the Puente Grande prison, until his escape in 2001, Arturo Guzmán played a key role in managing the Sinaloa cartel for his brother. Arturo Guzmán was assassinated at the La Palma maximum-security federal prison in 2004.

CHAPTER 29

The Election

J osé Reyes Ferriz walked out of his oak-paneled office, through an ample foyer and a conference room, to his personal elevator. It was the fourth of July 2010, a day of national elections in Mexico, elections that most pundits viewed as a referendum on Calderón's drug war policies. Reyes Ferriz was on his way to vote. In a number of states, including Chihuahua, governorships were up for grabs, in addition to congressional seats and mayorships.[1]

The PRI slate for the Chihuahua elections had been set the night of March 9 at the Westin Soberano hotel in Ciudad Juárez, when the representative of the party's National Executive Committee, Adela Cereso, had arrived from Mexico City to meet with the contenders. Typically, the exiting governor had great influence over the selection of candidates, and José Reyes Baeza had his lineup: Héctor Murguía would replace him in the governor's slot and Víctor Valencia would be the party's candidate to be the mayor of Juárez. But Reyes Baeza had not counted on César Duarte, who had recently completed his second term as a federal deputy in congress, where his skill at working with other political parties had earned him the influential position of president of the Chamber of Deputies. Duarte, who had the support of Mayor Reyes Ferriz, was well liked within the party at a national level. Much to the governor's dismay, Cereso told him that César Duarte, not Hector Murguía, would be the PRI's gubernatorial candidate. Duarte had succeeded in outflanking the governor's plans.

Cereso then convened the six aspirants for the Juárez mayor's job, one of whom was Víctor Valencia, who'd arrived at the meeting under the impression that he had the position sewn up. Cereso announced to the group that Héctor Murguía would be the party's "unity" candidate to be mayor of Juárez. Furious, Víctor Valencia stormed out of the meeting in protest. Duarte strenuously opposed Murguía's candidacy, but was given no choice: it was a bone thrown to Reyes Baeza, who'd been preempted in terms of the gubernatorial succession.

Foiled in his campaign to secure his party's nomination for the governor's slot, Murguía had accepted the consolation prize: he hoped to land his second stint as mayor of Ciudad Juárez, where he'd been mayor between 2004 and 2007, the term immediately preceding that of Reyes Ferriz. The animosity between the mayor and Murguía was such that Reyes Ferriz decided to back the PAN candidate for mayor, a man named César Jáuregui, rather than Murguía.

Everything about César Jáuregui communicated that he came from a modest background. Early in the campaign, Jáuregui had appeared on *El Malilla* (*The Bad Boy*), a local TV show popular among the maquiladora workers and working-class Juarenses. El Malilla, the host, was fast-talking and quick-witted in a streetwise sort of way, sparring with his guests in his customary short sleeves, jeans, and skullcap. El Malilla's language was chock-full of street slang, his manner Mexican urban hip-hop; he exuded working-class sensibilities. All of this would have seemed to stand in contrast to Jáuregui, dressed in a pressed baby-blue dress shirt and slacks, but Jáuregui came across as a guy who was more comfortable with a beer in hand at a backyard barbecue than at an upper-class cocktail reception. He was chubby, with short-cropped hair and the look of the sharp-witted elementary-school kid who had found his place in the peer group despite an absence of cool.

Jáuregui invoked his class origins by telling El Malilla that his background was "of the people." He wanted to help people in their communities, in their barrios, he said. He told El Malilla that the reason improving public transportation was a priority for him was that he had grown up taking the bus back and forth to school. By the end of the show, Jáuregui had apparently passed the test; he received El Malilla's on-camera endorsement.

But the heart and soul of Jáuregui's campaign was less about public transport (a major concern for working class Juarenses) than the more pressing issue, the more obvious issue: the violence that had eviscerated Ciudad Juárez over the last three years. His pitch was consistent: a vote for Murguía was a vote for the dark narco-forces that were destroying the nation, not just the city. His campaign spots were thinly veiled accusations that Murguía was under the control of the Juárez cartel, if not an outright "Godfather."

"It's a horrible feeling, going through our city that has accumulated so much pain," Jáuregui said in one of his commercials. "With more than six thousand families in mourning because they've lost a loved one in a war that few can make sense of, we need a municipal president *a quien no le den línea* (who won't toe the line)." In the spot, the words "the line" echoed in reverberated accentuation, bringing home an obvious reference to La Línea, the Juárez cartel's feared shock troops. That reference was not lost on anyone in Juárez. But Jáuregui also took on the Sinaloa cartel, saying that the city also did not need someone who would "sell it short." The specific phrase he used, however, was a play on words, because *achaparrar* means to shorten or to make short, and everyone knew that El Chapo's nickname meant "shorty." The message that Jáuregui wanted the voters to take home was that he would not deliver the city to either La Línea, that is, to the Juárez cartel, or to El Chapo Guzmán. In one of the campaign's face-to-face televised debates, Jáuregui directly accused Murguía of being a Juárez cartel operative, citing a report that had appeared in *El Universal*, a respected Mexico City newspaper, claiming that Murguía had purchased eleven million pesos worth of property on behalf of the Juárez cartel. He also cited a purported DEA report linking Murguía to La Línea (neither of these reports has ever been confirmed). A visibly furious Murguía threatened to sue Jáuregui over the allegations.

Though Héctor "Teto" Murguía presented himself as a populist, his background was upper class. He had started out running family businesses over thirty years ago, and at the time of the campaign he was president and general manager of twelve different companies, in addition to serving on the board of directors of several banks. But his public persona was that of a guayabera-wearing ordinary man who talked *norteño* slang and felt a kinship with the working class.

The Juárez mayoral campaign was a referendum on the local narco-war and the violence it had spawned. Jáuregui's views on Murguía were widely shared in Juárez. This was the same Murguía whom *El Diario* had accused of making Saulo Reyes rich with insider deals and who had imposed Reyes on the municipal police, making him its director of operations. Jáuregui insisted that electing Héctor Murguía was tantamount to delivering Juárez back into the hands of the Juárez cartel.

In the days prior to the election, Murguía's numbers were up and it was looking like the old guard was going to be back in the driver's seat in Juárez. That eventuality created a great deal of uncertainty as to the future of Calderón's project in the city. In his campaign spots, Murguía had attacked the federal police and the army, accusing them of committing rampant human rights abuses and of wreaking havoc upon the city. The federal forces were making things worse, not better, Murguía argued, calling for them to leave Juárez. On one radio show he'd mocked the "*chilangos*," a term of derision for people from Mexico City (most of the federal police were from the Federal District), making fun of their Mexico City accents and describing them as useless. José Reyes Ferriz made no effort to mask his dislike of Murguía. "He's absolutely nefarious," Reyes Ferriz told me.

One might have thought that such antics would alarm the citizens of Juárez, but throughout the city there was an emerging nostalgia for the ancien régime. The old days might have been laced with corruption, but the violence had been mostly "private" and limited to the narcos themselves; it had rarely spilled over into the public sphere, much less into every nook and cranny of the city, as it had over the last three years. The idea that a vote for Murguía was a vote for the Juárez cartel, whether or not it was true, had lost its toxicity. Like the national elections, the municipal elections were, in effect, a referendum on the city's stomach for continuing the fight.

■ ■ ■

As José Reyes Ferriz left his office to cast his ballot, members of his security detail were posted at the door to his office and at every door along the way to the elevator. As the mayor approached, Roberto, the head of the security detail, punched in the code that opened the elevator door. Two other bodyguards in bulletproof vests, carrying AR-15 automatic rifles, flanked the mayor. Roberto had managed the Ferriz family's security since the early 1980s, when Reyes Ferriz's father had been mayor of Juárez. Roberto was like family; his balding gray hair and sad brown eyes gave him the look of a kindly grandfather, but with the demeanor of a man whose entire identity was bound up with the concept of security.

Throughout much of the country, the elections were fraught with fear, but this was especially so in the numerous states where the narco-traffickers held sway. The prior week, in the border state of Tamaulipas, the leading gubernatorial candidate, Rodolfo Torre Cantú from the PRI, had been executed along with most of his entourage at eleven in the morning as they made their way to a local airport during a final campaign swing. Calderón had described his assassination as "an assault against democratic institutions."

In Juárez, for days now the cartels had been threatening to attack and kill people at voting precincts and to assassinate candidates. I'd spent an afternoon at the electoral center where workers were preparing ballot boxes to be delivered to the various precincts, and it was evident that people were nervous. No one knew what to expect. Under the circumstances, it took courage, not just a sense of civic duty, for these men and women to do their jobs. Just two days earlier the cartels had left signs all over the city threatening to behead Mayor Reyes Ferriz and execute his wife and children.

This very morning the mayor had awoken to the news that in Chihuahua City five men had been executed and left hanging from bridges. As in recent elections in war-torn Iraq and Afghanistan, in parts of Mexico elections were being conducted under the threat of mass violence against citizens who showed up to vote. It was full-bore narco-terrorism: the intent of the cartels was to intimidate and frighten the populace and thereby shape electoral outcomes, in a context in which some experts were saying the number of narco-candidates was unprecedented. Such efforts would have their intended effect: in Juárez only about a third of the electorate would turn out to vote.

The mayor was in constant touch with the commander of the Juárez garrison, assessing the state of security. "*Mi general,*" Reyes Ferriz said, taking a call on his cell phone. "What else is going on?" A call from the representative of the federal forces informed him that there were renewed threats to burn polling places and shoot voters and candidates. "We're on alert," the mayor responded.

For José Reyes Ferriz and his team, there was tension in every move. Everyone knew that the threats were real. One could see it in the eyes of his security detail: they approached the mayor's movements with the same deliberation that combat soldiers use when traversing open terrain in a war zone. The security challenges were daunting, but showing up at his precinct to vote was an obligation that came with the office of mayor. This was especially true given the circumstances; public figures all over the country would be out today performing their civic duty. There wasn't even a discussion of the matter: the mayor had to appear in front of the cameras and vote.

Three of Ferriz's security detail stepped into the elevator with him and descended to the first floor, which opened to a private garage where three Suburbans lay in wait. The mayor's Suburban, with the highest armor rating, had the door to the back seat open, with a guard posted next to it. Once the mayor entered the vehicle the engine was fired up and the garage doors opened. The lead car exited the garage into the city hall parking structure, where a fourth Suburban was waiting for the convoy outside. This vehicle led the way through the garage and into the street, where it assumed a blocking position: the body of the vehicle was perpendicular to oncoming traffic. The mayor's car roared into the street past the blocking car and onto Malecón Boulevard (near the spot where Enríquez and Redelfs had been assassinated a few months prior), en route to the mayor's precinct. The other three Suburbans followed, one occupying the right lane so that no one could pull alongside the mayor's vehicle (the favored *sicario* modus operandi for executions), and the other two trailing close behind. Each of these other vehicles was carrying four bodyguards, armed with an AR-15 and a pistol each. The rear seats of the two trailing Suburbans had been configured so that they faced backward, making it easier for the security team to monitor the rear of the convoy and detect approaching danger.

On the way, the mayor received a call from César Duarte. "Things look good," he told Duarte. "There's a lot of enthusiasm out there," he said as the convoy happened to pass by the enormous home, replete with indoor swimming pool and tennis courts, that was built in the 1990s by Amado Carrillo Fuentes, the notorious head of the Juárez cartel. The home was so close to the U.S.-Mexico border that man with a good arm could almost throw a baseball from the rooftop of the house to the Rio Grande. The mayor made no mention of the death threats or the hanging bodies in Chihuahua City, but he did interrupt the gubernatorial candidate: "Don't say it," he said to him at one point. "I'm on a cell phone." It was the ever-present wariness that one comes to know so well in Juárez.

When the caravan arrived at the polling place, a public school, a half dozen of the mayor's bodyguards exited their vehicles and secured the area. Some attempted to blend into the crowd, pistols bulging from beneath their untucked shirts. My impression from the communications was that the detail also had people in place at the site prior to the mayor's arrival. When everyone was in position, the go-ahead was given for Reyes Ferriz to exit his vehicle. He was met by a crush of journalists who followed him to the school's gate before he continued into the school, escorted by a single bodyguard, to cast his ballot. Roberto stayed at the entrance to the school, sizing up every person who entered.

While the mayor was voting, a man pulled up in a pickup truck and parked across the street. When he exited the truck, one of the mayor's people thought he'd spotted a gun in the man's belt under his shirt. The security team closed in on him and three of them stopped him before he could enter the schoolyard. They had him surrounded, hands on their own guns, as they engaged him in an agitated exchange. The man claimed to be a state ministerial police officer, which is why he was armed, he said, flashing his police badge. There was a flurry of communication among the people in charge of the mayor's security, who were both in the various vehicles and deployed around the school. Finally, the mayor's people escorted the man to his pickup truck, where he deposited his gun before returning to the school, presumably to cast his ballot. The incident left everyone on the mayor's security team feeling unnerved.

Before long, a suspicious car that had been spotted earlier became the focus of concern. The car was parked under a tree across the street in an empty lot toward the end of the block, some thirty yards away. "They've been there for over an hour and a half, which makes us suspicious," the mayor's driver told me. There were three men in the vehicle—an aging, beat-up van—and nothing about them suggested that they had come to the school out of civic duty. "They're *halcones* (hawks)," the driver said—the eyes and ears of the cartels. The hypothesis was that they were there monitoring the mayor's activity. One of the mayor's SUVs was moved and positioned between the entrance to the school and the suspicious van. "Our people are on them," I was told.

Just then, word came that the mayor was exiting the polling place. The same group of reporters met him at the gate and the mayor stopped briefly to answer their questions, but he was pressed by Roberto and the bodyguard who'd been escorting him to board his vehicle, which had now moved up to the school's entrance. The mayor's team was jittery, given the presence of the presumed *halcones* and the armed man they'd intercepted. Nerves settled noticeably once the mayor was safely inside his armored Suburban, and so did the communications chatter among his people.

Back at the Municipal Presidency, the mayor and I followed the elections on the fifty-two-inch flat-screen television that hung from a wall in his office. His assistant had brought us lunch (hamburgers from the Arby's across the street and coffee from Starbucks). Duarte was no surprise for governor; he'd been ahead in the polls all along and cruised to an easy victory over his opponent. But even though Murguía had also been ahead, there had been a thread of hope that Jáuregui, his opponent, would pull ahead. That hope evaporated quickly once the exit polls began to come in: "Murguía's got it," the mayor told me, with obvious resignation. He hit the mute button on the remote as if he'd had enough, leaving silent images to bounce across the screen.

We sat in silence for several minutes. Not long after, as if others had arrived at the same conclusion, Reyes Ferriz received a call from someone at the Juárez Federal Police command center. "All of the top commanders are flying to Mexico City on Monday morning," the mayor told me once he was off the phone. "They are going to deliberate about what comes next. They don't want to work with this guy," he said, in reference to Murguía.

But like it or not, Héctor Murguía was back. The word on the street was that people thought he might be able to broker a peace between the Juárez and the Sinaloa cartels. They were fed up with the violence; they wanted someone to tone things down. Three years of killing sprees, extortions, and rampant crime coupled with a year and a half of near–state of siege with army and federal police roadblocks all over the city had exhausted the populace. As July 4, 2010, drew to a close, the heat of the Chihuahuan desert was heavy on the city where Héctor Murguía had just been reelected mayor. José Reyes Ferriz's term was set to expire three months hence. When I asked what he planned to do when he left office his response was vague, as if he were pondering that very question and had yet to come up with an answer.

■ ■ ■

The mayor of Juárez is a creature of habit. On the morning of Saturday, October 10, José Reyes Ferriz awoke at 5:30 a.m., as was his custom. After looking at the LCD screen on the nightstand to check the household cameras, he ambled down the stairs and unlocked the bank vault door. A metallic groan accompanied the opening of the fortification that separated the landing at the foot of the stairway from the living room and the entry to the house. Padding his way into the kitchen, the mayor poured himself a glass of orange juice before sitting down to his laptop at the dining room table and starting his morning ritual of scanning his favored news sites, which were preset to pop up when his computer came to life. For three years he'd considered this his daily homework: it was his job to know what was taking place in Juárez and elsewhere in Mexico and what people were saying about it. Always, the first site was the federal government's daily news bulletin, announcing everything from new developments in federal law to the most recent presidential appointments. This was how Reyes Ferriz kept

José Reyes Ferriz delivers his final state of the city address, October 2010. Photo copyright © Ricardo Ainslie.

a finger on the pulse of what was going on in Mexico City. Next he read *El Diario*, the most important paper in Juárez, whose circulation was ten times that of its nearest competitor, *El Norte*. *El Diario*'s coverage of local and regional news was by far the most extensive and accurate, even if the paper's views did not always align with the mayor's. Reyes Ferriz eventually got up to make himself a cappuccino from the espresso machine in the kitchen before finishing off the round of news with the Chihuahua newspapers, then *Excélsior*, *El Universal*, and *Reforma*, the leading Mexican national newspapers. He saved the American press (*USA Today*, the *Washington Post*, the *LA Times*, and the *New York Times*) for last. The lead story in *El Diario* that morning was the transfer of power to Héctor "Teto" Murguía; today was the last day that José Reyes Ferriz would be presiding over the city of Juárez.

When the urge struck, Reyes Ferriz got up from the table and went to the kitchen to cook up some breakfast. His favorite was eggs with *machaca*, strips of dried beef that are a regional specialty. He called his wife and children in El Paso every morning at this time to check in on their day. By the time he finished his morning routine of reading, breakfast, showering, and dressing, it was eight o'clock.

Over the course of his three-year term the mayor had been extremely circumspect about his relationship with Governor Reyes Baeza. In the countless press conferences and hundreds of interviews that he conducted over that interval, Reyes Ferriz had taken pains to shape and parse his words so as not to have a direct, public confrontation with the governor. The reasons were multiple, but it came down to the fact that in Mexico governors are exceedingly powerful and control many essential resources within their states. Any mayor, even the mayor of an important city like Juárez, had to factor in the governor's predilections in everything he or she did and said. To do otherwise was certain to make it almost impossible for a mayor to govern, a recipe for making a mayor's life miserable in infinite ways. Reyes Ferriz needed the governor's cooperation for funding the city's operations and projects, but he also needed to work with the governor on the political front, given that they belonged to the same political party. These considerations had precluded open conflict with the governor. However, the previous day, José Reyes Ferriz had chosen to stop playing this game. Both men were leaving office, and it was time to end the charade. The mayor arranged a meeting with three local journalists during which he placed a significant part of the responsibility for the enduring chaos in the city at the governor's feet, thereby publicly breaking with the governor. Reyes Ferriz accused the governor of blocking the mayor's efforts in myriad ways, but most egregiously by refusing to help fund Juárez's security needs and refusing to augment the presence of the state police in Juárez. Indeed, the mayor noted that the governor had repeatedly rebuffed him in his efforts to obtain state support for everything from law enforcement to public works.

Reyes Ferriz also accused the governor of protecting Patricia González, the state attorney general, whose ineptness or otherwise-motivated inefficiencies had resulted in judicial processes that were so defective that they had yielded successful convictions of only 2 or 3 percent of those arrested by municipal, state, and federal authorities. In a state with the highest crime levels in all of Mexico, González had presided over a legal system in which massive criminal impunity was the order of the day. Even by Mexican standards this was a travesty. There was no way to fight a war against the cartels when, no matter the evidence against them, most who were apprehended were back on the streets in a matter of days. As an institution for fighting crime, the Mexican legal system was as effective as trying to hold water in a sieve. It was an open secret of scandalous proportions, yet the Mexican Congress and the state legislatures continued to do little about the systemic failures of a dysfunctional judiciary. What should have mobilized local and national outrage was mostly set aside, the numbing aftereffects of a profound sense of helplessness: after nearly a decade of much-trumpeted judicial reform efforts in Mexico, *sicarios* and other drug cartel members, as well as kidnappers, extortionists, and ordinary criminals, were all but assured a free pass out of prison. And only a fraction of the criminals were even caught in the first place. Reyes Ferriz recounted to the journalists the many times he had privately complained to the governor about the state's attorney general, complaints that had had no impact. The governor was shielding Patricia González, Reyes Ferriz asserted.

José Reyes Ferriz described his conflicts with the governor as having multiple sources, among them the fact that the governor had energetically backed the candidacy of Víctor Valencia to succeed Reyes Ferriz. The mayor viewed Valencia as disreputable, and he and key allies had succeeded in blocking his political aspirations, notwithstanding the governor's support for Valencia. The story of the mayor's conflicts with the governor and the state attorney general was on the front page of *El Diario* that morning. As Reyes Ferriz readied himself for his final day in office, he knew city hall would be abuzz with it.

One of the last things the mayor did every evening before signing off was to confirm the next morning's departure time with his security team. Reyes Ferriz slept with a guard posted at the door to the house and a municipal police patrol car in front of the house. When the rest of his security detail arrived in the morning, the overnight crew joined the convoy, leaving the house with them. The morning exit was considered one of the riskiest moments of the day, given that the majority of kidnappings and assassinations took place when the target was leaving home: ambushes are more easily set along familiar routes. There were only two ways in or out of the mayor's subdivision, and the several miles down the Juan Pablo Segundo thoroughfare also made vehicles easy prey. Many executions had taken place along this very roadway. So mornings were always the most tense for members of the security detail. The mayor could see the tension in his bodyguards' faces and he felt it, too, as they took up their assigned positions and made their way out of the house and into the streets of Juárez.

The mayor's convoy roared out of the gated community and headed for the Presidencia Municipal for what was anticipated to be a simple, straightforward event. Although the new mayor had already been sworn in, Reyes Ferriz was still officially responsible for the city until the end of the day. The *entrega de poder*, as the formal handing over of power is called, was to begin at 10 a.m. and consisted of the mayor's team meeting with the city auditor and his people to review the inventory of equipment that the municipality had provided during Reyes Ferriz's term. Everything from cell phones to computers, office furniture, and decorations had to be checked off the inventory lists. Reyes Ferriz had anticipated that the entire process would take at most a couple of hours, but over the course of the morning all of his staff, as well as city council members and others who had been part of his team, filtered into the spacious, dark-paneled office to say good-bye. Everything that the city had endured, the grim state of the war, the seemingly endless assassinations, and the reign of terror that the cartels had brought upon the city somehow swelled the atmosphere of this good-bye, giving it an especially somber cast. Many of the men and women who came to bid the mayor farewell had worked together for years, some even prior to Reyes Ferriz's term. The camaraderie engendered by shared tribulation was clearly in evidence: the mayor's people had endured a great deal over the course of the last three years, more than any of them could have imagined at the time they'd signed on. There was also evident relief: Héctor Murguía would now be responsible for addressing the city's profound ills. The bureaucratic and tedious mechanics of checking serial numbers on everything in the office that was not the mayor's personal property, the mundane elements of the ritual of passing the torch of power, had become the pretext for a bon voyage reception for Mayor José Reyes Ferriz.

Reyes Ferriz left the Presidencia Municipal for the last time hours behind schedule, knowing full well that it was unlikely that he would ever return. Certainly returning to Juárez anytime soon would be akin to signing his own death warrant. Everyone knew that. Still in his armored Suburban, the mayor and his convoy headed back to the house to pick up his personal belongings. There, all of the men who had comprised the mayor's security detail congregated in the living room for a final good-bye. For Reyes Ferriz it was a moment filled with emotion. His life had been in the hands of these men for three years, and that meant that their own lives had been on the line as well, even more so: with the exception of the mayor's driver and the man who rode shotgun next to him, the other members of the security team rode in unarmored Suburbans whose sides and windows could be easily pierced by even small-arms fire, much less the ever-present assault weapons preferred by the narcos. Every time they walked out the door, every time they entered a restaurant or even stopped at a stoplight, the team had been fully conscious of the real possibility that a *sicario* commando group might make an assassination attempt. The threats had been persistent and brutal: severed human heads in trash-strewn lots, severed dog's heads with notes, and countless poster-board signs threatening to behead the mayor and kill his family. In a city where that kind of blood was seen on a daily basis, such threats were real; they spoke to declared intentions, not idle notions. Reyes Ferriz's life and the lives of these men had become deeply entwined, producing that rare intimacy borne of sharing moments of great fear and anxiety, but also the profound intimacy borne by the passage of simple, ordinary time: riding in vehicles together day in and day out, chatting or overhearing phone conversations between the mayor and his wife and children, or the ever-present conversations with state and federal authorities, including the president himself. The bodyguards were posted at meetings, they took up strategic positions at restaurants, and they counted on each other as they watched the back of the man they knew to be at the top of the cartels' target list. The only time the mayor was not with some subset of these men was when he crossed the river to attend a meeting or visit his family (at which times they met him at the bridge upon his return), or when he turned in for the night and made his way up the stairs, locking the bank vault door behind him. These men had safeguarded his life, and he was grateful to them. As a memento, in the living room of the house in Bosques de Aragón, the mayor gave each member of the security team a plaque acknowledging their service and thanking them for their courage and dedication.

As of the end of the day, the mayor would no longer have the protection of the municipality. His security detail was disbanding. Some, like Roberto, who had been the head of security for the mayor's father as well, were retiring. Others would be incorporated into the recently reorganized state police. Following the good-byes in the mayor's living room, the convoy left the house, headed for the Lerdo-Stanton Express Bridge, traveling along the Juan Pablo Segundo throughway that ran parallel to the Rio Grande. The mayor was in his armored Suburban, while the other Suburbans trailed behind. One of his men followed in the mayor's personal car, a red 2006 Volkswagen Passat. When they arrived at the bridge the convoy stopped one last time. The mayor exited the security of his armored vehicle and gave Roberto an *abrazo* before waving good-bye to the rest of the men who had been his trusted guardians for three long, hard years. He then stepped into his own car.

Pressing down on the accelerator, José Reyes Ferriz moved slowly into the sparse traffic crossing the bridge into El Paso. Evening had set in, and the lights along the bridge were already aglow. Below, the trickle of water making its way toward the Gulf of Mexico some eight hundred miles to the east was all but inaudible. Reyes Ferriz was alone now, finally set free of the war and violence that had left nearly seven thousand dead in his city over the last three years. Behind him, the lights of Juárez were also aglow, bright against the desert evening, like so many diamonds cast into the night.

Notes

1. Like governors, mayors in Mexico cannot succeed themselves. They get one three-year term, so Reyes Ferriz was not in the running.

Epilogue

Not long after the July 4, 2010, elections, attacks on the federal police in Juárez increased. Numerous officers were killed while off duty or on their lunch breaks. Near Villas de Salvárcar, federal police were lured into an ambush by a report that several young women were being abducted. When a patrol arrived at the scene, *sicarios* opened fire on them from various perches, killing and wounding several officers.

The most troubling incident was an Iraq War–style terrorist attack that took place on the evening of July 15, 2010. The previous day, the federal police had captured Jesús Armando Acosta Guerrero (aka El 35), the third-most important leader of the Juárez cartel and the head of La Línea. The following day, the federal police received a call to the Emergency Response Center reporting that there was a wounded police officer on the street at the intersection of Bolivia and 16 de Septiembre Streets. As a federal police convoy headed for the scene, they noticed that they were being followed and called for reinforcements. Arriving at the scene, they found a wounded man, bound and in a police uniform, lying beside a green Ford Focus, but as they approached, the car exploded. The blast was of sufficient force as to be heard for several kilometers around and windows in the immediate vicinity were shattered. Triggered by a cell phone after the federal forces had been drawn to the scene, the device was sophisticated, and the likes of it had never before been seen in Mexico. The toll was four killed: a federal police officer, a municipal police officer, one of the emergency responders, and a bystander, in addition to a score wounded, including six federal police. The car bomb was in retaliation for the arrest of Acosta Guerrero and it was the first time such tactics had been used in Juárez. A narco-message left near the Red Cross later that day, signed by La Línea, warned of more such attacks to come. A week later a car bomb with a much larger quantity of explosives was similarly set up, although this time the federal police succeeded in disarming the car bomb before it exploded.

Months later, on the evening of January 24, 2011, Héctor Murguía, the recently reelected mayor of Juárez, was having dinner with the spokesperson for the Catholic diocese of Ciudad Juárez. Just down the block, two of his bodyguards were standing on the corner of Cuitláhuac and Tlaxcala Streets, waiting for the mayor to wrap up his visit. It was around eight thirty in the evening.

Nearby, at the Hotel Santa Fe, which was serving as a bivouac for some of the federal police, a taxi driver pulled up to the agents standing guard and informed them that there were civilians armed with assault weapons two blocks away. A contingent of federal police left the hotel with the intent of checking out the suspicious men—the mayor's bodyguards, unbeknownst to the police.

Reports differ as to what happened next. The federal police say that when they approached the two men and asked them to identify themselves, one became belligerent and raised his weapon. The federal police shot him twice at close range as the other bodyguard threw himself to the ground.

Héctor Murguía offered a very different account of what had taken place. According to him, the federal police had approached his bodyguards while he was still dining with the priest. The two men had identified themselves as municipal police officers assigned to the mayor's security detail, but the federal police had shot the officer without provocation.

Hearing the shots, the rest of the mayor's security detail spirited him away in his armored Suburban, "following the security protocol for such situations." However, not long thereafter, the mayor and seven of his bodyguards arrived at the Hotel Santa Fe, where they blocked the entryway, and, armed, exited their vehicles. Murguía addressed the federal police who were standing guard, demanding an explanation for the shooting and the arrest of the officer responsible for it. Murguía claims the federal officers cursed and mocked him, and when he identified himself as the mayor of Juárez, Murguía claims he was told, "You aren't anybody here, son of a bitch!"

The standoff was tense and volatile, as an angry Murguía confronted the federal police and both sides trained their weapons on one another for an extended interval. It was only defused after a federal police commander and Murguía settled things down. Murguía subsequently called a press conference, where he asserted that the federal police had murdered his bodyguard "in cold blood." "If this is what the federal authorities do to a bodyguard who identified himself, lowered his weapon, and raised his hands in a gesture of peace and they killed him . . . What must be happening to ordinary citizens?" Murguía remarked. "God only knows how I wasn't killed," he added. In the incident's aftermath, two federal police officers were arrested and charged with homicide, abuse of authority, and improper behavior.

Several months later, Mexican federal police fired on the convoy of the new Juárez chief of police, Julián Leyzaola, as he headed for the municipal jail following the execution of seventeen prisoners who were members of the Artistas Asesinos. Members of the rival gang Los Aztecas, armed with assault rifles and handguns, had assassinated them. These incidents, as well as another in which Murguía claimed that federal police had pointed their weapons at members of his security detail (Murguía was caught on tape berating the federal officers, jabbing his finger into their chests, telling them that he was in charge of Juárez, not them) made it more than obvious that enormous strains existed between the municipal authorities and the federal police.

From the time of his campaign, Héctor Murguía had called for the withdrawal of the federal forces. By early summer of 2011, he seemed to be delivering on that campaign promise: he announced that there would be a "gradual withdrawal" of more than five thousand federal police from Juárez by the end of September 2011. In the year since the federal police had relieved the army and taken charge of the city, the tally of the dead had dropped noticeably (from an average of eight and a half executions per day to six), but killings remained at war-zone levels. A source within the federal police told me that an unspecified number of federal agents would remain in Juárez "to conduct operations relevant to federal offenses." However, the Juárez municipal police would henceforth have responsibility for areas of the city's security "which by law fall under their purview." The decision was further evidence of a profound rift between the municipal and federal authorities, although neither publicly acknowledged it as such. What was undeniable was that the federal forces did not have anything that resembled an ally in Héctor Murguía. If their relations with José Reyes Ferriz had at times been strained, Calderón's security cabinet no doubt now longed for the days when they felt a sense of collaboration with the mayor of Juárez.

■ ■ ■

In May of 2011, I met with a Mexican intelligence officer at the Centro de Investigación y Seguridad Nacional, CISEN (he asked that he not be named). He outlined for me the reasons he believed that Mexico was winning the war against the drug cartels. At the time the Calderón administration came to power, in December 2006, there were five major cartels operating in Mexico: the Sinaloa cartel, the Juárez cartel, the Tijuana cartel, the Gulf cartel, and La Familia Michoacana. Those cartels were operating relatively free of interference from Mexican law enforcement or the Mexican Army. In some parts of the country they controlled significant territory and the institutions within that territory. His summary reminded me of Eduardo Medina-Mora's statement, when I'd interviewed him in London, in which he'd emphasized that at the time that Felipe Calderón launched the war, Mexico had no choice as to what to do; the cartels were no longer simply organized crime groups conducting their business, they had become a threat to the Mexican state.

The strategy of "disarticulating" the cartels has been largely successful, the CISEN officer told me. The command and control structure of the cartels has been decimated and the cartels severely fractured. Twenty-one of the thirty-seven individuals on Mexico's Most Wanted list had either been apprehended or killed.[1] Of the five original cartels, two of them, the Juárez cartel and the Tijuana cartel, were mere shadows of their former selves (the Juárez cartel continued to control the important border crossings in Chihuahua, and their war with the Sinaloa cartel continued in the state's cities and rural areas, but the national scope of the Juárez cartel had been significantly reduced). The Gulf cartel had split into two warring factions, with Los Zetas, their armed wing, now fighting to take control of the Gulf cartel territory. La Familia Michoacana had atomized into small bands. The Sinaloa cartel, under the leadership of the mythic El Chapo Guzmán Loera, had always operated more as a federation of closely allied organizations, with Guzmán at the head. The Beltrán-Leyva organization had broken off from El Chapo in 2008 and had been at war with him ever since. Ignacio "Nacho" Coronel, a powerful leader within the Sinaloa cartel, had been killed in 2010. And there was evidence of ruptures between groups in Durango, the heart of El Chapo's territory. The cartels had been eviscerated by a combination of federal operations and internecine conflict, the intelligence officer summarized.

The CISEN agent told me that one factor making it increasingly difficult for the cartels to operate was that they were being hunted by a variety of Mexican military and law enforcement agencies. The Mexican Army and Marines operated independently of one another, and Mexican federal police had quintupled in size to a force of 35,000 officers (and U.S. sources described their cooperation with American law enforcement as unprecedented). Each of these entities was pursuing the cartels, sometimes collaboratively, sometimes independently, and each had taken down important cartel capos. There were too many players tracking down the cartels and it was costly and difficult to pay all of them off. For example, even though the Beltrán-Leyva cartel had been paying the head of the organized crime unit in the Mexican attorney general's office $450,000 dollars a month to provide information about investigations and operations, Mexican Army special forces had arrested Alfredo Beltrán Leyva in January 2008. His brother, Arturo Beltrán Leyva, was subsequently killed in December of 2009 by the Mexican Marines. The federal police had also taken down top Beltrán-Leyva operatives.

A source who had served as a security advisor for President Calderón during the first two years of his administration suggested an additional variable making it more difficult and costly for cartels to ensure the control and protection to which they'd long been accustomed. Prior to 2000, in PRI-controlled, pre-democracy Mexico, what was decreed at the top levels of government was enforced all the way down to the poorest municipalities. That made corruption efficient. Well-placed bribes at the top controlled everything up and down the line. Today's playing field was much more complex, given that there were so many actors. Mexico's fledgling democratization had increased the cartels' cost of doing business. Once a country where a single party controlled everything, today Mexico's three most influential political parties controlled governorships and municipalities, making it more cumbersome and expensive for the cartels to control local and regional institutions. In response, the cartels had turned to raw intimidation, murdering mayors and attempting to influence electoral processes more directly.

The Mexican government was perhaps right in its assessment that it was "winning the war," if by winning they meant arrests of cartel operatives and the fragmentation of cartel operations. There had been unprecedented seizures of cash, weapons, and drugs over the course of the Calderón administration. The problem was that these successes had had no appreciable impact on the one index that mattered most to the Mexican public: the level of violence and the overall climate of lawlessness in some regions of the country. In fact, destabilizing the cartels had generated more violence and more crime, not less. Therein lay the paradox facing the government's efforts, a paradox that was not easily explained to a Mexican public for whom, in many communities, ordinary life consisted of daily fear of what might happen to them or to their loved ones each time they left their homes.

In addition to the bloody cartel-on-cartel warfare (the Sinaloa cartel attempting to seize control of the Juárez *plaza*, the Zetas attempting to take over the Gulf cartel's areas of operation, etc.), there were two additional factors behind the tidal wave of crime and violence in Mexico. One was the emergence of the Mexican retail drug markets that had begun slowly in the mid-1990s after the United States' Operation Hold the Line started making it more costly for the cartels to move product across the border. By 2000, Mexico, which had been a transit point for drugs but not a major consumer of them, was experiencing a precipitous rise in addictions and drug-related crime problems. The majority of deaths across the nation were due to gang-on-gang disputes related to the local retail drug business. Thus, some of this violence was more akin to the Bloods and the Crips killing one another off in the streets of South Central Los Angeles than cartel-upon-cartel violence per se.

The fracturing of the cartels had also resulted in a proliferation of criminal bands engaging in ordinary street crime, including the lucrative kidnapping and extortion rackets. In Juárez, I spoke to shopkeepers and small business owners who were deeply afraid of the extortionists. People who did not pay the *cuota* were executed or had their relatives or employees kidnapped, or their businesses burned to the ground (both as a consequence for not paying and as a way of terrorizing others who were being extorted). These crimes were taking an enormous toll on citizens, which is why Calderón's popularity was sagging, notwithstanding his government's success in dismantling the cartels.

Though the dividing lines were anything but clear given who the players were, Mexico was now actually fighting two different, if interrelated, wars: the war against the cartels (which was under the purview of federal authorities), and an explosion of ordinary street crime (much of which was under the purview of state and local police forces). The Mexican government had had a significant impact on cartel operations, but organized crime groups had proven to have a tremendous capacity to adapt and to reinvent themselves. Meanwhile, local crime had become an enormous challenge. And even as the federal government succeeded in strengthening the federal police and the military as tools for fighting organized crime, the institutions for fighting ordinary crime, the state and municipal police forces, were still highly problematic: many remained infected by cartel influence and the traditional corruption that had been their mainstay for decades. As "ordinary" (though no less violent) crime exploded, the institutions charged with meeting that challenge were at best inadequate, at worst still participating and colluding with it.

The biggest failure of all remained the Mexican judicial system, a system so flawed and byzantine that it ensured criminals' impunity in all but a small percentage of cases. The fact was so apparent and so grotesquely obvious that no one could fail to see it, yet the Mexican Congress was either unwilling or unable to implement meaningful reform. Admittedly, the challenge was complex, involving both reforms to Mexican law enforcement (how crimes were investigated, how police were trained to handle evidence, questions of human rights, etc.) as well as judicial reform (how attorneys were trained and how judges and the courts worked to establish truth and culpability or innocence). But the Mexican Congress had dallied with these questions for more than a decade, and the outcome of those years of debate were far short of what the Mexican nation needed if it was going to be saved from the narco-disease by which it was being devoured from within. Instead, the absence of judicial reform in Mexico bordered on legislative malfeasance; it was unconscionable, but politics and personal agendas consistently trumped the greater good in these deliberations. No progress was possible without substantive reform. It was a matter of will, but it was also a matter of the Mexican public pressuring, insisting that legislators do the necessary work.

In late August of 2011, four vehicles pulled up to the entrance to the Casino Royale in Monterrey, Nuevo León, where they set fire to the establishment, trapping and killing fifty-two people inside. The act of narco-terrorism resulted in the greatest number of civilian deaths on record in Mexico.

President Calderón declared three days of national mourning, vowing to track down the killers. The federal attorney general's office offered a nearly three-million-dollar reward for information leading to the arrest of the culprits. In an unusual move, Calderón delivered a fifteen-minute speech to the Mexican nation. Especially noteworthy were the last four minutes of the speech, in which he directly and pointedly addressed the American people, the U.S. Congress, and the U.S. government. Calderón thanked the United States for its cooperation and for the information and intelligence that had helped Mexico "to capture dozens of organized crime leaders and hit their criminal structures." Calderón asked Americans to "reflect upon the tragedy that we are living in Mexico." It was partly a plea, partly a demand. "Part of the tragedy that we are living as Mexicans," Calderón said, "comes from the fact that we live next door to the greatest consumer of drugs in the world." (It was a play, perhaps, on the oft-repeated phrase apocryphally attributed to Porfirio Díaz following the Mexican-American War: "Poor Mexico, so far from God and so close to the United States!") Calderón called on Americans to reduce their "insatiable" drug consumption or institute "mechanisms" that would deprive the cartels of the profits derived from drug trafficking (a thinly disguised appeal for legalization strategies). Finally, Calderón addressed the fact that the cartels were armed with weapons that had been purchased in the United States. "There is no reason that hundreds of thousands of weapons are being sold to criminals," he argued. He urged the United States to close the "criminal" sale of high-powered arms and assault weapons. These weapons were going into the hands of criminals operating in Mexico and everyone knew it. The problem had a solution, Calderón argued. The United States "has done it in the recent past. Stop the indiscriminate and uncontrolled sale of assault weapons!" Calderón demanded.

Perhaps it was the onslaught of Hurricane Irene, which was preparing to hit the Eastern Seaboard the day of Calderón's speech, but in the United States Calderón's words, like much of what was taking place in Mexico, received scant attention. By the fall of 2011 the national tally of the dead since the beginning of the narco-wars was nearing fifty thousand, though no one could know the true number with any certainty.[2] In Juárez, the grim tally had exceeded nine thousand souls, and the counting appeared far from over.

■ ■ ■

One afternoon I visited a cemetery in the heart of one of Juárez's bloodiest neighborhoods. I'd been told that the violence was so transforming the city's culture that it was even altering the rituals around death. The man who oversaw the cemetery told me that funeral directors like himself no longer stood too close to the victims' families for fear that *sicarios* might come to the graveside and assassinate the deceased's relatives along with anyone who happened to be standing near them. It went against the grain of his job of providing comfort, he said, but people in his line of work saw no alternative. Recently, a van full of men wearing sunglasses had pulled into the cemetery just as a funeral was getting underway. The funeral director and his crew had panicked. "They looked like *sicarios*," he told me. It turned out they were only a mariachi band contracted to play at the graveside. But the panic was testimony to the edginess that had come to reign over everything. Implicit in the funeral director's lamentation was the connotation that civilization itself seemed to be unraveling. I left the cemetery feeling disquieted.

Less than fifty yards from the cemetery entrance, I happened upon a group of six young men. In Juárez, in this neighborhood, the reflexive assumption was to assume that they were *cholos* or NiNis. All of them were under twenty, some sporting tattoos. But they were holding musical instruments, not assault rifles. The musicians (three trumpet players, two percussionists, and a bass player) were playing tropical *cumbia* music outdoors, in the driveway of a house. They told me that they were called Banda La Palmera. "We're playing at a party tonight!" they added, almost in a chorus. There was an innocence in their excitement that I found refreshing. That day I had been to two executions prior to visiting the cemetery, and I'd been feeling the press of the city's violence. The *cumbia* group dissolved those emotions. These young men were full of life. It was a serendipitous gift, I thought. In this forlorn neighborhood, surrounded by so much death, the musicians were evidence of the resilience of the human spirit.

Two years later, there was a glimmer of light. As October 2012 drew to a close, the tally of the dead for the year was running slightly more than 700, the lowest murder rate since the drug war had begun in 2008. Local tax revenues were up (a sign that people were going out to restaurants and making purchases in stores), as were building permits and real estate sales. Some credited the purported victory of the Sinaloa over the Juárez cartel, others the success of Mexican law enforcement, still others the rebounding maquiladora industry enjoying the fruits of a post-recession American economy. There had also been unprecedented investment in the city's social fabric. Whatever the reasons, the turn made it possible for some to begin to hope that Mexico's most brutalized city had perhaps seen the worst of it.

Notes

1. At the top of Mexico's Most Wanted list was Joaquín El Chapo Guzmán Loera. Following the 2011 execution of Osama Bin Laden, INTERPOL listed El Chapo as the most wanted man in the world.

2. People who had been lifted and disappeared were not in the tally, for example, and every month or so a mass grave was discovered in some part of the country containing victims who had been dead from weeks to years. Given the absence of adequate investigations, it was often a matter of conjecture whether any given murder was a cartel- or gang-related execution.

Interviews

Interviews with Mexican Academics and Government Officials

Anonymous (officer, Centro de Investigación y Seguridad Nacional [CISEN])
Sigrid Arzt, Commissioner of the Mexican Federal Institution of Public Access to
    Information (IFAI), former Security Advisor to President Felipe Calderón
Luis Astorga, Universidad Nacional Autónoma de México
Manuel Balcazar Villareal, Coordinator of Special Projects, Presidencia
Enrique Betancourt Gaona, Secretaría de Desarrollo Social
Juan Buenrostro, Communications, Secretaría de Seguridad Pública
María Josefina Linda Carreón Chairez, Presidencia
Fernando Castillo, Director of Communications, Procuraduría General de la
    República
Jorge Chabat, Centro de Investigación y Docencia Económicas
Carlos Cristóbal Flores, Inspector, Federal Police, Juárez
Genaro García Luna, Director, Secretaría de Seguridad Pública
Agustín Marciel, Mexican Consulate, El Paso, Texas
Eduardo Medina-Mora, Mexican Ambassador to the United Kingdom, former
    Federal Attorney General
Adriana Obregón Andría Vásquez, Advisor on Social Policy, Presidencia
Lic. Lizeth Parra, Director of Communications, Secretaría de Seguridad Pública
Alejandro Poiré, National Security Spokesman (Mexico), Secretary of National
    Security Council (Mexico)
Facundo Rosas, Director of the Federal Police, Secretaría de Seguridad Pública
Juan Ramón Salinas, Communications, Secretaría de Seguridad Pública
Guillermo Valdés, Director, Centro de Investigación y Seguridad Nacional
    (CISEN)

United States Interviews

Fred Burton, Stratfor Global Intelligence
Howard Campbell, Ph.D., Department of Anthropology, University of Texas at El
    Paso
Michael Lauderdale, Ph.D., Department of Social Work, University of Texas at
    Austin
Tony Payan, Ph.D., Department of Political Science, University of Texas at El Paso

Interviews with U.S. Government and Law Enforcement Officials

Diana Apodaca, Special Agent, Public Information Officer, Drug Enforcement
    Administration, El Paso Field Division
Joseph Arabit, Special Agent in Charge, El Paso Division, Drug Enforcement
    Agency
Robert Lindemann, Homeland Security Agency
Sergeant Joel "Purple" Peña, El Paso Police Department
Greg Thrash, Resident Agent in Charge, Drug Enforcement Administration, Aus-
    tin, Texas

Index